THE NATURE OF BELIEF

Est il pas temps désormais de chanter
Un vers chrestien qui puisse contenter
Mieux que devant les chrestiennes oreilles?
Est il pas temps de chanter les merveilles
De notre Dieu? et toute la rondeur
De l'univers rempli de sa grandeur?
Le payen sonne une chanson Payenne
Et le chrestien une chanson Chrestienne;
Le vers payen est digne des payens
Mais le chrestien est digne des chrestiens.
Doncques du Christ le nom tres sainct et digne
Commencera et finira mon hymne.

RONSARD

THE NATURE OF BELIEF

By M. C. D'ARCY, S.J., M.A.

CAMPION HALL, OXFORD

LONDON
SHEED & WARD
1931

FIRST PUBLISHED JULY 1931
BY SHEED & WARD
FROM 31 PATERNOSTER ROW
LONDON. E.C.4
IMPRIMI POTEST
HENRICUS KEANE : PRAEP. PROV. ANGLIAE
NIHIL OBSTAT : GEORGIUS D. SMITH, S.T.D.
CENSOR DEPUTATUS
IMPRIMATUR : EDM. CAN. SURMONT
VIC. GEN.
WESTMONASTERII 20 MAII 1931
PRINTED BY THE STANHOPE PRESS LTD.
LOVE LANE, ROCHESTER

FOREWORD

THOUGH many books have been written on the subject of belief I do not think that it has received as much attention as it deserves from those competent to deal with it. The reason may be that it has too many sides and touches on too many problems, living and dead, and that any writer on it has to bear in mind the historian, the lawyer and the psychologist as well as the philosopher and the theologian. This, certainly, has been my own chief difficulty, and if, as I hope, I have succeeded in presenting belief in the light of a few main principles, I fear the success may have been won at the expense of simplicity of treatment. The reader asking for bread may have to complain that the mills work very slowly. Nevertheless I would urge that the subject merits serious thought and a longer consideration even than what I have been able to give to it in this small volume. To those who are disconcerted by the density of the following pages I may say that the portions of the book more difficult of assimilation come at the beginning —in the second and third chapters. The philosophic argument in them has been deemed necessary to remove false assumptions and prejudices and to open the way to a positive theory of belief. I should like the reader to read that argument, but, if it prove too abstract, I suggest, rather unwillingly, that it be skipped and the book resumed at or after the chapter on the *Grammar of Assent*. What follows contains all that I have most at heart to say of positive value on the subject of belief.

It remains that I should acknowledge my debts and express my thanks to the many who have helped me in the writing of this book. My debt to Cardinal Newman will be obvious, and with his name I join that of the late H. S. V. Bickford. Mr. Douglas Woodruff and Mr. Christopher Dawson have made me valuable suggestions, and I have benefited by discussions on psychological questions with Dr. C. Burns. I owe more than I can say to Mr. T. F. Burns of Sheed and Ward. All the drudgery of revision and improvement was undertaken most generously by him, and without his co-operation and advice this book would have taken far longer to reach a state fit for publication.

M. C. D'Arcy, S.J.

ANALYTICAL CONTENTS

CH. V: THE BASIS OF BELIEF (p. 147)

A Critique of the Grammar of Assent (1)

CH. VI: THE ILLATIVE SENSE OR INTERPRETATION (p. 165)

A Critique of the Grammar of Assent (2)

CH. IX: THE LIMITS OF BELIEF (p. 271)

CH. X: DIVINE FAITH (p. 295)

CHAPTER I

THE PRESENT CONDITION OF BELIEF

*Ce n'est pas particulièrement par des institutions politiques
que se manifestera la ruine universelle, ou le progrès universel ;
car peu m'importe le nom. Ce sera par l'avilissement des cœurs.*

BAUDELAIRE: *Fusées.*

THE lights of great cities go out, and there is a howling
darkness to all appearance.   But always since men
began, the light of the pure God-knowing human
consciousness has kept alight; sometimes, as in the Dark
Ages, tiny but perfect flames of purest God-knowledge,
here and there; sometimes, as in our precious Victorian
era, a huge and rather ghastly glare of human "understanding".   But the light never goes out.

D. H. LAWRENCE: "On Human Destiny."

Assorted Articles.

Now I want
Spirits to enforce, art to enchant;
And my ending is despair
Unless I be relieved by prayer.

SHAKESPEARE:

Epilogue spoken by Prospero.

CHAPTER I

THE PRESENT CONDITION OF BELIEF

RONSARD'S poem, quoted opposite the title page, represents my own beliefs, but it is not my intention in this book to argue at length in favour of the contents of the Catholic religion. The trend of the argument necessarily brings into evidence certain truths which converge on the Christian religion, indicating that the Catholic faith is the way of entry into complete life. But I cannot hope to prove this satisfactorily for all readers, and I would ask them to keep in mind the limited scope of my essay; otherwise they may confuse means and end and fail to look for what, perchance, may concern their own problems. I wish to show that it is better to believe than to disbelieve, and by "better" I mean both more rational and more profitable. That there are no real grounds for scepticism and despair, that all the scientific discoveries and philosophies make no breach in the walls of perennial belief, is the argument of the chapters to come. In this chapter I assert that belief of some sort is profitable, and even essential. For introducing the word "profitable" or "valuable," some apology is required. The hard thinker may be irritated and exclaim, "I ask for reasons and you give me expediency instead," and a host of others may receive the impression that, like many other defenders of religion, I mean by belief a valuable experience which cannot stand the test of reason. Such an impression would be lamentable.

I know that the word "value" has been very often misused and that earnest and good people, alarmed at the arguments against belief, have seized upon it as a weapon of defence. I admire their integrity, but cannot follow their lead, and I mean by "valuable" here, a truth which is also a good—as one might say that it is true that the mind is higher than the body, and it is good for civilisation that this truth should be practised. When Socrates, in the *Republic* of Plato, was forced to argue on behalf of justice, he made two points against his adversaries: the first, that men ought by reason to act for justice's sake, and the second, that it was to the advantage of each individual that he should be just. Let the example of Plato or Socrates be cited to avert the wrath of the hard-headed thinker.

There are special reasons why I should begin a discussion of belief with a reminder of the importance of the issue. Professional philosophers, having a definite and limited study, quite rightly leave out of consideration all factors which might interfere with the examination of their particular problems. A Hegel does not want to be disturbed in his writing by the noise of a battle of Jena. But I am not writing as a professional philosopher. Life is more than philosophy, and the welfare of human souls comes first when one has to think and behave as a man amongst fellow-men. This is true at all times, and surely not least, when, in the opinion of many, that welfare is in peril.

There are many who think that we have reached a critical point in the history of Western civilisation, and, naturally enough, they have turned their attention to the value and permanence of prevalent beliefs and disbeliefs. In order to provide a setting in which the arguments of the chapters to follow may be better understood, and in order to allay any suspicion that I am exaggerating the importance of the subject to be treated, I will call to mind some of these contemporary witnesses of the Crisis in the West, as it has been called. In the first place it should be observed that they represent a large body of opinion, and are not, therefore, to be regarded as Cassandras, who speak without a brief and to ears that are deaf. They witness to the fact that many are suffering from that condition of mind called anxiety, and that it is rapidly ousting the confidence which prevailed in the years before the war. Just as the sturdy assurance of the average Englishman thirty years ago in the financial prosperity of this country, is yielding rapidly to a fear of economic collapse, so in the realms of politics, morality and religion beliefs have been shaken and are no longer trusted. We are face to face, as a result, with a dangerous condition of mind, one which some would regard as a herald or symptom of defeat, others as a warning that we must recover some lost faith or set about making another. Whatever be the remedy for it, and whether the reasons for gloom be unduly exaggerated or not, the point is that the state of mind exists and as such has its dangers—for instance, the danger of restlessness or panic.

From some measure of agreement in their observation of the facts, there are many modern writers who are attempting to tell us whether the reasons for anxiety are justified and what remedies are applicable. Herein they pass from fact to theory, from observed data to supposed causes, and it would be too much to expect unanimity in their conclusions. I will put aside explanations which depend, as I believe, on radically false principles. The theory, for instance, that civilisation depends entirely on material laws or economic causes is one which I cannot now stop to dispute. The next

B

chapter will be devoted to proving that mind is other than matter, and, however dependent on the body, cannot be judged entirely by the latter. It may well be conceded that economic conditions play a more important part in the rise and fall of a culture than has been admitted by historians in the past. But that part must be checked and corrected by the continuous presence of beliefs and ideals, and it is to these latter we must turn if the present historical situation is to be appreciated. On the same grounds, much of what a writer like Spengler says must be dismissed. He makes his cycles too rigid and is too anxious to fit the facts and phases of history into a predestined scheme. It will be more profitable to study writers who regard movements and changes in history as tendencies for which human wills are, partially at least, responsible. Examples can be drawn from writers of the most widely divergent outlooks; who are nevertheless in agreement in their witness and have criticisms to offer and remedies to suggest. The late Léon Bloy, M. Julian Benda, Mr. Wyndham Lewis, M. Jacques Maritain, M. Nicolas Berdiaeff, Mr. Christopher Dawson—these with many others come readily to mind, but here I must confine myself to short scrutinies of only a few.

The views of Bloy are extreme and few will accept them without qualification, but they have this special merit, that they are quite independent of any contemporary fad or fashion. He stepped out of another age and was horrified by what he saw. In his own words he was "the Grand Inquisitor of literature marching proudly under the laughter of hate, wrapped in the dazzling beggary of a dream." Ever forceful in his language, he described the principal evils of his time as mediocrity—"that power which can uproot the

Himalayas," and, as the expression of this mediocrity, a widespread *bourgeois* ideal in manners, learning and religion. Thus, referring to scholars, he speaks of "the sawdust of history carried each day by the commonplace cabinet-makers of *l'Ecole des Chartes* to the basket of the guillotine—where the great concepts of Tradition are beheaded." "Religious metaphysics," again, "is no longer permitted to-day, save on the condition of being an *apéritif* preceding a feast of dirt." The one remedy for him is that poverty of the spirit inculcated by the Gospel and shown forth in suffering and the Cross. No good work can be done by one who wishes to make the best of two worlds. "An artist can work only on two kinds of tables, either on one that is worth fifty thousand francs or on one worth fifty sous." In accordance with this philosophy he inveighed against what he called the English shopkeeper's religion. "The Judge will say, I was hungry and you gave me not to eat, and a thousand pork butchers will say, 'that is all very well, but Lent did us real injury';" and in bitter satire he offers a new social order, which includes the erection of a massive gold cross on the Eiffel Tower at the expense of the City of Paris, and the abolition of universal suffrage.

As can be judged from these extracts, Bloy was not likely to win popularity, and undoubtedly his habit of exaggeration, the virulence of his language, and what some would call his mysticism, have prevented many from taking him seriously. But since his death his importance has come to be more and more recognised, and there is no denying the influence of his views on a number of writers of repute. It is, moreover, easy to separate the wheat from the chaff in his writings, and to estimate his point of view. It comes to this: that the modern world has ceased to believe wholeheartedly in the extremes which Christianity has its mission to present as contrasts: poverty and riches, the Cross and comfort, humility and pride, the supernatural and the natural, Heaven and final perdition. Bloy called this unwillingness to face eternal facts, to grasp this sword of division, to bear with a faith which wounded while it healed, the *Esprit Bourgeois*, and he predicted a time when the poor would rise in wrath against those who have taken away from them their one hope in adversity. "The poor have stood erect at the foot of the Cross since the first bloodstained Mass of the great Good Friday—in the midst of darkness, stench, dereliction, thorns, nails, tears and agonies. For generations they have whispered into the ear of the divine Victim and . . . all of a sudden, there is revealed to them with a jet of electrical science the gallows fallen to dust, where the teeth of beasts have devoured their Redeemer. . . Zut! Very well! They are off to amuse themselves!"

M. Benda is as discontented as Bloy with the present beliefs of the West, but he does not hark back to religion for a remedy. Spinoza is nearer to his ideal, and he expresses his point of view in the pithy sentence: "*Spinoza était ivre d'éternité, les seculiers sont dans leur rôle en étant ivres de contingence.*" He would have all those whose duty it is to cultivate the best and direct the people, lovers of what is eternal; and by eternal he means those values which are reached by the intellect, which abide and control life. Those whose duty it is to maintain these values have, to his mind, betrayed their cause, and abandoning their principles have joined hands with the worshippers of sentiment, passing vanities and popular cries. The sure sign of decline is when reason is made to minister to instinctive needs and arbitrary desires, when everything is left a prey to the contingent. There is always strife between the eternal and the contingent; the austere discipline of intellectual study and statement whether in science, art or philosophy, and the craving for immediate satisfaction. That the former should be interrupted and suffer is normal, but that it should be prostituted with the consent of the learned to the ends of passion and prejudice is an abomination, and it is this abomination which is praised as the glory of our present state.

M. Benda develops this thesis by reference to philosophy, politics, education and kindred topics. We need not follow him in this development. His summary is concise and we are at no loss to discover what is his judgment of the age we live in. For different reasons he reaches the same conclusion as Bloy, and the concurrence of two such differently-constituted minds is not without significance. The force of their conclusions is, moreover, enhanced when we recall that Mr. Wyndham Lewis, in England, acting as an independent witness, and M. Maurras, in France, no lover of the Jews or Spinoza, arrive at the same verdict. M. Maurras, as is well known, has railed for many years against the featureless democratic ideals of the past century. They are for him nothing more than the cries of the rabble against law and order, the letting loose of sentiment and feeling from the control of mind. The Graeco-Roman world was built with stone and laid out in severe design; it had an apex in one ruling principle and a variety of orders. All that is enduring and constructive in the West has been inherited from this world, and our modern tragedy consists in this, that we have deserted the tradition and welcomed the superstitions of the East, and made overtures to the barbarians, who think in terms of numbers and brute force.

To Mr. Wyndham Lewis the vice we suffer from is that we close our eyes and open our ears, that we discard space and embrace time, and so, instead of standing still and contemplating, we are for ever moving on and exulting in the empty form of progress. This commendation of space-forms at the expense of music is not just the prejudice of a painter and draughtsman; Mr. Wyndham Lewis is using the example of his craft to embody a philosophic principle. The eye is the faculty of vision, and vision is in language and in thought associated with the intellect. It is the eye which perceives the pattern, which measures objects, and, in contrast with this, it is the ear which records the rhythm of movement and makes of it a pleasurable sensation. The eye is objective, the ear subjective; in vision we contemplate, in hearing we experience. And so, by a very natural transition from the organs of sight and hearing, Wyndham Lewis defines and contrasts two philosophies: the one of intellectual sight and order, of reality as it is in itself, and the other of time, of experience, of relative values and of reality as it appears in sensation. The philosophy of time, he holds, is the disease of our present generation; it is a child-cult, a bad mixture of primitive barbarism and tired nerves. It shows itself in every department of life, in votes to "flappers," in the "movies," in impressionism in art, in relativity in morals, in the *élan vital* of so many modern philosophies, in Bertrand Russell, H. G. Wells, James Joyce and the rest.

With an industry and an ingenuity beyond belief Mr. Wyndham Lewis has collected evidence from all quarters in support of his thesis that Western man has succumbed to the cult of time. Assuming his evidence to be cogent, what are we to understand by this fixation of mind? Some critics have been unable to make head or tail of the book, *Time and Western Man*, but surely the philosophy implied in it is not obscure. The boast of

Western civilisation is that it has seen the Universe in the light of certain principles due to Christianity and Greek Metaphysics and Roman order. It has, to use the formula of Aristotle, formed itself by "right reason." To Socrates was due the discovery that beyond the ever-changing panorama of the senses could be discerned a world of stable and imperishable forms. Plato worked out this discovery and distinguished between the world of sense, which was ever in flux and therefore only half real, and the objects of the intellect which made possible science, morality and religion. This distinction of two spheres—modified by Aristotle and Christianity, so as to allow for good, even in the lower sphere—has been the inspiration and virtue of Western thought. Against the centrifugal tendencies of the lower, the restless urge of instinct, the momentary enjoyment of sense, the sovereign power of the spirit has waged never-ceasing war and has taken for its honour that it could reduce the motive of these forces to order and direct them by high purposes. But as soon as the highest function of man is overcome by fatigue, or by temptations from the ancient serpent to over-reach itself, the forces of barbarism gather and descend like Attila on Rome. Wyndham Lewis is but repeating in his own way under the titles of Space and Time the old distinction, and he claims that the regard for the ecstatic and amorous satisfaction in sensation and fleeting experience, the worship, in fact, by artists and philosophers alike, of the relative, are the characteristics of our present epoch and the signs of its decadence.

Those who have been persuaded by this analysis will find corroborative evidence in the most recent declarations of scientists and theologians. We are being told with increasing emphasis that the old formulae of science have lost their efficacy, that the scientists are all mounted on peaks of Darien in their laboratories. As I am still giving the impressions of others, I can without scruple refer to the constant use made of the names of Eddington and Whitehead, and quote the latter to the effect that science, at least since the advent of Hume, has based itself on a false abstraction and sinned grievously by taking the numerable element in sensation as a measuring rod of the intelligible. What Mr. Whitehead desiderates is a new Plato, who will bear in mind the distinction between an empiricist science of physics and metaphysical philosophy, between sensation and knowledge. Parallel with the movement in science is the change of attitude amongst modernist theologians. Once upon a time they scorned the introduction of metaphysics into religion and relied almost wholly on the test of experience. Many of them are now ill at ease with this point of view, and are heading a movement away from the heart to the intellect, from the conception of an immanent to that of a transcendent God.

The close correspondence, both in the past and the present, between the tendencies in Protestant theology and science has been noted by M. Maritain and explained by one cause. That cause can be summed up in the Reformation. The Middle Ages were a period of faith supported by Thomism, and it is the essence of Thomism to trust reason and to distinguish it carefully from sense. At the Renaissance faith and Thomism disappeared, to all intents and purposes, in the cultured circles of Northern Europe. In place of metaphysics a new method, which may be called that of mathematical physics, came into vogue and by its successes secured a permanent hold upon minds. There was nothing inherently wrong in this method, but by evil fortune it aggravated a vicious error. In the decline of the Middle Ages a philosophy of Nominalism had made ground, and Nominalism consists in saying that the general ideas of objects which we form have no real relation to their proper nature, but are just labels or counters or symbols for the series of data we perceive with our senses. This view may strike the reader as probably right, and at any rate as harmless. M. Maritain —here I would agree with him wholeheartedly—looks upon it as a pestilential error. If it be true, then we have no truth save in sensation, and it will not be difficult to show that sensation cannot bear the weight put upon it, and that therefore there is nothing left but a bleak scepticism or an assurance based upon some intense experience. What happened can be told shortly. The scientists, on the rickety foundations of this Nominalism, went on for centuries content to manufacture symbols like atoms and electrons; the religious folk, distrustful of the intellect, fell back on inner experience, at first confidently, and now with supreme misgiving in many quarters. M. Maritain tells both alike that they are mistaken, that it is high time they took up a philosophy worth considering and built their natural beliefs on intellect and their religion on a faith which is intellectually watertight.

It would be easy to continue giving illustrations of a kind of criticism of contemporary thought and conduct in line with that of M. Maritain and the others quoted. But I must leave the rather fascinating if facile task of catching resemblances between, and assigning common causes to, apparently heterogeneous data, and making a unity of the generalisations of critics and philosophers. We have enough for our purpose. There can be no doubt that many are alarmed at the present state of our civilisation, that they are contemptuous of the shibboleths which served their fathers and are looking for a philosophy of life which will bear criticism. Men are always inclined to exaggerate the evils of the age in which they live, but it is not difficult to match the pessimism of modern writers with forebodings in the literature of the late nineteenth century. Have we not Mallock asking, Is Life worth Living by the ideals then in vogue, and also Samuel Butler's mordant irony and laughter at much so-called progress? Perhaps Newman, because of his Catholic outlook, may not be taken as a fair witness, but Carlyle may be cited. "That intellect do march if possible at double quick time is very desirable; nevertheless, why should she turn round at every stride and cry: see you what a stride I have taken! Such a marching of intellect is distinctly of the spavined kind. . . Intellect did not awaken for the first time yesterday; but has been under way from Noah's Flood downwards; greatly her best process, moreover, was in the old times when she said nothing about it." Again, we are inclined to think Ruskin typically Victorian and old-fashioned, but it is surprising how fresh his comments on morality and social conditions read. If such men were witnesses against their own time they were also prophets crying out against ours.

For parallels with the present situation we have, I think, to go back to the break-up of the Roman Empire or the decline of the Middle Ages. We seem to be at the end of an epoch which began at the Renaissance. Such an impression of history as this is not quite worthless— as I shall argue later, impressions or interpretations can be a valid form of knowledge. I base my judgment on a vast number of concordant pieces of evidence. First, the late war was of a kind which cannot be treated as other wars. It shook civilisation to its foundations, and, what is more, it has forced man to reflect and ask himself "what kind of a being am I that could commit such an act and how comes it that such a folly was possible?" In the scorching light of indignation many supposedly fair ideals have turned black. Secondly, the insurgence of Fascism and Bolshevism has given the direct lie to that liberal philosophy which has been the breath of men's nostrils for generations. Thirdly, the intellectual tradition of Christianity which was affected at the Reformation but kept alive by sentiment, habit and good will, has, as so often happens with lingering effects, vanished suddenly. Religion in the West (except, of course, the Catholic faith, which, as all will agree, has continued its traditional beliefs and remained independent of the successive changes in European philosophy) had been for a long while like a great tree without live roots; it seemed to be secure and many rested on its branches, but now it lies on the ground. If this statement be doubted I beg the reader to ask himself whether any definite religious faith now permeates literature, literary criticism, education or the principal doctrines of our day. Many still practise some form of religion and even go to church, but few have a definitely religious outlook and all have grown accustomed to the expression of views which once would not have been tolerated. There are no signs of a crusade against a body which is far more virulently anti-Christian than the medieval turk. If ever a protest is raised by a believing Christian against anti-religious and—from the point of view of Christianity—immoral propaganda, a chorus of ridicule greets that protest. So great is the change that most would be surprised if one were shocked by a book championing evolutionary ethics or economic materialism. Novelists—and they serve as a good test—seldom write for a believing public; they take for granted that their readers will be as themselves, that is, human beings without a definite standard of morals, without preconceived conceptions of truth, who will readily agree with anything said to them provided it arouses their feelings of sympathy.

To illustrate this truth, we need only contrast the reception of Mrs. Humphrey Ward's *Robert Elsmere* with the newspaper's headlines for Dr. Eisler's recently translated book on Christ, or, if it be thought that the Victorians were unduly sensitive, plant Dr. Johnson down in Fleet Street. The limit of his tolerance was that you could always toss snails over the garden wall if your neighbour was a dissenter, but he would believe himself in a more barbarous region than Scotland if he were to come again.

I know well that there have always been atheists and antinomians, but that is not the point. They existed, indeed, but we have only to think of the suspicion in which a comparatively harmless man like Wilkes was held, and the boycotting of a Shelley and Byron, to realise that beliefs and standards of conduct still counted for something in their time. And, if any doubt still lingers, the reader has but to consult the letters and correspondence of men and women in any century before the present. Those of us who are not historically minded, and are apt to read the present into the past, must be constantly taken by surprise when reading the letters of some gallant or worldly rogue to his wife and family. Without affectation he will speak of God and providence, take for granted an after life, a Heaven and a Hell, and end his letter with pious words. Such letters are rare now and, from the pen of similar characters, inconceivable—and it is in the recognition of this difference that we can most easily reason the truth about our own present beliefs, the truth that we have no fixed belief and creed.

I do not think, therefore, that the judgment of the critics is mistaken as to the facts nor, when allowance has been made for exaggeration and personal equations, are they so wrong in their diagnosis of the causes. They assume, however, that the breakdown of belief and of an intellectual belief is an evil, and though this may seem obvious to many, the justice of the assumption will be seen better if we consider the meaning of belief. We all have a rough idea of what we mean when we use the word "belief," and we can leave most of the problems connected with it to the chapters to follow. Not all beliefs fall short of certainty; nevertheless, the word is rarely if ever used for the certainty that comes from direct knowledge or perception. We *see* a colour, we do not *believe* it, but we may well believe that the colour is bad for the eyes or the nervous system. That is to say, belief stretches beyond the visible evidence, and so it is that we speak of belief in progress or some policy or remedy or philosophy of life. For a similar reason we apply the word "belief" above all to our regard for persons and their word. "I believe in him and I believe in what he says." Sancho Panza, despite all, believed in his master, and Don Quixote believed firmly in the ideal of gallantry and devotion. Two facts emerge from this analysis: the first, that belief has an object; the second, that though the belief may very well be based on rational grounds, it is usually accompanied by a feeling of confidence. The reason and the emotion co-operate with one another and vary in their respective strength. When a Scotsman invests money in a Company, his belief is, in all likelihood, well grounded in reason; the belief in British Israel, on the other hand, is possibly more enthusiastic than rational. The emotion can persist against all the evidence of visible facts, because, as stated above, in all cases belief goes beyond seeing, and for the same reason a belief can remain rational when all the appearances are against it. The celebrated Tichborne trial furnishes an example of emotional belief. Here, the mother of Roger Tichborne kept an inexpugnable faith in the survival of her son, and welcomed a claimant with impostor written all over him. In contrast with this we can take the example of a traveller who by study has made sure of his right direction, and, nevertheless, is tempted at a certain point to retrace his steps because the landscape looks strange and the turning indicated does not seem to lead to his journey's end.

In nearly all cases, then, belief goes beyond immediate perception and is to be contrasted with vision. Hence, it is natural and legitimate to speak of belief in crusades and causes, in changes to come, in the effects of what we can prescribe with certainty from philosophies of life and from religion, and it is with these larger conceptions that we are dealing when we say that belief has fled and that the flight spells grievous loss. It is surely no light matter that man should lose confidence in his highest powers and in the existence of a God who can save. Historically the latter precedes the former, for pride is reckoned amongst theologians as the first sin; and it is far more likely that a confidence in one's own strength should lead to the discarding of God, as a youth grows too old for a nurse, than that recognition of weakness should spell denial of Omnipotence. The misfortune is that after the first wave of exaltation in his human prowess man has a reaction to despair. When Nietzsche, through the voice of Zarathusthra, whispered with awe and joy that we have slain God, he was breaking the news of the Superman to the world. Pearse, too, in late years told how once, as he knelt by the cross of Kilgobbin, it became clear to him with an awful clearness that there was no God. "Why pray after that? I burst into a fit of laughter at the folly of man."

But there are different endings to the story of the two men. No one can help feeling pity for the last days of Nietzsche, and it is rather to the fate of his spiritual children that I would refer. The days of the Superman are over, and the inheritor of his greatness is the "free man." "Blind to good and evil, reckless of destruction, omnipotent matter rolls on its relentless way; for Man ... it remains only to cherish, ere yet the blow falls, the lofty thoughts that ennoble his little day; disdaining the coward terrors of the slave of Fate to worship at the shrine that his own hands have built."* Such is one ending, a belief rooted in unbelief as honour in dishonour; the other ending is that of a recovered faith: "He has revealed His face to me, His face is terrible and sweet. I know it now. His name is Suffering."

If we accept the sequence: belief in God, disbelief in God, belief in man, disbelief in man, we shall find we have approached the same conclusions as M. Maritain, Mr. Wyndham Lewis and many others. Generalisations are notoriously unsafe; they are, as Bacon said, of no more aid to practice than Ortelius' universal map to direct the way between London and York. Nevertheless, it cannot be denied that for a long while after the Renaissance metaphysics were out of fashion, and that many non-Catholic theologians preferred to rely on a faith acquired by experience and independent of reason. The intellectual basis, therefore, of a belief in God and religion was taken away. Next, we find a succession of philosophies and political theories which assign to man a power he did not previously realise that he possessed. In literature, liberal culture and romanticism take precedence of classicism. In the

* Bertrand Russell, *Philosophical Essays*, p. 70.

nineteenth century the multiple and hitherto indistinct
lines of development converge and make in one direction; and this direction is noticed by many of the
leading thinkers and deplored. There is a kind of
belief throughout the century, but it is one in which the
factor of feeling, sentiment and experience is more
conspicuous than that of reason resting in a metaphysic;
and if the heart of the people is still sound even their
orthodox teachers are already wilting before the glare of
the Huxleys, Spencers and Mills. As Mallock remarked
through one of his characters, "Materialism once came
to the world like a small street boy throwing mud at
it; and the indignant world very soon drove it away.
But it has now come back again, dirtier than ever,
bringing a big brother with it, and Heaven knows when
we shall get rid of it now." The implied aspersion on
science in this remark is typical of the great Victorian
moralists, and it suggests a lack of assurance in argument. There are exceptions of course; Newman's
Grammar of Assent, to which I shall refer again later,
contains a positive philosophy and creed, and Balfour's
Foundations of Belief saves much from the wreck caused
by materialistic science and scepticism.

It is, however, no unfair criticism, I think, of the
Victorians, to say that their assents were due more to
high sentiment than to intellectual certainty, and that
the reader may judge for himself the truth of this
criticism I will ask him to compare Malory's *Morte
d'Arthur* with Tennyson's, the work of the primitives
with that of the Pre-Raphaelites, Dante's *Divine Comedy*
with the *Earthly Paradise* of William Morris, or, in order to
summarise the change from the days of faith to our own
times, compare the fourteenth century as described by
Sigrid Undset, in her *Kristin Lavransdatter* with Mr.
Galsworthy's Saga of the Victorian Forsytes, the pre-war

Jean Christophe and Mr. Aldous Huxley's representation of modern society in *Point Counter Point*. This last book confines itself to only one section of the community, and may be thought to amount to an exaggeration so gross as to be caricature. It is, as I have said, easy to see rakes everywhere and generalise on slight evidence. Good is so ordinary as to pass unnoticed. The judgment of Mr. Huxley, nevertheless, is corroborated by that distinguished German novelist, Thomas Mann : "Humanity seems to have run like boys let out of school away from the humanitarian, idealistic, nineteenth century, from whose morality—if we can speak at all of morality in this connection—our time represents a wide and wild reaction. . . This fantastic state of mind, of a humanity that has outrun its ideas, is matched by a political scene in the grotesque style, with Salvation Army methods, hallelujahs and bell-ringing and dervish-like repetition of monotonous catchwords, until everybody foams at the mouth. Fanaticism turns into a means of salvation, enthusiasm into epileptic ecstasy, politics become an opiate for the masses, a proletarian eschatology; and reason veils her face."*

"Reason veils her face" and we are lost in unbelief. Grant that this is saying too much there is enough left over to justify my opening assertion that it is better to believe than disbelieve. Belief is the natural end of beings possessing minds, and if they allow their minds to suffer an eclipse, then, in the ensuing darkness, it is no wonder if the *gens lucifuga* of the soul, the creatures of darkness, emerge. No doubt, even in the act of foreswearing reason we employ it, and we think and reflect now as always, but it is one thing to use our royal

---

* "An Appeal to Reason," by Thomas Mann. A speech delivered in Berlin on October 17th, 1930, published in the *Criterion*, April, 1931.

C

faculty and another to honour and rejoice in it. In an age of doubt man sows and does not reap; he has no courage in his convictions, he is like one beset by scruples who loses his sense of values and power of steadfast judgment. The evil of unbelief is that it must shut its eye to the forms and patterns of truth inscribed in the universe, and retire to the inner sanctuary of the mind, there to rest in uncertainty, in the presence of a fugitive self and the broken idols of its hopes. For a time, perhaps, the world of inner feelings and experience may take the place of external interests as confidence in self so often succeeds the worship of God. But psychology is a poor substitute for religion and metaphysics —was it not of the English philosophers that Nietzsche said, "I am told that it is simply a case of old, frigid and tedious frogs crawling and hopping around men and inside men as if they were as thoroughly at home there as they would be in a swamp"?—and psychological experience is apt to prove the happy hunting ground of the faddist and savage and to culminate in utter pessimism.

Belief is positive, an act of affirmation in which the soul expands. If, as should be the case, it flows from reason or apparent reason, it provides a foothold for comparison, a standard of values and a desire for further truth. It is no accident that those ages which were confident in their beliefs were at the same time most vigorous in their creative art and full of the spirit of wonder, the sense of the ridiculous, the reverence for what is high. Loyalties are a form of belief and attachment is a consequence, and on a background of truth assumed or known it is possible to paint a Divine Comedy. What is more, only on condition that some truth is accepted can advance be made. If even the beginnings are uncertain we must turn hither and thither and begin all over again. This is the lot of Sisyphus, a damned soul, and not of the lover of wisdom, whose joy it is to explore the mystery half unveiled and to advance with knowledge of his direction and in love with what he already sees.

I have purposely, in the foregoing, left the content of belief vague, as I am not at present arguing explicitly for any one definite belief. Necessarily, certain possibilities have been excluded, such as a belief in disbelief or materialism; and, because of the association of the word "belief" with religion, and the common fear that scientific discoveries are washing away ancient boundary marks, I have been obliged to stress the value of what once was held as true and to contrast it with the materialism incidental to science but paraded by certain men of science. I hope this will not be misunderstood as prejudice or begging of the question. The aim of this chapter has lain solely in the contention that belief is better than unbelief, and that it must have an intellectual basis. It is now time to examine some of its necessary contents and justify its reasonableness.

CHAPTER II

THE POSSIBILITY OF TRUTH

As for the possibility [of metaphysics] they are ill discoverers that think there is no land when they can see nothing but sea.

BACON.

> Sure He that made us with such large discourse
> Looking before and after, gave us not
> That capability and god-like reason
> To fust in us unus'd.

SHAKESPEARE: *Hamlet IV*, 4.

HE must have little spirit who thinks that a spirit is nothing.

ST. BERNARD.

CHAPTER II

THE POSSIBILITY OF TRUTH

SO many accepted beliefs have been, within living memory, challenged or overthrown that doubt about the very foundations of knowledge has become widespread. Our first task, therefore, is to restore confidence in the intellect, a task made easy by the fact that no reasoning process can be doubted save by reason, by the exercise, that is, of a faculty whose light cannot be put out. Unfortunately this process is not by any means certain of success with particular individuals. A mind can become so distracted by intemperance of thought or prejudice that it is unable to concentrate on what is being said; the simple meaning of terms is disregarded and viewed in a context to which it is not relevant, or else it is enshrined in some favourite image and then lost to sight. For instance, let the word "thought" be mentioned; immediately the listener translates it into a remembered phrase such as that thought is a vivid sensation or the behaviour of the brain, and he will go on to confuse it with some image—a ray of light, a spark, a vibration. Another cause for failure in reasoning is what has been called an anxiety-state. Those who suffer from this are unable to make up their minds; they have had their balance upset by some shock to their old convictions, and as a consequence they oscillate to and fro; like the traveller in a strange bed they cannot make up their minds to rest in a fixed position. Where this malady is due to "nerves" or obscure emotional causes the doctor is more likely to be of aid than the philosopher.

Where doubt and suspense of judgment invade a whole society, because of mass suggestion or repeated failure, the disease can be treated by reason, provided the sufferers do not love their own misery. The first step is to show that the mind is not material. The truth of this is self-evident, and there is not a single person who denies it in practice. It is only when the question is put to a man, explicitly as a problem, that he begins to hesitate; and even then he will hesitate only if he finds that he has already committed himself to a general theory which does not square with the obvious answer, or because he remembers adverse arguments or is now presented with them. A proof, therefore, must proceed either by displaying the radical difference of mind and matter in definition and examples, or by a convincing *reductio ad absurdum*. Our own body is a fair example of what we mean by material. Now the body of a human being has this in common with a lump of clay or coal-gas, that it can be measured and is therefore quantitative and made up of parts. If, then, there be anything we can think of which, of its nature, defies measurement and division into parts, that thing cannot be defined as material; it may be called immaterial or spiritual. The question, then, is whether there be anything of this kind. An obvious claimant is thought. To make this term precise we must consult our consciousness and distinguish the various possible meanings of the word "thought." If I say "I am thinking of my reader," there is first the activity of thinking, as when we say "I am thinking hard" or "I am meditating on a problem"; when this is over I can speak of it as my "past thought," "my former reflections." Secondly there is the subject of the thinking, that is the "I."

The use of the word "subject" suggests both activity and passivity. The thinking is an activity of the subject and the subject is to some extent affected by the nature of his thought. He grows wiser, for instance, and if the activity of thinking be immaterial it will necessarily follow that the agent or author will also be immaterial, at least, in so far as he is a thinker. Thirdly there is the object of my thought, let us say, the reader. To escape irrelevant problems let us assume that I know precisely who he is. The reader is an individual being distinct from everybody else, and although he is the object of my thought he is quite unaffected by the fact that I have him in mind. If he were grasped by my thought in the same way that a coin is grasped in the hand, then his body and soul would be in my possession, and in that of nobody else, and the thinking, like the grasping, would be material. But is this conceivable? No doubt, in some sense I have the actual reader there before my mind: I do not confuse him with anybody else; I can describe him and conduct myself towards him without error; I know him for what he is; my thinking is true thinking. But there is a distinction between the reader as he is and the reader as thought of. The mind can possess itself of objects as truly as a hand can possess a coin, yet without taking hold of the object physically in the same way that the material hand holds the one individual physical piece of money. The coin is or is not in my hand—that is a fact and not a truth; and the presence or absence of a reader is a fact. Now these facts are spoken of as true only when they become the object of the mind and represent the facts as they are, or—shall we say, if the word "represent" is disliked— when the object as an idea is identical in some way with the object as a fact or event.

There is the closest connection between thinking,

thought, and the thinker; so close that one word is often
made to do service for all. In many books of philosophy
the thinker is described and hidden by the word "mind,"
and in everyday language we use "thought" indiscrimin-
ately, for the thinking or the content of the thinking.
This shows how closely related the three are. The
content is not of an alien stuff from the thinking; it is
rather the thinking at work and in act, and it appears
at the end like the flower or fruit on the tree. That is
why a favourite word for the result is "concept." As
with the herb or tree, an external cause has been needed
to fertilise it; but there is this striking difference, that
the mind can be fertilised by any object, and the
product is a living and spiritualised replica of that
object. This being so, we can concentrate for the
moment on this object or product of consciousness in
our attempt to determine whether thought is material
or immaterial. We have already concluded that the
reader, though he is known truly for what he is, cannot
be the material content of consciousness. This might
be urged as a negative proof that thought was immaterial. There is, however, an objection in the way.
It is possible and has been held by certain philosophers
that the content of consciousness is a material image of
the real object. By physical means, as in a photograph,
the appearance of objects can be reproduced, and there
is, so it is argued, no reason to suppose that the idea is
anything else than a particularly subtle and delicate
image produced by the organism. But, in fact, this
difficulty helps to bring out the immaterial nature of
thought. Thought is not the same as the image. We
are bound to explain it in terms which resemble those
of an image, because it has a certain analogy with it,
and in our language we are always at the mercy of
material symbols. First of all, if we examine our con-

sciousness, it is easy to see that image and concept are not the same. They are both there occupying different rôles. I can think of the reader and at the same time I can have an image of him. The image is not the reader as known, nor do I ever dream of confusing it with him. Often enough I may ignore it completely, and, when I do call one up, it is as an aid to thought and not as a substitute for it. Moreover I can turn my attention to the image and think of that, yet surely no one will maintain that all I am doing is having an image of an image, and that if I like I can go on with such images *ad infinitum*.

More conclusive still is the fact that in thinking of a real object one does not take any notice of one's thought as a content of consciousness distinct from the real object. It is the medium in which one thinks, a medium so immaterial that it offers no resistance, but serves as a passage of communication between the mind and the thing. In the direct act of knowledge the mind is busy with the real object; it is only on reflection, in the examination of its work and prize, that it becomes aware of its own concepts. Now all this separates the concept entirely from the image, if by image is meant a material reproduction or photograph. And there are other decisive differences as well. A concept has this peculiarity: it is never of the singular. When I think of the reader of these lines the concept "reader" which I am using is applicable to an indefinite and inexhaustible number of readers. It is what is technically called a universal. If another person glances at these lines, he too must necessarily fall into the category of "the reader," just as all those sitting in a library with books in their hands are so many units with one name. Strange as this must seem to those who hear it for the first time, there is no escape from the concept, and the

concept is invariably universal. Were there but one
sun, as once was thought, one unique individual, I
should still have to think of it as a specimen of a type
which was indefinitely multipliable.

Now this feature which characterises a thought-object
separates it radically from the image, and from anything material. An image is bound to be particular. This
fact we take for granted when, for instance, we open an
album of photographs. There may be likenesses common
to many of the photographs, out of which we can construct a *tour de force*, as Mrs. Virginia Woolf has done in
Orlando; and the opponents of the intellect argue that
the concept is nothing more than such a composite
image, a kind of compendium or *précis* of a number of
objects. But a moment's consideration will show that
such a compendium differs essentially from a universal.
The former is the result of leaving out or fusing. (In
a composite photograph, for instance, we obtain a
portrait which is untrue of any individual, and in the
compendium enough is included to get a mass effect.
It may be all that is wanted for a special definite purpose. Sometimes the image is used as symbol, as in
advertisements. In this case the image remains particular because it is the image of one definite thing, but
by a recognised convention it is made to stand for a
general idea.) But the universal is not formed by such a
process of elimination, nor as a universal is it actually
and explicitly concerned with every individual that
falls under it. When I say "man," I have done justice
to every single man, and unlike the image, my concept
is true of every human being. The image is tied to
time and space; but the universal concept is independent,
yet realised in every time and space. What is more,
everything new that I discover in men and women is
contained in the notion of humanity. Thus the mind of

man can make its way through the litter of sense to the natures or essences of external things, which are concealed from the bodily eyes and seen only partially with the eye of the intellect.

And now, having tried by an analysis of the immaterial and the material to show their irreconcilable difference, let us see some of the absurd consequences of denying what ought to be accepted as self-evident. The denial itself is either true or false, but who can measure this alternative in terms of matter? Certainly the thinking would not take place if our brain were taken out, and our meditation would come to an abrupt end if a thunderbolt struck us. But it does not follow from this that the brain, or anything material, is the cause of the thinking. We are justified in saying only that almost all the evidence accumulated proves a connection, a connection such that the working of the mind may be said to be conditioned by the body. To go further would be to commit oneself to holding that the brain behaves far more strangely than Dr. Jekyll and Mr. Hyde, that it is what it is and is also something else, and that there is no correspondence between the two. To escape this difficulty Mr. Julian Huxley has invented the name "mentoid." But this mentoid is a hypothetical monster which fits no observed facts and only multiplies difficulties. We are forced by the hypothesis to give a mind to those lowest of God's creatures which have never, so far as we know, showed a glimmering of intellect, and evolve out of them a being who opens his mental eye to the absolute and fixed ideas of duty, truth and beauty.

So the brain cannot be just a physical organism composed of grey and white matter and at the same time the recipient, catalogue and system of the whole universe; it remains that in possessing universal knowledge the mind is in some sense in possession of all things. Or, to go further with the materialist view, we are to suppose that the brain is not only itself and the content of the universe as well, but the awareness of the brain and the awareness of the mental content! The fact is that the material organism is here now in space and its past is actually no more, but since it is also mind it is floating above space and time, stretching back to the past and gazing into a future which is present to it in its thought; or perhaps, regardless of its changing physical state, it is pondering over some problem in mathematics and carrying on an argument the steps of which could not exist or have efficacy were they not all present and pointing to the answer to the problem.

We may clarify our notions of mind and brain by considering an example of their spheres of operation. Take the *Divina Commedia* of Dante. In its composition the poet's physical organism was active and could be described in terms of measurable movement. That movement, if it was identical with the thought, ought to be the poet's thought-content—the subject-matter, with its meaning and the thousand and one subordinate themes falling within the general structure. But there is no common measure between the movement of the matter as explained by science and the world of beauty conceived. The consciousness of the brain is something completely different from its structure, and it makes not the slightest difference to the scientific explanation of the brain what world of ideas or fancies the possessor of the brain happens to be contemplating. The biologist, when he gazes at a brain preserved in a jar of spirits, does not say, "I am quite at a loss; an esential element is missing; I have not the mental side of that brain before me; I do not know what its thought was, and so I do not know whether it is a brain." The truth is that the brain is a complete whole without any reference to the content of consciousness, and to know the content of consciousness would not make a particle of difference to the scientific definition of the brain. Further, to return to the example of Dante, still another factor would have to be included, namely the consciousness of the poet of the content of his mind. This is to put an impossible strain on the meaning of "brain"; it is as if we were to ask a glass mirror to be the image reflected in it and the awareness of the person who is gazing at his reflection. These difficulties, moreover, are increased if we consider not only Dante but his readers. The ideal of the latter is to understand and enjoy a poem of the Middle Ages written in Italian, and if we are not utter sceptics we must see that this is possible. Imagine then a thousand and one persons of different countries, costumes, habits of speech,—physically, that is, as varying as men can be from each other,—and yet all enjoying the same thought, the same beauty, the same scheme of ideas, originally conceived by Dante!

If the distinction between mind and matter be blurred, no room is left for truth or freedom. The scientific discoveries which are employed to prove that the mind is material become nothing more than a movement of the body or brain, and the knowledge of the body, of the brain, of persons and of everything, is to all intents and purposes just a certain disposition of the material constituents, whatever they be, of the brain. Change them, and my knowledge is changed; make knowledge material, and all the objects of thought, including the brain itself, become illusory phantoms. There is no criterion to distinguish the true from the imagined, phantasmagoria from facts; there is no reason whatsoever which can be given why any order should appear in thought, why facts should be consistent or follow any sequence. One might pretend indeed that they followed fatally in an order determined by material laws, so that I am bound to say what I am now saying, but even this suggestion must be ruled out, seeing that I know of those material laws only by thought, and the evidence of my thought has been discredited.

Such then is the absurdity to which the materialistic position is reduced. It should be noted that the point of the refutation is not that the mind is completely independent of the body, but that they are distinct in nature. The human being who thinks has a body as well as a mind, and strictly speaking it is the man who thinks and not his intellect. How spirit and matter can be combined in one being, and what effect this psycho-physical unity has upon the thinking, must be studied later.

Having vindicated the mind, we are now in a position to examine its claims and its beliefs. It is because of the possession of mind that man has lived such a different life from that of the animals, which do but live and go about their proper business, searching for food and propagating their species; caring not a whit for virtue or beauty, for the past of their race or some far-off event of bliss, for culture and the joy of learning the secret of nature, for the building of castles in the air, the invention of toys and new devices, or for voyaging beyond the pillars of Hercules or scaling the Himalayas.

The more one considers the work and history of the human race, its art, science, philosophy and religion, the more infinite does the gulf appear which separates it from all other orders of living beings. Yet mankind has again and again shown itself uneasy about its powers and prerogatives; doubt has followed rapidly on success; philosophies have prescribed doubt or scepticism, and, as we have already suggested, it is common nowadays to find even the first principles of reason reduced to probable assumptions. Against this tendency it is necessary to work by reasserting the native capacity of the mind to know truth, and, though it will involve some repetition, it is this claim which must now be examined.

Universal scepticism ignores the contradiction inherent in it. There can be no question of doubt or scepticism unless we have some conception of what truth is, and in the very act in which reason abdicates it declares its sovereignty. To make this matter clear, however, it is necessary to be certain of our terms. The word "truth" is used in several senses. When Pilate asked "What is truth?" he was not doubting whether he was speaking with Christ; he took for granted a number of facts like that, of which he was sure. His cynicism was due to his professed inability to answer the riddle of life; and when we ask what that means it resolves itself into the question of the end or purpose of human thought and desires, and the end of the universe at large. When a man is struck down with an illness in the prime of life, when human endeavour meets with disappointment through no fault of its own, when virtue goes unrewarded and ideals remain unfulfilled, the mind, which of its very nature seeks for causes and a meaning in what happens, turns back upon itself, questions the very possibility of knowing, and casts the shadow of its disappointment upon truth. This sense of the word "truth" is of the utmost importance, and will detain us later when the connection between knowledge and purpose, intellect and desire, will have to be settled. Clearly "truth" in this meaning presupposes a number of truths, and it is with these latter that the problem of knowledge is concerned.

D

In knowledge we are aware of an object, and in our judgment, which is the complete and proper act of knowing, we make an assertion which must be either true or false. What is the worth of this act? There are some who minimise it as far as possible. They say that it teaches us little or nothing about the nature of reality, if indeed there be such a reality. It is like the antennæ of an insect, a delicate instrument evolved to protect and develop the life of the species. A less extreme view is that the human mind, at any rate, faced with a real world, adapts what it experiences to its own structure, and so builds that world of law and order of which all of us are conscious in some fashion. No theory of this kind, however, is satisfactory, because the author of it invariably assumes more than his account allows. *He has suppressed the factor which does all the work.* Without that factor the theory would vanish away, bereft of its substance. How, for instance, can we say that our ideas are like or unlike reality, if we have no knowledge of the features of reality? And why should the propounder of a theory of this kind advance it so proudly, if he has no sure criterion for knowing whether it possesses any probability or not? Only by knowledge can we know whether there be such a thing as knowledge. If we tamper with it we had best keep silent—and even silence is consent, an admission of something. We must away, then, with any talk of mind as an instrument or a practical instinct, and cease to hoodwink ourselves into words which we belie by our very speech.

Our only course is to consult knowledge itself and see what it teaches us. It is a sovereign power, and, like the snakes in Ireland, scepticism cannot live in its kingdom. Whenever the mind is active there is some object before it, and the end of the activity is to discover the nature of that object. In this search we are certain that the thought is no impediment, but the means —the only possible means—of attaining success. It is of the nature of the mind to give us reality; it does not invent or play a game; that it leaves to the imagination. If, therefore, we meet with disappointments and difficulties, they are not to be attributed to any inherent defect in thought. It is, as I have said, irreproachable, a heavenly child, and any critic would have to borrow from its perfection to criticise it. We must look elsewhere if we want to find out what ails human thinking. Again, when it is functioning properly, it is able to recognise its own act. That is to say, when the intellect grasps the nature of its object—sees, for example, how and why two and two make four—it is also aware that it is thinking truly, and when questioned it can point to the evidence for its conviction. The justification of knowledge, therefore, is to be found within itself and its criterion is the evidence in each particular case.

In this account the word "knowledge" has been used as synonymous with certitude. To avoid confusion one or two distinctions must be drawn. By "knowledge" is meant either the thinking of an object, without specifying further whether it be certitude or opinion or deliberation or suspension of judgment; or else the type and pattern of all thinking, which gives us certitude and truth. It should be observed that all the other modes presuppose this latter and have no meaning without it, so that it is the prototype and guarantee of belief and opinion. Truth may be described as the conformity of the mind with its object. Our judgment has the quality or attribute of truth when the mind is aware that it knows something about the object as it is in its own nature. This awareness is also called certitude. Some writers distinguish further within certitude by pointing to a state of consciousness which we all experience when,

though we have not the slightest doubt that we are
right, we yet in fact are wrong. This cannot be knowledge or truth, because in knowledge we know why we
are right and why the opposite cannot possibly be
true.

We can always avoid error, though we cannot, alas,
always know what we should like to know; for this reason
some writers have made a distinction between correctness or rectitude of judgment and knowledge of reality.
It would be unwise to press this distinction, as it might
lead to what would very easily become a false separation of the two—and in fact it has been so misused by
certain philosophers. Taken with caution, however, it
succeeds in throwing light on the processes of our mind.
If we take care we can always be infallible. Others may
look on us as a dumb ox or a canny Scot who never
ventures beyond the evidence. If we are ignorant, we
can know that we are ignorant—a proof, so Socrates
thought, of a rare wisdom. If we have grounds for an
opinion, we are perfectly correct in advancing an
argument as an opinion, and even if later the facts are
found to be other than we supposed, our infallibility
is left intact, because an opinion does not claim to be
the truth. Does this mean that it is sufficient for knowledge to say that it is, or can be, immune from error?
Infallibility is a negative gift, and does not tell us whether
we know anything of the nature of reality. The answer
to this question has already been given in the statement
that opinion and belief have no meaning unless some
truth is already presupposed. We could not tell whether
our ideas were in the slightest degree like reality if we
knew nothing of the nature of reality. This ought to
give the *coup de grâce* to the sceptic and pessimist; but
they flourish, because they sigh for what they have not
and despise what they have.

For any fruitful study of the nature of knowledge and belief, we must start, therefore, with the certainty that we know something of reality. As the dove from the Ark, the thought flies out and brings back tidings of land; and this information, once gained, gives a direction and a standard with which to compare all future thought, so that it might seem that there should be no limit to our discoveries and that we should in time be able to map out the whole universe. Such a hope is sure to be disappointed, and it is to this strange infirmity which attacks human thought that we must now turn.

If it is true that knowledge as such cannot play us false, it is equally obvious that all is not well with it in practice. The mind is safe only with the very simplest statements and the most immediate experiences. When asked to show its paces it circles round the obvious, saying "I am sure of the principle of contradiction; I cannot be talking and not talking at the same time; to be means to be and is different from not to be; if I see blue I am certain that I see blue." This is a poor showing for an examination, for it comes to saying that about self-evident propositions the mind can have absolute certainty. And yet let it be said in parenthesis that, little as it is, it is something, and it ought to suffice to end once and for all the foolish talk about necessary or provisional assumptions. Self-evident truths are not assumptions; they display the power of the mind working unrestrictedly on material suited to it, and in such knowledge the mind cannot fear contradiction because it knows why the facts are as it says, and that the opposite is not only unlikely but impossible. By a curious and obstinate habit, however, we love to see an accumulation of evidence, and we feel tricked when it is not forthcoming. It is perhaps due to our natural timidity that we take refuge in numbers—I shall suggest another reason later—but it is also an act of insanity. Take, for example, some self-evident truth; if we imagine that we are dissatisfied with it, and ask for more evidence, we must, whether we know it or not, be asking for some still more evident truth to buttress it with; but that means that we are merely substituting in our minds another self-evident truth for the one that is staring us in the face—a truth, besides, which is totally unnecessary. It is as if, like the policeman in the court, we urged that the witness could not give evidence because he was dead and had pawned his clothes. If we deny that there are truths which are self-evident we implicitly declare that there is nothing which is or can be evident, for truths do not prosper by taking in each other's washing.

To return to the number of self-evident truths. It must be admitted that, though they may be more numerous than might at first be supposed, they are still regrettably few. That is the first sign of the subordinate character of the human intelligence. What we do in daily life to overcome this handicap is to argue out conclusions which necessarily follow from what is self-evident or immediately experienced, and to do the best we can with beliefs. We are stimulated to belief by our confidence in the integrity of the mind, and, as I hope to show, our confidence is not misplaced. Beliefs do not necessarily fall short of certitude. Truth nevertheless generally requires much diligence, and costs labour and toil, because, as the proverb says, it lies in a well. And since there is no reason why nature and the world of spirit should of themselves be obscure, we must explain that obscurity by the shortsightedness of our mental eye or by some film darkening our vision.

Without retracting anything already said about the infallibility and perfection of mind, we have to find some cause for the checks which human thinking invariably encounters. Since the impediment does not reside in the object or in the nature of thought, it must be sought in the agent who does the thinking. Now certain causes can be diagnosed immediately, as they are manifest in our daily experience. Our reason rarely works impartially. Even in mathematics and the most abstract sciences the scholar grows hot on the trail of the answer, and if he be not careful oversteps his premises or forces the evidence. We need not follow the psychologist into his divisions of the feeling tones and states, the emotions, sentiments and passions; it is sufficient that all are well acquainted with their influence on judgment. As always happens, some philosophers have exaggerated this influence to the extent of saying that thought is nothing but the servant of our wishes. It may in all likelihood be their ally, so that thought and desire are as brother and sister to each other; but such an alliance leaves each autonomous. In all the minor issues of life desire may play the traitor, generating prejudice instead of truth, but the proof that thought is not fatally injured is that it can correct the error and in time allow for the personal equation.

More interior to the mind itself is the abstract life it is forced to lead. The "pale cast of thought," the "bloodless categories," the "shadow-world of ideas," the "icy and dead splendour of the world of mind"— how many expressions there are which bear witness to the shortcomings of human thought! The philosopher in the legend is the wise fool spinning cobwebs while golden girls and boys dance in the sun, and the scientist is bound to confess that all the juice and quality have been squeezed out of nature to leave a dry concept, which may be, to change the metaphor, only a pointer-reading. And besides, our knowledge is gained with much difficulty, by looking before and after, by multi-plying data and experiments, by suggestions which have to wait on verification. Universal as the experience is, it is none the less surprising that learning should be a long and difficult process and involve a drudgery most distasteful to schoolboys. Humility is said to be a virtue of those who are truly learned, and there is reason for all to be humble when we consider how small still is the stock of human knowledge after so many centuries of study. Were the ideal of knowledge within our grasp we should hear no more of the sceptic and pessimist. But the opposite is the truth. Science walks like a blind man tapping out his way with a stick, and the classic literature of the world speaks again and again of frustrated hope and the evening darkness of speculation.

This characteristic of human thought calls for an explanation. Such a sense of imperfection could not exist were there not a glimpse of a better state and a perfect kind of knowledge. This ideal has been called intuition—and by that is surely meant an act of knowing which moves straight to its object and sees it as it is. More than that; the object known must become ours in the most intimate way conceivable. It must not remain a stranger at our gates; it must be known even as we are known. Now this last condition suggests an answer to the problem of human knowledge. What is to come is difficult and may best be shown by examples. The philosophers and mystics agree in singing the praises of a state which is an experience and a union. The former, however, often spoil matters by wrapping up their discovery in some impossible theory. That distinguished English thinker F. H. Bradley, for instance, maintained that the ideal lay in an experience which ended the distinction of subject and object. He hit on a truth, but ruined all by denying that this experience could be reached by intellect. Time and time again, because of a misunderstanding or undue suspicion of the intellect, a similar mistake has been made, by recourse to a mystic sense, an *élan vital*, an ineffable Nirvana, a heightened sensibility. The mystics usually have not bothered to take sides, though, owing to a bad tradition, some of the German and English, like Jeffries, have shown a preference in their language for what M. Paul Claudel has called the *anima* as opposed to the *animus*. Needless to say, our latest travellers to mystic Pisgahs, such as Mr. Middleton Murry, disdain truth save in so far as it is beauty; and even that strange genius, D. H. Lawrence, had too much affection for what he called his night-time self. Discontent with our separatist and abstract conceptual thinking is responsible for these revolts against an immortal faculty which alone can scatter clouds and light up darkness, giving insight, understanding and union. We shall never grasp even the meaning of our present knowledge unless we look upon it as prophetic of a more perfect form which it is capable of realising.

To make this clear, take any average man; he has received a certain education, and now we find him able to attend to and appreciate a number of subjects and to bring to their study a formed mind and fair judgment. Now what do we mean by this formed mind? On analysis it must mean at least this, that what he has previously learnt is present as a force or form determining his judgment, acting, as it were, as a light wherewith he sees the object to which he is attending. It has been absorbed into his character and is part of his life. We have to distinguish it carefully from what is contemplated; this belongs to the objective side of knowledge, the other to the active or subjective side; and though there may be a self-awareness accompanying all our thinking, that awareness does not get in the way of the object we are studying. But all the while we are studying, a subtle process is going on; the stuff, so to speak, of the object is being sucked in by the mind and so passing into the life of the mind—thus, for instance, one who at first knew nothing about architecture after a time becomes architecturally minded and brings to the study of some detail a stock of learning which makes itself manifest in his judgment and appreciation. This is what we mean by a wise man. The learning he has acquired has not been barren; it has grown and organised itself in his mind into a unity, so that in the presence of a new object innumerable relations occur to him, and he is able to read in it far more than the ordinary man; because his mind is unified he sees reality as a whole; he is at one with himself, and his condition is approaching that of intuition. The difference between an idiot and a wise man has been described as lying in this, that the first has one idea which devours or is dissociated from the rest of his mind, while the second has one mastering idea which embraces and systematises all the rest. The mental life of the idiot contracts, that of the wise man expands, and in this expansion the personality is more and more integrated.

This development never attains its end in this life. There is always process and always a veil of darkness hiding the nature of objects and obscuring the knowledge that one has of oneself. To take the latter first. What we learn and experience passes into our life, but not in such a way as to be fully active. We speak of habits and dispositions, and however vague our answers might be if questioned about them, we are sure the words do not make nonsense. Psychologists have written learnedly about them, but not infrequently they fail to realise the light they throw on the nature of the self and our mental life. A generation ago it was the fashion to treat the self as identical with consciousness. Now the fashion has swung to the opposite extreme; consciousness is minimised, and all the talk is of the unconscious. But the habits give us an important clue to the truth about ourselves.

We are more than our self-consciousness, but we ought in a complete state to express ourselves, all that we are and all that we know, in a supreme act of self-consciousness. At present our nature consists of a subject which is growing, and growing by acts of knowledge of other things and subjects. This outer world is reproduced in our life, and we thus become richer and at the same time more personal. But at any moment of this growth there is to be found something that is actualised and something that is in us but only in a potential state. Our nature slumbers within us, to be awakened, please God, some day. In the meantime all that we are shows itself in the *way* we think and behave, in the pose or posture or complexion of our mind, and in our habits, the way we might or could think and behave. If our nature came completely to life, burst into flower, the right term for such an act would be "self-expression." Notice that in such an act the rôle played by the various parts which we distinguish in an act of cognition—the subject thinking, the thinking, and the object thought of—would be altered. The object would not lose its colour and characteristic, but it *would* cease to be just an object cut off from the act of thinking, a *pensiero pensato*, to use Gentile's phrase, a corpse hanging on the gallows of the mind. Instead of being a limit to our thought the object would be fused with the experience and have the right to be called the self-expression of the subject. The lover in the Persian tale, when asked who he was, replied "It is thou!"

In complete knowledge the mind is absorbed in what is near and dear to it, and this absorption is its own life expressed and enjoyed. Introspection is no longer needed, because in the realisation of all things we ourselves have also become fully alive. When an actor or an artist is engaged upon his work, self-consciousness acts as a hindrance; yet perfect acting and perfect art are as truly self-expression as the expression of the part played; which shows that ultimately the two fuse. The flame shows its force and its brightness in consuming its object; were that object to stamp the flame with its own colour and the flame to live consuming but not destroying, we should have something like an adequate picture of the life of the mind at its highest. Activity, that is, without anything left over, everything turned into live experience or expression, nothing in my thought which is not wholly mine, as much mine as the "I" in my thinking— this is the epiphany of the soul's life, when all within becomes light, and there is no longer the shadow of division between the subject and the object, the "I" and the "me," the thinker and his thought. The soul sees itself in the very seeing, and all else which its nature comprehends in the one saturating exhaustive experience. Gone now are those half-lights, the chequered glimpses of our nature seen through the foliage of sense, those projections of the self, the mists which lie around the objects of our thought, making them remote and vague. The nature of the self, like the bow of Ulysses sings at the touch of the master, and in that singing are to be heard the forms of all known things re-echoing.

Recent German philosophy has employed a word, *Erlebnis*, that will serve excellently to bring out the characteristic of thought which I have tried to explain in the preceding paragraphs. Croce's theory of expression, which consists in saying that the spirit creates, and beholds what it creates in one individual æsthetic experience, also bears a resemblance to the truth, but the interesting analysis he makes is spoilt by the intolerable philosophic setting which he gives to it. In his emphasis on the close connection between the form or design of the beautiful object and the formation or expression of it by the onlooker, he recalls Gerard Hopkins's remark: "But as air, melody, is what strikes me most of all in music and design in painting, so design, pattern, or what I am in the habit of calling *inscape*, is what I above all aim at in poetry." Croce provides no natural form, and here he is fundamentally in error; but granted this natural form, the part of the artist is to express it in terms of the medium he is using, and by a form seen and experienced. So too with thought; our mind is held fascinated by the object, and gives itself to it unconditionally. This is the way we gain information. But this surrender is, by the mysterious law of our nature, a victory; by this death we live. The mind, while losing itself in its object, is all the while actively converting itself to the likeness of it, by the strange alchemy of thought assimilating this new thing; and behold, at the end there lives in the mind a thought expressed or generated, a piece of autobiography or correspondence with itself. In knowledge, therefore, we communicate with a world which is not ourselves, and at the same time, make and discover our own history. In human knowledge at the present moment there is incompleteness, whether we look without or within; in perfect human knowledge there will be no more mysteries within, and what is without will shine in the light of the soul's lamp, so far as that light can comprehend it. But all human thought, even the highest, has its horizons; there are realms which it cannot encompass and mirror in its nature, be it the most candid and clear. God alone measures reality by what He is, and in His essence sees all things vividly or faintly resembling His truth.

Enough now has been said to show why human thought is open to criticism, and also why we should not turn in discontent to some other strange power to relieve the situation. There is no salvation save in truth, and the royal road of truth is by the mind. God generates the Word which is Himself, one in substance, and the truth of all things. We, when we reach our consummation, shall conceive a word one with our nature and fit to tell the truth about all that is proportioned to the truth in us. In the meantime we conceive a thought, and are glad if, like a Cook's guide, it can show us something of the world and help us on our journeying. Impatient at the stiffness and slow rambling of our guide, we are tempted to choose other showmen— the instincts, or the heart. The latter is sometimes right, though it is blind; the former ought to have reason always in tutorial attendance. When these two boast of their discoveries, they have not been, as they say, alone. By themselves they tend to wander off the track; yet they are quite capable of enticing people to follow them, because many forget or do not notice that they are acting on false pretensions.

To many this may sound hard doctrine; they will say that there are many occupations in life which at first sight do not seem to require much book-learning or clerical training. And if reason were what modern educational ideals suppose, this objection would have force. By an unfortunate habit we have come to accept a false distinction between thinking and doing or making; the thinking, we are told, gets us nowhere; the way to succeed is to bank on something else than the intellect. So, possessed by some demon of folly, men rush ahead and fall down the precipice, and those who witness the spectacle shake their heads and say that the fault is due to ignorance, and that the only way to cure it is by more and more education. The result is, as the author of *Fantasia of the Unconscious* has written, that "our poor little plants of children are put into horrible forcing-beds, called schools, and the young idea is there forced to shoot. It shoots, poor thing, like a potato in a warm cellar. One mass of pallid, sickly ideas and ideals. And no root, no life. The ideas shoot, hard enough, in our sad offspring, but they shoot at the expense of life itself. Never was such a mistake. Mental consciousness is a purely individual affair. Some men are born to be highly and delicately conscious. But for the vast majority, much mental consciousness is simply a catastrophe, a blight." The effect of universal education may be exaggerated in this quotation, as is certainly the attack on ideas, but the indignation is surely not groundless. We have forgotten the wisdom of the Greeks, who were well aware that the mind is not confined to the purely theoretical, but is active also in the sphere of conduct and art. Mind is characteristic of the human being, and it is not the mind which thinks but man. Now man has a body as well as a mind, and his normal behaviour should involve both. When the two work harmoniously together, obviously the mind is developing and as it ought to develop. "Art is science incarnate," and the mind of children, as of most men, lives far more in the concrete than in the abstract. But by a vicious policy, based on a false division, the work of the hands is neglected, and intelligence is defined in terms of science and the reading of books. The product of this education has no means of self-expression; he has no means of digesting the vast amount of information, of translating it by a personal art, and so he turns into an introvert or lets the swelling number of ideas burst into some bigotry or fanaticism. It is not "Alas! poor Yorick," but "Alas! poor Hamlet." The failure to comprehend the close partnership between handiwork and thought has produced an intellectual proletariat which is sub-human.

> "I have loved colours and not flowers:
>   Their motion, not the swallows' wings,
> And wasted more than half my hours
>   Without the comradeship of things."

And there is not much to choose between this dilettante and the social idealists and the readers of the Sunday newspapers; they are all the fruit of a tree without roots.

These comments on our modern education are not really a digression; they bring us to the conclusions which the analysis of truth has suggested. The majority of men were never meant to be scholars and to over-strain their heads with meditation on philosophy. They would do much better to meditate upon a Person and, having committed their ways to His providence, to be shrewd and wide-awake and go about their lawful occasions. We were always intended to live under authority, and, as we shall see, we cannot escape altogether what is a fundamental law of human life. And this is no such misfortune, as is sometimes supposed. Were the practical life deprived of all contact with the intellectual, it would indeed be in evil plight, but, as we have seen, this is not the case; to suppose that it is is precisely that modern error which has made such havoc of our education. It may well be, then, that a good practical life will count for much in the search for truth, that if the direction of the march be right a study of all the milestones on the way may not be necessary for all. More than this, as man is in search of his own soul, of truth and happiness, we should expect that even in his most disinterested studies, in the life of thought itself, desire will have its say. That this often happens no one can gainsay. Desire has a trick of racing ahead, and like a child calls on its elder brother, the mind, to follow it. It is folly at times to listen to this cry, and desire should never be allowed to run out of sight, but if there is an answering call in the blood, if all that is best in one leaps to respond, then it is the purest wisdom to go forward, because, as St. Augustine said, there is an inclination deep down within us which is the love of God: "We ascend Thy ways that be in our heart and sing a song of degrees."

The presence of this desire is to be seen in the lives of those whom all would admit to be good men; it can be seen too in conscience and duty. Here desire is the fuel of knowledge. We must not, however, exaggerate its influence so far as to make it a substitute for reason. There are judgments we pass which are without any explicit desire. The mind confronted with certain evidence cannot hesitate. We have dealt with this aspect of human knowledge already, and there is not a jot or tittle of this old law that should be changed. It is the plea of Modernism that the heart's needs and desires can escape the sanction of fact and be treated as of high station and worth, though cold reason look askance. Modernism has lost much of its attraction since the coming of psycho-analysis. If the latter be, as some claim, a philosophy of life and more than a method, then it is an insidious foe not only to Modernism, but to all systems as well that base their faith on reason. Hence, before entering upon a discusssion of faith and belief, it will be necessary to show that the discoveries of psycho-analysis have not invalidated the claims of reason.

E

The position that we have reached so far is that the mind carries with it its own credentials of truth. The truth we possess is, however, but a passable and commonplace version of that we long to have; if we seek the reason for this, it must lie in the fact that our nature is not in its full vigour, a living act illuminating indivisibly what is within and what is without. In all our thought and action we can detect this *Erlebnis*, this striving through friction and effort to state ourselves and make our statement of the meaning of the universe. "Think you that wisdom is other than truth, in which the supreme good is beheld and possessed?" Beheld and possessed: both these notions run together, and both must be mentioned if we are to understand the consummation of knowledge and the life of the soul. We cannot be put off with any counterfeits of reality, we must see things as they are, and that reality must also be our good, our refreshment and our peace. In philosophy and science we proceed in order that we may see and we reject as far as possible any interference with the pure light of reason. In belief and faith reason is still active, but in degrees varying according to the subject-matter we permit the help of other factors, such as desire. Never, however, can these other factors make up completely for the absence of the clear and compelling evidence of reason, with one exception—supernatural faith. In this one case the reason is not so determined as to lose its liberty, yet its certainty is absolute. How this can be we must try to show in the succeeding chapters.

CHAPTER III

BELIEF

MAN has a prejudice against himself; anything which is a product of his mind seems to him to be unreal or comparatively insignificant.

SANTAYANA.

He who Doubts from what he sees
Will ne'er Believe, do what you Please.
If the Sun and Moon should doubt
They'd immediately Go out.

BLAKE: *Auguries of Innocence*.

CHAPTER III

BELIEF

IN the preceding chapter I have attempted to establish the ground of belief. Without such a background there is little use in the discussion, for belief must have an assured position from which to advance. There may indeed be gardens of the Hesperides, fair islands beyond the pillars of Hercules, promised lands which lie beyond the confines of our known world, but it is vain to search for them if our ships and home and all else are but the phantoms of our imagination, and our very imagination a monstrous birth of lies.

Belief, as already explained, carries us beyond the obvious in experience and the self-evident in propositions. This might seem at first sight to be a misfortune, but actually it is not. There is very little that we can know with the certainty of absolute proof; there are many things we can know on an evidence which it is silly to doubt. The lawyer examining documents has to take for granted that the writing is that of certain persons, though they are not present; even if they are present there is room for error, but the error is in its likelihood so infinitesimal that he pays no attention to it. Now beyond the certainty qualified by evidence that is the property of lawyers and scientists and antiquarians, and all that tribe which perforce or by taste has recourse to dry-as-dust methods, there is the world of everyday conversation with its news and its good stories, the world, too, of risk and trust and speculation and daring. We should travel no distance if we had to examine every-thing under a microscope and view with suspicion all testimony till it had been proved up to the hilt or by our own experience.

It is enough that we should have some truths which are constant and undeniable, and the power to learn other truths or draw near to them, using the mind as a measuring-rod with which to judge their relative near-ness or farness from the ideal that the mind craves. All that falls short of demonstrable certainty has been included under the word "belief," and it will be readily seen that the various states of mind which are thus classified have no relation with one another save in their reference to truth. Doubt, for instance, means that something we thought to be true is now seen to rest on insufficient evidence, or that in our search for knowledge we realise that the evidence before us holds us up. If, however, there is some evidence pointing in one direc-tion which is not contradicted by other facts, our state of mind inclines to an opinion; and as the evidence grows in strength we reach to probability. Let it be repeated, as of some importance, that there is nothing whatsoever common to these different states of mind except their relation to the constant, truth or certainty—a state, therefore, which must be already understood. Another misunderstanding, which is all too prevalent, lies in the assumption that probabilities if multiplied can make a sum equal to truth. Like the scholar who wrote an answer to as many questions as he could to make up for the defect that each answer was only third-class, the man with nothing but probable opinions will never have anything but probabilities, though he swell them to infinity. Either the man in the dock forged the cheque or he did not. There is no probability in facts or events; they are or they are not, and the probability in my mind or yours has nothing to do with the fact. When we speak of "probable" events we are using an expression which all readily understand; but it is incorrect. The word "probable" belongs to the state of mind of the man who is thinking of those events; if justified, it shows what he has a right to think; but the way he happens to think when he does not know the reality has nothing to do with the reality. What he is thinking might turn out in the end to be quite untrue, while a man who knew next to nothing and yet ventured an opinion might by chance have hit on the truth. The truth when discovered removes from the picture all the opinions and the probabilities; they are of no more service, as the state of mind is completely changed.

Belief, therefore, is used to cover a large number of different states of mind, which have this single common feature, that they fall short of demonstrable certainty. I do not say that this conventional and generally accepted statement is a wholly satisfactory description; indeed part of the aim of this book is to correct it, and I have already supplemented it with another use of the word "belief" which turns on a distinction of the immediately felt and experienced and the invisible. By an odd inversion of the word belief, the much-abused man in the street is apt to say that seeing is believing. This prejudice—for after all it is nothing more—has been supported by some well-known systems of philosophy. They have lent their aid to propagate the idea that sensation is the only form of experience in which we can have certainty. Consequently the intangible, the invisible, all in fact that belongs to the realm of spirit, may be an object of faith, but it in no wise falls within truth. This, when taken literally, is clearly nonsense, for the simple reason that in every sensible experience there is also some knowledge of what is not sensation. There is at least an awareness of the attitude of our own mind, and also that the sensation is of something which may not always be present. No doubt our knowledge of the immaterial and the invisible lacks the warm, palpitating reality of what we immediately experience when in contact with the sensible, but this coldness and distance are no disproof of the certainty of their existence. Poor folk that we are, we like to have our logic touched by a burning coal, but that implies a defect in our humanity, not in our intellect. Hence, if, in order to contrast direct experience with knowledge of the invisible, we use the word "belief," for the latter we must be careful not to underrate this belief, and reckon it necessarily uncertain.

After these general remarks about belief we now come to that form of belief which has so much overshadowed the others that it has taken the name as its own property. This form goes also by the name of faith, and on analysis seems to mean a state of mind, usually formed on testimony, which plays the rôle of absolute certainty, though it cannot readily present its credentials for so acting. We may strongly believe that a friend of ours is not the kind of man to rob a bank or murder his father, but if asked for proof of our belief we have very little to give. There are innumerable facts of history which we believe, though we are quite hazy in our knowledge of the periods in question and the authorities for our statements. More than this—a countless number of facts that we take for granted in everyday life rests on the testimony of others. It would seem absurd to counsel others to be cautious in accepting them, and yet we could be quickly put to shame if we were asked to justify our confidence.

Men are not ruled entirely by logic; they divide themselves up into parties and factions; they take part in

BELIEF   73

movements, political, social and religious, and their
actions are governed by a kind of belief that we may
call "interest," which finds a place, not only in the large
canvas of history, but, in the life of the individual also.
Many interests mean little more than an attraction to
something; some persons love colours and so show an
interest in natural scenery and one aspect of painting;
other are interested in collections of various kinds.
But often enough, when the subject permits of it, such
interest breeds another kind of liking. For instance,
our interest in our fellow countrymen may lead to a
great belief in their future or lead us to enlist in some
social crusade for their betterment. In an interest of
this kind our desire blends with our understanding, and
so our belief in our cause or crusade will be the product
of the two.

Very many beliefs are intimately bound up with
desire, and are thus to be distinguished from those
attitudes of mind which are purely intellectual. The
latter are notional. But it must not be thought that
because the former, to borrow a distinction of Newman,
are real, the intrusion of desire is necessarily a hindrance
to truth. The common verdict of mankind is strongly of
the opposite opinion. There have been many jests made
at the expense of the don, who is supposed to have
theoretical knowledge and no living interest. Ridicule
has been poured on Kant because he seldom varied
the routine of a musty old scholar and could be quite
put out when a student cut off the coat-button at which
in his lectures Kant was accustomed to gaze. There was
something inhuman in the talk of a Brougham or a
Coleridge, something silly in the over-ponderous judgments of a Herbert Spencer. Wives are apt to be disappointed when love is treated as a theorem, and children seldom conform to the demands or hopes of a

Pilgrim's Script. The old tag, "Learning comes, but wisdom lingers," is a variant on the same theme, and there can be little doubt that to the end of time the generality of mankind will prefer sympathy and understanding to erudition.

Nor is the reason of this far to seek. The awareness of the existence of something does not mean that we shall be able to appreciate its worth. The world is full of varied beauty and excellence, star differing from star. It takes time and trouble to discover this many-splendoured thing. Many are content to remain admiring their own perfections, and when they are drawn outside themselves they are sometimes so swept away by the object on which they set their heart that they are oblivious of all else. Hence it is that some have sought a short cut to complete understanding by giving rein to their loves, persuaded that love will meet with perfect knowledge at the end. Whether this is true we are not yet in a position to decide. It sounds more dangerous than the plan of those who set their heart on the primal love and trust that in its light the truth of all else will be perceived. But before we discuss this there is a formidable enemy lying in the path, who must be removed if belief of this kind is to have any value at all. In the discussion of truth the main obstacle was, as we saw, a doubt of the very existence and power of mind. If mind be of the stuff of matter, or so closely interwoven with the body as to be nothing else than an expression of it, then there is an end of truth, and the whole building of science and philosophy comes tumbling down. Now we have a more insidious foe—a foe, too, who is more within than without. He says that of course there is a life that is other than the physical, a life that is the source of all our activities and has a mighty influence on our bodily states. The world has always recognised this, and the world has so far been right. But with the development of knowledge we have at last reached a stage in which we can give a true account of this psychic life and even state it scientifically. The clue to the truth is the recognition of the all-importance of desire. Whereas before it was thought that the combination of thought and desire left both the activities autonomous, now investigation has proved that desire is not only an active agent but the sole efficacious agent; where thought was supposed to act calmly and disinterestedly we now know that desire was at work in subterranean ways. What happens on the threshold of the mind is not the whole story; there is another life which goes on behind the scenes, and it is this life which is responsible for what happens to us consciously.

This is the doctrine of many psycho-analysts. I do not say method but doctrine, and to be quite fair to the general body of psychoanalysts, let us say doctrine of a certain school. The method it employs does not concern us, and it ill becomes those who allow themselves to be treated for mental troubles by physical remedies to quarrel with doctors who suggest that the cure may lie in mental treatment. We are far too ignorant of the details of the relation of the soul with the body, the psychical with the physical, to refuse any new methods that are credited with successes. But, as so often happens, a hypothesis which has nothing except a provisional and practical value has been erected into a philosophy. It is this philosophy which we must examine, not in its entirety but so far as it bears on the problem of belief. The psycho-analyst tends to regard what he calls the Unconscious as of more importance than the conscious. The unconscious is the Stock Exchange, and the conscious is little more than the newspaper report of its proceedings, with the inner history of what has happened left out. The life of the mind is thought of in terms very similar to that of the energy of the body, only it is psychical energy. This, it must be allowed, may be a useful image, but it should be remembered that it is nevertheless little more than a metaphor. Quite legitimately psychologists have followed the lead of physical science and assumed hypotheses which have a methodological value.

The dangers of the hypothesis adopted by the new psychology are many. Amongst them may be mentioned, first, that the mind is less adapted to comparisons than any other form of reality; second, in speaking of a psychical life which is real though not conscious, we are all the time drawn to think of it as conscious. Hence the habit of some theorists of inventing a region called the unconscious in which everything happens as if it were conscious; there are movements and events that we could not conceive of intelligibly without reading into them conscious acts. The instincts are troubled at being frustrated; they become ingenious in their attempts to get past a censor; this censor is very much on the *qui vive*, and so forth. We listen to all this and swallow it without realising that by ingrained habit we have been introducing the forbidden consciousness into our image of the drama. The psychologist has been doing the same, committing the very sin of transference against which in his writings he is for ever warning us. This personification or mythology is one of the main faults of modern psychology.

Thirdly, there is a similar danger in substantiating and materialising what we have to recognise as just not substance. Both consciousness and unconsciousness are made into subjects, and the various energies are thought of as tides or clusters of forces which act with a power of their own. Much of this is a world of make-believe,

especially where it is a question of sensation and knowledge. In knowledge ideas are treated as if they were
like rabbits in the burrow of the mind or self. It would
be inflicting too great a penalty on the reader to embark
on an analysis of what we meant by ideas, but a little
consideration will show that ideas exist only as thought
of; they have no separate existence, no manner of
behaving of their own. A very bad tradition, derived
from Hume, is responsible for the confusion of ideas
with images, for long chapters in books of psychology
explaining the growth of something which does not exist,
and for the latent or explicit assumption that we start
inside ourselves, have a remarkable history and make a
guess that there is an external world into which we can
project our fancies and sensations. The truth is that we
start with an external world, that we know it, and that
these psychologists raise the drawbridge of the self
only after having crossed that bridge an infinite number
of times to store the citadel with knowledge about
itself.

Such, then, are some of the dangers. Now in this
modern psychology the soul is thought to consist of
psychic energy seeking self-satisfaction. To some this
energy is one, to others it is multiple. In the first case
it is the *libido*, and all the variations we are aware of
must be traced back to one source; in the second there
are many primary instincts, and life at its best consists
of the expression of these in a harmonious and systematised union. Just as the welfare of the body depends
on the interplay, the equilibrium of its various parts, so
the health of the psyche can be defined in terms of the
proper functioning and balance of the principal impulses.
Much of the life of these instincts is carried on below
the level of consciousness; in fact Freud declares that
"those which are conscious are merely isolated acts and

parts of the whole psychic entity." All that we do and think and desire is therefore the outcome of these unconscious impulses. The attempts that we make to explain our conduct are nothing but "rationalisations," excuses which are untrue and valueless. The fundamental desires rule the day; when thwarted they form complexes, dammed-up streams seeking an outlet, causing pestilence within and upsetting the balance of forces.

If this explanation were the last word on the nature of the self, clearly there would be an end of discussion of truth and its relation to belief. It is therefore essential to clear the way for truth before turning to find out whether this new psychology has any light to throw on the nature of belief. The question turns on whether reason is so subordinate to unconscious impulse as to be always a rationalisation. By rationalisation is meant, in this psychology, an explanation or excuse offered for one's actions which is different from the true cause. This very definition gives an answer to our question. If we can know the true cause, and if there is a distinction to be drawn between the true cause and the rationalisation, it must follow that we can know the truth. This knowing the truth can have nothing to do with the impulse, as it is itself the knowledge of what the impulse is and of its relation to what we are saying—unless indeed we say that there is an impulse to know what is true. To speak of an impulse to know and know truly does not, however, get us any further; it can only reinforce the fact that knowledge is not affected by anything else than knowledge and truth. The new psychologist tells us that all our conduct is governed by the movement of the impulses to self-satisfaction. If reason were nothing but a means in the process, then truth would have to be defined by the satisfaction of the instinct, and this could easily be shown to lead to the denial of truth altogether. If an escape is made from this by adding that there is a satisfaction in knowing the truth, the fact can well be admitted; but the admission makes truth and not satisfaction primary. We cannot say that for the sake of satisfaction twelve times twelve will make one hundred and forty-six; we are compelled by the evidence to say that it makes one hundred and forty-four. To rely on a theory of instinctive satisfaction in the matter of knowledge is to play with ambiguities. Let us grant that knowledge gives satisfaction; let us grant even that it gives us the supreme satisfaction, because it is the end of our nature to have knowledge and so possess truth; but it is quite a different kind of satis-faction from that afforded by the instincts. These latter are private and selfish; lust and the appetite for food and the desire for domination are conditioned by nothing save their own fulfilment. For knowledge it is the reverse; the intellect is the slave of truth; it desires to enjoy external objects as they are in themselves, and to do so it must sacrifice all self-seeking, abide patiently by the evidence and so learn the unvarnished truth about the nature of the external object.

The power of the mind to judge and to judge the nature of its own act makes it independent of the conscious or unconscious forces. The new psychologists themselves admit this in fact; they are bent on dis-covering the true working of the human psyche, and in their researches they are relying on the intellect and in their conclusions they are, as they think, judging truly. Were their own theory entirely true their judg-ment would have itself to be a rationalisation, and so they would have cut off the branch on which they are sitting.

The question of knowledge, therefore, remains un-affected by the findings of the new psychology. If there be rationalisations, there must be reason, as otherwise we should not be able to tell the difference between excuses for conduct and the real motive. If there be distortions there must be a right order dimly or clearly perceived; if baleful complexes are produced by fears and the failure to face reality, there must be a reality to which we can adapt ourselves. It may be true that in a far greater majority of cases than was usually assumed men are duped by subconscious desires, that they assign wrong reasons for what they are doing, and that they project their states of mind and desires into external objects and ideals. There are many apparent instances of this projection, when hope becomes certainty and desire a faith in the objective existence of some character or quality or ideal. The lover sometimes finds the beloved with all the beautiful qualities he adores; a fond mother is inclined to turn geese into swans; and in revivalist religious bodies emotion tends to do duty for truth. Such examples, however, do not justify the psychologist in averring that our judgments of existence and value are always due to projection. This fallacy has its origin in the false assumption already criticised, that we begin from within and project our feelings and our ideas into an unknown world external to us. Thus it is said that we project into external objects the idea of causality in some sense experienced within us, and endow others with life and human characteristics. Apart from the fact that this is a completely wrong analysis of the nature of thought, there is no explanation offered why we choose particular objects and not others as caused or living or personal. There must be something in a cat or a fly which leads us by projection to fancy it as living in preference to a table or a fire. Even if we take an example more favourable to the theory of projection, say the idea that God is liable to anger, it can be argued

that the mistake, if it be a mistake, consists not so much
in projection as in the failure to realise that not all
beings possessing personality have necessarily the
emotion of anger. The same is true of most of the cases
of projection; an object is presupposed and we refer to
it what it does not deserve. We blame the lover for his
ecstasies; but—who knows?—he may see more than we
do with our jaundiced eyes. Hate and love are passions
which are blind, not to the object on which they are
intent, but to all else that might modify their impression of it. Hence if the object were beauty itself, our
neglect of all else would not matter, and so it may be
that the contemplative and mystic are right when they
seek God alone and claim to find a hundredfold.

Summarily, then, the new psychology has nothing to
teach about the nature of truth, and the act of knowledge and its content are bound to escape its meshes.
With an ill-judged enthusiasm many of this school have
ignored this fact, and by venturing beyond their subject-
matter have muddied the waters. Psychology does not
touch the question of knowledge in its strict sense, and
only indirectly affects the problem of belief. It has for
its task to investigate the station of the self, marking out
the various termini, the platforms, the rails and signals,
the engines and coaches; it will also have something to
say of the traffic; but about the source of the goods and
the destination it must be silent. Assuming an external
world, psychologists can show, by looking within, the
effect produced, according as feeling, thought, or desire
play their respective parts. Their concern is with the
health of the psychical self, and in taking this as their
criterion they again assume certain distinctions of better
and worse which they think they understand and take
for granted that others will understand. The full
explanation of words like "good" and "reality" and

F

"development" and "error" and "wrong" belongs to other branches of philosophy. Their criterion, as I have said, is health or equilibrium, the balance of the various instincts and activities in the system of the self. Hence for their purposes they ignore one side, and that the most important side of the life of man, and treat notions like "truth" and "goodness" only so far as they relate to the life of the human self. Just as in biology a poison might in certain circumstances be to the benefit of an ailing body, so too from their point of view a lie might appear to benefit the mental health, or the release of the libido might free a psychical congestion. The sacrifice of youth and promise by, say, a Julian Grenfell or Rupert Brooke, for the sake of duty would be bad in the eyes of a psychologist, and there could be little meaning in the Gospel text of cutting off one's hand if it scandalise, and going maimed into Heaven.

It is possible, therefore, to exaggerate the conflict between the moral order and truth as perceived by the mind and the ideal of the new psychology. There are indeed extremists in the latter camp, but as pseudo-philosophers they can be left out of account. It could, I think, be shown by an inspection of examples that the two ideals corresponded, and that in the long run they were bound to converge. This is the reason why psychology can serve as a very useful handmaid to a theory of morality and belief. The broad unalterable outlines given to us by knowledge can be filled in by a study of character, habits and instincts, and the discovery of approximate laws governing psycho-physical actions and everything else in the human constitution that is in any way determined. We may go further and argue to the validity of experience by its effect on us. From all times this has been done with precautions. Peace of soul, for example, is taken as a test of the value

of certain experiences, and one of the ways of distinguishing between incipient madness and exaltation
of the soul, between false and true mysticism, is to watch
the effect upon the personality. Where there is impoverishment and disintegration, there we can safely conclude
that illusion and falsehood are present; and *vice versa*.
The fruits, too, of psychological research go to confirm
the ancient doctrine of the dependence of spiritual
insight on the spiritual condition of the soul. This is a
doctrine of profound significance, the best expression of
which is to be found perhaps in St. Augustine: "If you
love the earth you will be a clod; if you love God you will
become divine." The intellect is the power to see things
as they are and to possess them, but it is the man who
judges, and in all judgments of worth he is exhibiting
himself and interpreting through the light or darkness
of his own character. The mind is like water that seeks
its own level; it keeps to the measure of its desires, fixes
its gaze on what is connatural to it, and is at home there.
If the desires are evil it returns to its own vomit, if they
are noble in the purity of its heart it sees God. This
doctrine, to which I will return again as essential to a
proper understanding of belief, is one of the most sure
lessons to be drawn from the new psychology, and when
it speaks of the influence of the unconscious on our
conscious decisions and judgments, it is fair to explain
this in the manner just mentioned.

Before proceeding, however, there are other points in
the new psychology which need explanation. Though
we take it as proved that the evidence it offers cannot
affect the sovereign rights of reason, this evidence seems
to offer a disturbing testimony against the integrity
of beliefs. Let us begin by laying down what a sane
philosophy has to say about the relation of desire and
reason, independently of what has been said by recent

schools of psychologists. The mind has two chief spheres in which it can operate, the theoretical and the practical. The theoretical has nothing to do with the direction to carry out or stop some action. The mind wishes to know or to state some fact of knowledge, and this is its sole purpose. In the pursuit of metaphysics or mathematics or ancient history I am anxious to learn the truth, and if, for instance, after having read over many times a chapter from Whitehead's *Science and the Modern World* I think I follow its general meaning, then I have achieved the end which I set out to attain. The same could be said of the study of the recent theories in physics, and, for the matter of that, of elementary mathematics. Opposed to theoretical knowledge is the judgment we make when some action has to be taken; here we are generally, if not always, confronted with alternative courses, and in the decision we rule out all the alternatives in favour of one. This practical decision is not vague or general, nor a formula or statement of a principle; it is necessarily concerned with a definite, particular action. In this it shows itself distinct from another type of judgment, which might be called juridical. A judge in court is there to deliver a practical judgment. On another occasion after dinner he might be asked for an expert opinion on a point of law. The interest in this case is theoretical, even though the subject-matter bears on human action, that is to say, on what ought to be done. To keep these two kinds of judgment distinct, it is well to have different names for them, to call the theoretical a juridical judgment and the other a practical judgment.

This being the sphere of the intellect, the question now arises what place desire has in its operations. From the time of Aristotle onwards it has been customary to make a distinction between voluntary and free action.

In English there is no hard and fast terminology for
these two types; indeed, our language has tended to
separate the intimate connection between will and
desire, so stubbornly upheld in the French *volonté* and
vouloir and the Latin *voluntas* and *velle*. The easiest way
is to begin with the word "involuntary," which suggests
an act done without intention, a gesture or slip of the
tongue or *faux pas*. A *voluntary* act is one done by the
will with a knowledge of the end. As we say, "You
knew what you were doing; you knew that those words
were offensive to X and you uttered them." Wish or
will and thought have gone together to produce the act.
Nevertheless they are not sufficient of themselves to
make it necessarily a free act. A father on seeing his
child drowning might leap into the water to save it,
and all the same not be free. A lover may sing the
praises of his beloved, drawn irresistibly by what he
conceives to be her beauty; he knows what he is doing,
he wants to do what he is doing, but he also cannot
help himself. For an act to be free the agent must be
conscious, at the very moment of willing, that he could
act otherwise. This means that the object does not
attract him irresistibly, that it does not contain all that
he could possibly desire. If it did then no other object
could possibly compare with it; he could have no
grounds for choice. Whenever he finds himself faced with
alternatives, drawn one way and another, it is a sure
sign that neither could give him his heart's content.
He can stand off and judge the insufficiency of both
alternatives as they appear to him, and by this judgment
he declares that his choice will be a rational act, which-
ever side he chooses, and that his choice is free. From
this it can be seen that freedom of choice lies between
two extremes which at first sight resemble each other.
A monomaniac having but one idea in his head loses

his freedom and is like a donkey looking at a carrot. Dante also exults in his loss of free will when his "mind was smitten by a bright beam, which contained the object of its desire." But that man is no idiot whose desires and will are "guided, like a wheel revolving uniformly, by the Love which moves the sun and other stars."

Free will may be exercised in two different ways. We may refuse or consent to attend to some agenda— this may be called freedom of attention or election— and we can pick and choose when the agenda are put before us. In the first case we are like the head of a firm who will not attend to business, or the child who will not listen to the various suggestions for a holiday. In the second case, which is freedom of choice or selection, we have two definite and positive alternatives before us, such as a game of golf and work at our desk. At certain times of our lives we fall back on the freedom of attention because we know or fear that if we yield we shall have no opportunity of exercising our freedom when we are faced with the facts. A fanatic or bigot does not want to hear the arguments on the other side. But supposing that he is persuaded to listen, what will be the relation of his desire to the evidence? That is the question. If we take experience, it does seem undeniable that certainty and desire have much to say to one another; nevertheless are we not bound to maintain that judgment must rest with the intellect alone and that it is essential to get rid of prejudices and the personal equation?

No solution to this question can be given unless the distinction between the voluntary and free act, already given, be kept in mind. There are some modern writers who are so obsessed with the notion of liberty that they make it the be-all and the end-all of human activities.

This is quite preposterous. Not content with teaching the malignant doctrine that education has for its end liberty of thought, they set originality and so-called personal beliefs above truth. They make a double mistake. Truth cannot play second fiddle and liberty is the servant of wisdom and should finally be absorbed in the love of it. The second error is in imagining that pure liberty exists. To withhold wise influence and direction is only to leave the child a prey to other influences. Nobody is immune from influence and suggestion, so that to sweep and clear the room of the soul means in fact to leave the door open to quacks and cheats and sophists. The truth of the matter is that the end of learning is knowledge, and the mind is uneasy until it attains certainty. Now in certainty it is the evidence confronting the mind which tells the reason that its work is done and gives it peace. And in such a condition, when for instance the scientist with a lightening of the heart sees the conclusion shining forth from the evidence or the premisses, there would seem to be no room, as there is no need, for freedom. The conclusions of the speculative reason in the domains of natural science and philosophy are, therefore, incompatible with freedom.

But—and this is often forgotten—this veto on liberty does not necessarily extend to will and desire. It is part of our misfortune that we cannot help making hard and fast divisions, where reality is far more delicately adjusted. We speak of thought and desire as though they were neighbours gazing at each other over their garden walls. These two conspirators are, however, far more intimately associated, and we have only to emancipate ourselves from our arithmetical imagination to see that they are both distinct and inseparable. Their relations are very intricate and at times baffling, but this at least should be clear, that there is a certain happiness in thinking. The mind, like every other activity of ours, is a function with a definite object, namely to know the nature of reality. Study is a pursuit, whether it be of a crossword puzzle, a problem in chess or mathematics, the character of Mary Queen of Scots, or unemployment. We grow cross when we get stuck, and merry as the end comes in sight. This pleasure is the sign of the presence of desire, and therefore in thinking as in every other activity desire must be active. Moreover, when a human being is active, no matter whether it be in reasoning or playing tennis or walking, he is aware of this activity as his own, and he derives a sense of pleasure from doing well. This suggests that there is something in him which is bent on furthering what is to his own good, a will of which he is conscious when it is successful, as we might imagine a British Supermarine aeroplane to take pleasure in the perfection of its movement, were it conscious.

But this account, while it proves the presence of desire, does not make precise the relation of it with the intellect. The natural answer to this is that the intellect precedes and starts desire. When a friend wishes to excite our interest in some plan or patent, he has first to tell us what it is, and if anyone sees a general excitement he asks what it is all about. All this comes to is the sufficiently obvious truth that men in their senses know what they are doing and that knowledge precedes desire. In other words knowledge gives us the content of experience, and the character of that content excites liking or dislike, fear or love, hate or indifference. There are indeed apparent exceptions to this law, as when we feel fear and are ignorant of the cause, and there is the well-known theory that behaviour creates the appropriate conception. For the moment, however, let us rest with the general law supported by our normal experience, that desire follows knowledge. This sequence must not be thought of as necessarily one of time (as we have already seen the two are generally concomitant); nor again is it a sequence of causality, if we mean by that efficient causality. The knowledge that there is a stream of pure water near by is not the cause of our desire to drink in it; all that knowledge does is to provide our appetite with an object which will satisfy its cravings. And herein we perceive the marvellous nature of the mind. In creatures without a mind desire is awakened by the physical stimulus of some object, and the desire gorges itself with that physical object as a spider with a fly. (I leave out apparent exceptions to this, such as the migratory instinct of birds.) By mind, on the contrary, objects afar off are brought to the presence of the appetite, and that without any physical interference with the object. Where the mind is assisting some physical craving such as thirst, then the craving cannot be slaked without something material, such as water; but in spiritual desire the beloved object is possessed entirely and yet left untouched in its own nature. This is a digression. What it concerns us to notice is that thought does not cause desire but serves it by providing for it its food.

There is one great apparent exception to this doctrine. In many experiences, especially those of art and morality, the rôles seem reversed. The artist's desire runs ahead of his clear understanding; he is drawn on by a fever and reaches to he knows not what, longing for beauty which is incarnated in imperfect realisations, and learning by his imperfect sketches that he has not yet reached his goal. The same holds true of morality. The good man might be able to define his ultimate aim in vague and general terms, but that far-off ideal flickers or brightens according as he follows or neglects the highest that is near to him. Explain it as we will, there is no denying that men think and feel and judge by *what they are*. Ruysbroeck's answer to his visitors' question, "You are saints according to the measure of your desire to be such," suggests that desire is not only a force but an informant. The same truth is expressed in the proverbial "casting pearls before swine," or better still in the magnificent phrase of St. Augustine: "*Pondus meum amor meus*, my love is my weight." There is no explanation possible of this fact, I think, unless we admit what the new psychologists would call a spiritual *libido* in human nature, a native inclination or intent which lies behind the dispersed explicit desires of the mind and acts as their measure. In this sense desire would have priority over thought. Our thought would flicker out like a damp match were there no desire present. The object must in some degree attract and enlist our attention, for if it were to cease altogether to interest us we should cease to think, and our minds would remain inactive like sodden grass that will not take fire. For thinking at all, therefore, desire must be present, and the procedure of the two appears to be as follows. The initial act of thinking has desire as its efficient cause. The mind then provides our various appetites with food for their satisfaction, and at the same time makes more explicit to us our own nature, defining for it what is its good. Our nature still, however, exercises its authority to judge as altogether insufficient or partially sufficient the good presented to it in thought. This it does both by its knowledge of what is absolute and final in the abstract and by the dissatisfaction betrayed by our desire when anything short of its complete satisfaction is offered to it.

Does this contradict what has already been said of the purity of truth and its independence of desires and

personal wishes? No, because the desire which fires our
nature and is immanent in thought has a character
distinct from all others. It is obedient to something
greater and higher than itself; it cannot reach its end
unless it foregoes any possible private satisfaction
for the sake of learning what external reality forces
it to think and by conforming itself to a moral good
which is its law and not its own manufacture. Therefore
the former conclusion holds fast, that personal desires
cannot help to produce certainty in speculative thought;
the mind should be occupied with the evidence and the
evidence alone, and it is this evidence which compels
certainty. That God, as the absolute truth and absolute
goodness, stirring desire and thought and controlling
them, exists, is I think a necessary corollary of this
doctrine, but to make this step would take us beyond
the point so far reached. It is sufficient that we are
able to see that the intellect has a priority over the will
by first providing for it food for its desire, and that in
turn the will precedes thought by setting it in motion
towards its satisfying and appropriate object.

In the preceding paragraphs the speculative judgment
has been the subject-matter of discussion. A word now
is necessary on the practical judgment. As stated before,
this practical judgment is not to be confused with the
semi-practical or judicial verdict, which ought rather
to be ranked with the speculative. A judgment whose
whole purpose is concerned with action is manifestly
different from the theoretical, as many a too-wise man
has discovered when he has been tricked into expressing
his belief and has then been forced to act on his theory.
When a commander in the field decides that a particular
course of action must be followed, it is obvious that the
character or content of the judgment directly influences
the will. Again, though not so obvious, it is fairly clear

that the judgment in turn depends upon the will to act. In a sense we make up our mind and thereby make one line of action ours. These expressions bring out the nature of the change from the state of mind before decision to the state of mind after decision. We are no longer impartial; having chosen our bed we must sleep on it; having chosen our side we are identified with it. More exactly still, of two objects presented to us we have preferred one, and by our act of choice we have made it preferable; or in other words it is our act of free will which has made it to be the object chosen in preference to the other. That is to say our free will has had the deciding vote in the formation of our practical judgment. From another angle too this can be shown. As long as we dwell in the land of theory, we cannot act. Our practical choices are concerned with particular objects or courses of action which are never repeated. Every moment the circumstances change and our own mood and motives vary. Like a field-battery in action we must always have spotters or observation-balloons to signal the necessary changes in direction and range. The mind is a paralytic and the will is blind, and to meet any concrete situation the two must help each other out. The best examples of this collaboration can be seen in the domains of politics and art. We speak of the genius of the artist who hits upon just the right solution, a solution which could never have been found by rule of thumb. The professor in politics who relies on his study of past history to make generalisations and apply them rigidly to present affairs will go all awry. The great statesman sits lightly to the past; he has profited by his study of it in that he has learnt its lessons and brings them to bear upon matters in hand. But it is the alliance of this knowledge with an appreciation of the immediate particular problem which gives him discernment and the power to judge well.

For practical judgment always, and for speculative judgment in many cases, the formation of good habits is of exceeding importance. We judge by what we are, and the nature of our desires is the measure of our appreciation. This brings us back to the question of the unconscious and the teaching of the new psychology on the relation of desire and knowledge. Partly owing to current understatements of the nature of consciousness, but much more owing to the discoveries of processes below the level of awareness, the word "unconscious" has become the shibboleth of the modern psychologist. There is no good reason, however, to fear that it will oust the conscious from its post of honour. As we have seen, one has only to follow carefully the arguments used by psycho-analysts and others to see that they cannot help invoking the aid of the conscious and treating it as the consummation of human activity. All the so-called unconscious processes tend normally to express themselves above ground; the psychiatrists themselves act consciously, use the conscious thought of their patients, and always make the assumption that the cure lies in the exposure of the hidden trouble to the sunlight of the mind and reason. That is, it is taken for granted that the last and deciding act of the human drama must always be in the front of the stage.

What, then, is the meaning and importance of this Unconscious? I believe that the origin of the conception is as follows. We have always been aware that our thought was not the same as our nature, that the self was more than the consciousness of it or the act of thought at any definite moment. Our self often seems to us like a giant at the bottom of a volcano, able to express himself only in mutterings and smoke. We

lament that we are not in form in argument, that
thoughts will not come when writing, that shyness or
nervousness makes us tongue-tied and unable to think,
and we are glad that certain friends are able to bring
out what is best in us, to make us surprised at the
uprising in ourselves of high motives and generous
judgments. These and a hundred other experiences
make us aware that there is a world within us, part of
which we should like to enjoy consciously and another
part to banish altogether. The description of this world
has always been difficult, as we have had to choose
between words that suit conscious activity and words
that belong to the physical order. Now the psychology
of the last century laboured under an unfortunate
handicap, in that it accepted for the most part a very
narrow philosophy. It assumed with the empiricists
that experience was the beginning and the end of
knowledge. Consequently it found itself at the moment
of its full development bound to maintain the extraordinary doctrine that consciousness was the self or all
that had any right to be called a self. The upholders
of this view had jettisoned the notion of substance, owing
to their dislike of metaphysics. They were forced, as a
result, to explain all by sensation and experience, and
the self became nothing more than an experiencing
subject. The result of this was that a number of
psychologists proceeded to treat all else in terms of
physiology; others, convinced that physiology could not
account for all the facts, began to play with a new
hypothesis. Suppose, said they, that there is another
self on the model of the conscious self, but subliminal—
can we by this hypothesis control the facts of experience?
They had this in their favour, that they were copying
the old methods of the physicists, who had invented the
molecule and the atom on the model of a visible unit to

control the physical world which was invisible. Success
soon justified this new hypothesis, and with time the
vague image became more and more detailed, as a city
seen from an approaching aeroplane passes from a
smudge to a pattern inlaid with lines and squares and
conic sections.

As a working theory, therefore, the unconscious has
justified itself by its results. But if we ask whether the
hypothesis has revolutionised former views about the
self or added to our knowledge of it, no immediate
answer can be given. Certainly erroneous theories have
been corrected, laws of uniform concurrence have been
discovered, and supposed homogeneous units have been
broken up and shown to consist of heterogeneous parts.
But if I ask myself whether I now understand the nature
of myself which falls outside that of which I have
consciousness I find that my explanations are slipping
into metaphors or images which I have to correct by
the old knowledge which I and everyone else have
always had. The most that can be said is that the
general knowledge has been cleared of the confusion
almost always present in it, in the same way that our
sure though indistinct knowledge of the meaning of free
will or sensation or value can be articulated by a careful
and accurate analysis. If this faint praise sounds too
damning, let it be admitted that much can be learnt
from a study of repression and the working of the main
instincts. It would be silly to deny this—as silly, in fact,
as to deny the advances made in medicine and
physiology. But just as it is doubtful whether physiology
has made any radical difference in our conception of a
living body, or revealed to us the nature of the relation
between soul and body, so we are at liberty to hold that
our understanding of the nature of a spirit which is and
yet is not conscious remains just what it was.

Some would be inclined to agree with this criticism, but to argue that our notions, which are still in the embryonic stage, may yet turn out to be of decisive importance. At the present moment a useful distinction between the unconscious and the subconscious is coming more and more to be accepted. The first contains processes which never rise into consciousness; it may turn out that they are physiological, but for the time being they occupy a no-man's land. The second includes all the states stretching from the central point of attention to the periphery, the semi-conscious—states of reverie and mooning, twilight, dark night and hypnotic states. These are all grouped together as one, despite certain manifest differences. Of the manner in which they exist there are various explanations. I will quote that given by de Sanctis as representative of the more moderate views: he accepts the *Aktualitätstheorie*, according to which ideas, perceptions, feelings and volitions exist as dispositions, capacities for receiving impressions—"not potential dispositions, but dispositions which become realised, once the way is clear; dynamic tendencies, in short." One may take it as proven that every thought has its motor side; that there is nothing psychic without some sort of correlative "behaviour." The so-called motor vibrations of thought have, in fact, been discovered by experimental psychology in the vascular system, in the glands, in the phonetic muscles, in those of the fingers, etc. It must be added that mental activity discloses motor elements in morbid phenomena, deriving from the most profound depths of the sub-conscious. But Ribot's explanations de Sanctis thinks incomplete unless one adds that these kinaesthetic elements preserve in all of us a species of record of those contents to which they were once joined. This implies a particular kind of disposition and orientation. And if this be so, they can only be regarded as "differentiated," not generic, kinaesthetic elements.

In conclusion, then, we find ourselves able to assert—for the purpose of a clearer orientation—that the subconscious is made up of "dispositions" or tendencies, complete and dynamic, which may be conceived of as a sort of animated mould, ready to receive contents; but with this peculiarity, that each mould is specially adapted for the reception of some particular kind of content, and no other.

What is the influence of these subconscious processes on the conscious life? An appeal is sometimes made to examples and experiments to show that they ride the conscious life and that the explanations of our conduct are as mistaken as the efforts to keep still on a moving stairway. For instance, a patient in a hypnotic state is told to clap her hands when a friend enters the room. On coming to her senses, she is apparently unaware of this suggestion. Nevertheless, when the friend enters she claps her hands and explains her action with reasons which have nothing to do with the command of the physician. The inference from this recorded incident is that the causes of our conduct and beliefs may, far more often than we suspect, lie outside our conscious motives and reasons. Such an inference goes far beyond the evidence. In the first place, the situation is abnormal. For the argument to run we must hold either that the condition of trance is a common phenomenon in everyone's life, or that there is no difference between the state of mind produced by hypnotism and the ordinary functioning of consciousness in a healthy-minded man. *Prima facie* it is bad reasoning to argue from an exceptional case in which an extreme of dissociation has been deliberately produced. Moreover, there are many explanations which are consistent with the evidence.

There is no proof that the woman sifted carefully the motives in her mind. We are constantly giving an account of some action of ours which does not tell the whole story. We do not bother, we economise in explanations, we look for an apparently sufficient reason, not for the complete one. Besides, in the case quoted above, the possibility of a vague awareness of the antecedent suggestion cannot be ruled out; or again, as the reasons were given after the action, the woman might at the moment of the act have had a consciousness of its true reason which, owing to her condition, she afterwards lost. This latter occurrence is frequent even with normal people. They do something, and immediately after are distracted so that when questioned they say with a frown that they must have done it for this or that reason. In this they may quite easily be mistaken, as they are only inferring or guessing the true cause. We have only to compare this incident with innumerable small acts of ours to see that a new and strange hypothesis is not needed to account for it. Once a practical judgment has been made it perseveres, as we are wont to say, virtually. We decide to buy gramophone records in a neighbouring market town, and while on the way there we are not conscious of our resolve. It carries us on nevertheless, even though we may be at a loss for a moment to know why we are walking in a definite direction. So, too, to give one other example, our actions on rising may be determined by a decision taken before going to sleep, and some can even awake at an unusual appointed hour by premeditation on it the night before.

The unconscious, therefore, to judge by the evidence so far forthcoming, need not be regarded as a new portent. It divides into the subconscious, namely, all that surrounds the focus of attention, all the felt but not

differentiated content that we have not fully expressed
to ourselves, and that massive force of our character and
personality called disposition, habit, sentiment, instinct,
which either actually goes to the formation of our
thinking or might do so. In the quotation given de
Sanctis adopts the theory of potential dispositions, but
he is careful to distinguish them from what he calls
"the old philosophic conception of intellectual habits."
They are active or dynamic tendencies; . . ."the subconscious content cannot be described simply as organic
conditions but, according to our parallelistic hypothesis,
as physico-chemical conditions associated with psychic
energy," or to express it differently, they are 'psycho-
physical tendencies.' There is no reason to question
this activity, as long as the myth of active ideas below
consciousness is avoided. The hypothesis of psycho-
physical parallelism is less likely, but the appeal to the
combined action of the psychical and the physical is
surely right. Here lies the clue and at the same time
the difficulty. In human nature there are acts which
are intrinsically spiritual, such as thought, and actions
which are intrinsically organic, like the beating of the
heart. But between these two extremes there lie all
those intimately connected human acts which are, so to
speak, hybrid—sensation, memory, feeling—tone, instincts, acquired dispositions and apperceptive complexes. Of the way these work we are always acquiring
new knowledge; nevertheless, no sooner do we relinquish
the old names than darkness covers the field of study.
The truth is that we have clear knowledge only of
certain broad distinctions, and have to fill in the rest
with similes which belong strictly either to the world of
conscious thought or to organic activity alone.

In some ways the more moderate modern views of
psychology bear a resemblance to the Neo-Platonic and

Augustinian theories. The development of the former has gone hand-in-hand with medical practice, and on the analogy of the body the psychical has been treated as a living organisation with its laws of health and disease. This has led to the constant use of words like "balance," "equilibrium" and "harmony," and an emphasis on the impulses and their ideal unity and satisfaction in a complete self. Now in the language of St. Augustine the words "harmony," "proportion," "order" and "unity" are for ever recurring, and the whole weight of his thought lies on desire and satisfaction. And this is no accident. Thought for him is √ saturated with desire. *Nulla est causa philosophandi nisi ut beati simus.* And this movement to completeness of being and love is worked out in terms of the Pythagorean and Platonic kinds of numbers. The natures of physical effects consist of numbers or the likenesses of numbers, and the soul is both integrated and impressed by its harmony with these numbers. On the principle that like is known by like, the soul chimes in accord with them, and this resonance is the truth and goodness of the soul because the soul is conscious of its resonance and judges it by the absolute norms of beauty and its approximation to perfect beauty. What modern psychology says of the need of healthily functioning impulses and the dynamic dispositions fits in admirably with the thought of St. Augustine. In both there is the same preoccupation with desire, and if modern investigation has told us much about the structure within us, of the various complexes and the interrelation of conation, cognition and affective tone, of which St. Augustine was ignorant, his view in turn corrects and supplements the modern conclusions in two ways. First, in his assumption of a fundamental craving of our nature as human. The fact that character grows by integration, and thereby

alone safeguards its health, points to a definite and single
end and a single power which works indefatigably,
collecting, reducing, correcting, unifying. Some such
integrating power is often admitted, but its end is
shrouded in the vague word "personality." Personality,
so understood, is nothing but an equilibrium of forces,
and as such resembles the play of Hamlet without the
Prince of Denmark. The content of the end is omitted.
St. Augustine supplies this omission, takes, as it were,
the cover off the casket of the soul and shows us not the
libido of Freud nor Adler's will to power, but a love in
and through all other loves for transcendent beauty and
overwhelming goodness. And, secondly, he shows how
this perfect state is not to be found in the subconscious
(where only the first intimations are given), but in the
highest part of the self, that part where the self expresses
and meets itself, and in the act is found possessed rather
than possessing. Now the only place where expression
is found with the enjoyment of it is in consciousness, and,
what is still more pertinent, the only way to perfect
satisfaction is by the control of will and mind. All
psychologists are aware of the need of what is called
sublimation. This sublimation means that we consciously are fitting recalcitrant desires into the pattern
that the mind conceives and the will approves. It follows
that the ideal which integrates the disordered movements
of the self belongs to the conscious order and is in
conformity with the law of perfection, not of the mind
alone, but of the whole of our nature. Leibniz recognised this when he said that "man is not by nature an
atheist," for he saw that in every experience, even the
very first, the mind judges it and transcends it, reaching
out to some absolute standard, not indeed, as he himself
thought by an innate idea, but by an innate tendency.

Those who have followed the account given in a

former chapter of the nature of truth and the implications contained in the distinction of subject and object will be able to complete what has been said in the preceding paragraphs with a philosophy of the self. Man is a composite creature of soul and body. This union it is which explains the strange mixture or interaction of the conscious and the unconscious, the purely physiological and the psycho-physical processes which, because of our prejudice in favour of neat categories, seem to us at moments to be neither flesh nor fowl nor good red herring. What we call the unconscious is just the necessary condition of a spirit united with a body in process of realising itself. It has been pointed out that the culminating act of a spirit is to be itself in an undivided act of self-to-itself, an act of self-realisation or self expression, in which all that one is is actualised in the very form of the thought. The food or content has been vitalised, taken up into the life of the thought, so that what once was passive is now wholly active. In perfect thought I express myself and, in the same act, all that I have become. Now if thought is a way of becoming all things, in knowing myself completely I also know all things, so far as my nature or form is capable of containing all things. In the light of this perfect state the present struggle with its odd manœuvres, its reserves which are not in action, its wedge-formation in attack and concentration, its losses of contact, its slow consolidation of new positions becomes intelligible.

The human being is not born perfect, but has to develop—and develop, at least in part, by his own effort. This development is mainly in and through intelligence and will. The will moves towards what is good for man and the intelligence is both his highest way of life and the means of knowing what is good for him. There is then the immense surge or tendency to well-being, which we may call desire of the self, and the man then is in movement, in travail by desire, and passes by his own initiative from darkness to a knowledge of himself and his purposes. At any moment in this passage he is more than he is able to hold in thought and express, but this penumbra of the self, this opaque mass in the background is one with the conscious agent and has for its end to come to fulfilment in an all-embracing act of intuition. At present it acts as habit or character or apperceptive unity and form or disposition or tendency determining the way we think and the judgments we pass on social, political and religious questions. The form in which we think (which is the past content of experience absorbed into the self) is therefore a prelude or foretaste of a diviner state in which there will be no latent dispositions, no expectant unconscious, but instead full noonday consciousness. Now if man were the *chef d'œuvre* of evolution, the final authority and measure, then truth and goodness would be relative to his personal wishes. But this is not so. In conscience he finds that he is subject to standards which he did not make, that duty and apparent self-interest do not always coincide; nevertheless, he is also aware that fidelity to this absolute serves also his own welfare. Again, in knowledge he does not make truth, invent it by consulting his own convenience. He is in the position of a disciple and pupil, and he can possess truth only on condition that his mind is candid and he himself disinterestedly in love with what is other and higher than himself. In this docility of the mind and asceticism of desire lies the secret of human perfection. It is because man, to use the phrase of Scripture, is made in the likeness of God that he cannot be himself until his desire is satiated with God and by the beholding of Him in an intellectual intuition.

Modern psychology, therefore, far from cutting the ground away from a doctrine of belief and knowledge, lends it support. Certainly it offers a warning against accepting too readily excuses and explanations which are prompted by desire. It shows with new force that the self is far more than its idea of itself in consciousness and lays down rules for the healthy integration of the chief impulses. But of the nature of that integrated life and self-expression it can tell us nothing. Looking at its results with help from other sources of knowledge, we can see that truth is left intact and that it is the best medicine for troubles of the mind. We conclude therefore, that there is a fundamental desire of the self which cannot be appeased save by truth, and that in the practical order the rectitude of that desire may be used as a short cut to the attainment of complete knowlede and self-perfection.

CHAPTER IV

THE GRAMMAR OF ASSENT

AN ANALYSIS

L'abstrait est incessamment nourri du concret, le concret est incessamment éclairé de l'abstrait.

PEGUY: Lettres et entretiens.

Ce qui fait donc que de certains esprits fins ne sont pas géomètres, c'est qu'ils ne peuvent du tout se tourner vers les principes de géométrie; mais ce qui fait que des géomètres ne sont pas fins, c'est qu'ils ne voient pas ce qui est devant eux, et qu'étant accoutumés aux principes nets et grossiers de géométrie, et à ne raissoner qu'après avoir bien vu et manié leurs principes, il se perdent dans les choses de finesse . . . ce sont choses tellement délicates et si nombreuses, qu'il faut un sens bien délicat et bien net pour les sentir, et juger droit et juste selon ce sentiment.

PASCAL: Penseés.

CHAPTER IV

THE GRAMMAR OF ASSENT

THE way is now open for an undisturbed consideration of belief, or what Newman called Assent. Much
has been written on this subject since his day, but the
Grammar of Assent still remains the masterpiece which
no one can safely neglect. If I find myself unable to
accept all the conclusions of that book it is not because
of any lack of admiration for the author or liking for
his line of thought. Indeed, so penetrating is his analysis,
so closely in touch with experience, that one feels almost
invariably that what he says is right and that it is only
the framework of his language that causes difficulty at
times. For some reason or other his explanations do not
seem to have received the attention they deserve from
scholars and students of psychology and philosophy.
For this reason alone they deserve to be explained at
length, but in truth so pertinent do I find his views that
I cannot advance without their help. I will therefore
set them down, omitting, alas, for lack of space, much
that, if worth met its proper recognition in this life,
should on no account be omitted.

The *Grammar of Assent* hinges on two fundamental
distinctions, the first between real and notional assents,
the second between assent and inference. In the first
chapter he distinguishes propositions into questions,
conclusions and assertions, and remarks that a clear
prima facie difference between the latter two is that a
conclusion is dependent on its premises, and therefore

in some sense conditional whereas an assertion is unconditional or categorical. These divisions are not watertight compartments. Our usual procedure is to pass from one to another; we begin with doubt, raise a question, settle it for ourselves by argument, and, having convinced ourselves of some fact or truth, arrive at a state, which remains permanently with us, even when we have forgotten all the arguments, of belief. If we link the word "belief" with assent we shall notice that certain conclusions seem to remain just conclusions, while others pass into something which had best be described by another word. We hear for instance some abstract argument; it all seems to proceed very smoothly, but though it does not pass from one ear out of the other it cannot be said to be very real to us. To understand the reason for this we must observe that there are two kinds of propositions, the one which uses general or abstract terms—"man is an animal," "a line is a length without breadth," "to err is human"—the other terms which stand for individual things external to us— "Philip was the father of Alexander." These two different kinds of apprehensions may be called notional and real. It should be observed, however, that they are not mutually exclusive. When, for instance, a schoolboy learns by heart the line, *Dulce et decorum est pro patria mori*, it is for him a commonplace proposition, as it may well have been for the poet who wrote the line; "whereas it would be the record of experiences, a sovereign dogma, a grand aspiration, inflaming the imagination, piercing the heart, of a Wallace or a Tell." Life, indeed, consists in part of the passing of a notional lesson into a real experience and of experiences into generalisations which we pronounce with our lips. Manifestly of the two modes of apprehending, the real is the stronger, and therefore as Newman says, "inferences, which are con-

ditional acts, are especially cognate to notional apprehension, and assents, which are unconditional, to real."

In assenting to propositions we must to some extent
apprehend their terms, and the kind of apprehension
makes a difference to the strength, though not to the
absoluteness, in every assent. A child for instance might
assent to the statement that "lucern is good for cattle";
again, without assenting to a proposition itself, he can
assent to its truth—"that lucern is good for cattle is
true"—and he might go one step further back and
assert that "my mother's word that lucern is good for
cattle is true." In all cases there is some kind of apprehension, and it is necessary, therefore, to make an inquiry
into the nature of this apprehension. Two classes meet
us straightway. Our language may express both what
is external to us and our own thoughts, the one real and
the other notional. It is notional in the grammarian
and it is real in the experimentalist. An economist, for
example, is dealing with facts, whereas a clever schoolboy
might turn into English a French treatise on profits,
produce and public debt, with an apprehension of what
it was that his author was stating sufficient for making it
clear to an English reader, while he had not the faintest
conception himself what the treatise, which he was
translating, really determined. Evidence of the same
distinction is the practice of doctors of translating into
a notional vocabulary the shocking realities of disease
and physical suffering. Terms stand either for things
and are singular, or for abstractions, which are notions.

Real apprehension is present in experience or information about the concrete, as in the remark, "The prospect is charming." And if the immediate experience
be gone it can still remain with us by means of memory
or association. "I can bring before me the music of the
Adeste Fideles, as if I were actually hearing it; and the

scent of a clematis as if I were in my garden; and the flavour of a peach as if it were in season; and the thought I have of all these is as of something individual and from without. . . ." Such apprehensions form a vast multitude, and by means of them what otherwise might be only notional may be converted into what is real. The word *fire* in the remark that "there is a fire in London" may be to me not a common noun in my apprehension, but may recall to my memory the experience of a fire I have known elsewhere, or some vivid description I have read. Again by our inventive faculty we can form to ourselves new images, and of things which we have never experienced. "Thus I may never have seen a palm or a banana, but I have conversed with those who have, or I have read graphic accounts of it, and, from my own previous knowledge of other trees, have been able, with so ready an intelligence, to interpret their language, and to light up such an image of it in my thoughts, that, were it not that I never was in the countries where the tree is found, I should fancy that I had actually seen it." Such reconstructions are generally confined to the domain of perception, and even within that domain they are limited. "If I said that Mozart's melodies were as a summer sky, or as the breath of Zephyr, I should be better understood by those who knew Mozart than by those who did not. I can understand the rabbia of a native of Southern Europe, if I am of a passionate temper myself; and the taste for speculation, or betting, found in great traders or on the turf, if I am fond of enterprise or games of chance; but, on the other hand, not all the possible descriptions of headlong love will make me comprehend the delirium, if I never have had a fit of it; nor will ever so many sermons about the inward satisfaction of strict conscientiousness create in my mind the image of a virtuous action and its attendant sentiments, if I have been brought up to lie, thieve and indulge my appetites. Thus we meet with men of the world who cannot enter into the very idea of devotion, and think, for instance that, from the nature of the case, a life of religious seclusion must be either one of unutterable dreariness or abandoned sensuality, because they know of no exercise of the affections but what is merely human; and with others again, who, living in the home of their own selfishness, ridicule as something fanatical and pitiable the self-sacrifices of generous high-mindedness and chivalrous honour."

In addition to this experience, nay as if by one and the same action, we institute comparisons between the manifold phenomena of the external world, as we meet with them, criticising, referring to a standard, collecting and analysing them. In these acts we regard things not as they are in themselves, but mainly as they stand in relation with one another. Man, for instance, ceases to be an individual and is attenuated to an aspect, or relegated to his place in a classification. He is made a logarithm of his true self, and in that shape works with the ease and satisfaction of logarithms. This is notional apprehension, when that fullness of meaning accruing to language from experience becomes but a heap of notions, little more intelligible than the beauties of a prospect to the short-sighted, or the music of a great master to a listener who has no ear. We all remember occasions in our own lives when we have found that the idea we carried with us of some individual, some statesman or foreigner, has been shattered by meeting him in real life. Tyrants, monks, crusaders, princes in disguise, and captive damsels, how far removed from reality these types have been in the minds both of children and the mature!

The language of Newman so far shows an unmistakable preference for real as opposed to notional apprehension. Nevertheless, he says that each has its own excellence and serviceableness, and each has its own imperfection. The notional leads to breadth of mind and shallowness; the real to depth and narrowness. The first is the conservative principle of knowledge, the second is the principle of its advancement. "However, real apprehension has the precedence, as being the scope and end and the test of the notional. . ." Both may co-exist in the same mind, and they give an external character to assent. Assent is always unconditional, but though it has no degrees, there is a variation of vividness. The notional may approach to a mere inference, because of the absence of experience and the consequent dullness and inoperative character of the assent. How this is so can be best explained by examining still more closely assent to notions and assent to things.

The reason why assents vary in strength is that what is concrete exerts a force and makes an impression on the mind which nothing abstract can rival. The mind is ever stimulated in proportion to the cause stimulating it. Sights sway us as scents do not, and similarly with mental objects. I can be more arrested by the words of Christ saying "Give to him that asketh thee," than by the best arguments of the economist against indiscriminate almsgiving. It is not surprising, therefore, that real assents are stronger than notional, nor again that the notional is at times hard to distinguish from inference. A Christian's assent to the fact of our Lord's crucifixion could never be confused with the inference to that fact made by a historian or philosopher, whereas it might be very hard to distinguish the notional assent of a Stoic to the nobleness of the just man struggling in the storms of fate from an act of inference forced on him by his principles. No one but God knows whether certain rich churchwardens assent unconditionally to the social teaching of Christ or take in with one ear the premises on which it is based. This being so we can call it the normal state of inference to apprehend propositions as notions, and we may call it the normal state of assent to apprehend propositions as things; and it is not too paradoxical to say that when inference is clearest, assent may be least forcible, and when assent is most intense, inference may be least distinct—"for though acts of assent require previous acts of inference, they require them, not as adequate causes, but as *sine qua non* conditions; and while the apprehension strengthens assent, inference often weakens the apprehension."

Newman groups the assents to notional propositions under five headings, and they are interesting as showing his power of observation and analysis of mental states. The first he calls Profession. They are assertions made upon habit and without reflection, as when we call ourselves Liberal or Conservative or Labour because of our upbringing, or accept the circle of ideas in which we move. Thus many use the language and shibboleths of some prevalent scientific or philosophic theory, professing it without understanding it, employing words and phrases such as "progress," "civilisation," "jesuitry," "rationalism," "evolution," "relativity" or "the development of thought." This type, which thrives on thought at second hand, and so often assumes the airs of a master in Israel, is too common to need further description. Included also in this category are assents to what strictly is a matter of inference, as for instance that the stars are billions of miles away from the earth. Few of us have a notional, much less a real notion of a billion or a trillion; we cannot assent to a proposition of which it

H

is the predicate; we can but assent to the truth of it. Newman here digresses to discuss the assent we give to mysteries, but as his argument does not add anything material to his main thesis we can pass on to his next heading.

This heading is called Credence. "What I mean by giving credence to propositions is pretty much the same as having 'no doubt' about them." This form of notional assent comprises a great variety of subject matters. "From the time that we begin to observe, think and reason, to the final failure of our powers, we are ever acquiring fresh and fresh informations by means of our senses, and still more from others and books. The friends or strangers we fall in with in the course of the day, the conversations or discussions to which we are parties, the newspapers, the light reading of the season, our recreations, our rambles in the country, our foreign tours, all pour their contributions of intellectual matter into the storehouse of our memory; and though much may be lost, much may be retained." This kind of knowledge it is which gives us in great part our morality, our politics, our social code, our art of life. Newman is thinking also of his favourite type, the gentleman, the Aristotelian man of culture, who may be an expert in one branch of science, but in any case is able to converse sensibly and critically on all subjects, in history, literature, politics, philosophy and art. He has in mind as well religion as accepted by many of the English people of his day. "The reiteration again and again, in fixed course in the public service, of the words of inspired teachers under both Covenants, and that in grave, majestic English, has in matter of fact been to our people a vast benefit. It has attuned their minds to religious thoughts; it has given them a high moral standard; it has served them in associating religion with compositions which, even humanly speaking, are among the most sublime and beautiful ever written; especially, it has impressed upon them the series of Divine Providences in behalf of man from his creation to his end and, above all, the words, deeds and sacred sufferings of Him in Whom all the Providences of God consist." Nevertheless, the assent is notional and not real, and the state of mind is such that it deserves a special name—credence.

Such credence might seem to be identical with what is often called a man's "opinions," unless we reserve the word *opinion* for a probable conclusion inferred from premises. Newman, however, discovers another act or state of mind which is neither of these two, and it is to this distinct kind of notional assent that he gives the name of opinion. It is an assent to a proposition as probably true independently of the premises, and it differs from credence in that it explicitly assents to the probability of a given proposition, whereas credence is an implicit assent to its truth. Opinionated men, who say that they have a right to think as they please, reason or no reason, fall into this category, and the word is used in this sense in Catholic theology, when a distinction is made between faith in dogma and theological opinion.

Less convincing is the title, Presumption, chosen for certain other forms of notional assent. Some, too, of Newman's philosophical presuppositions peep out in this section, and as they differ from those defended in this volume they cannot be passed over. "By Presumption I mean," says Newman, "an assent to first principles, and by first principles I mean the propositions with which we start in reasoning on any given subject matter." There are clearly many such assumptions. He prefers not to call our trust in our powers of reasoning and memory principles, because, as he maintains, what we actually do is to trust particular acts of memory and reasoning, and this trust implies no recognition of a general power or faculty over and above the particular act. It is furthermore unphilosophical to speak of trusting ourselves. "Our consciousness of self is prior to all questions of trust and assent. We act according to our nature, by means of ourselves, when we remember or reason. We are as little able to accept or reject our mental constitution as our being." I cannot think that this is a satisfactory account. We surely do in some sense trust our intellect as a power. Whenever we are in an awkward predicament or emotionally disturbed we stop and think, and thus appeal to the reason as the one unfailing guide if we want to know the truth. Unless we were sure of the power of the intellect to give us truth, we should be lingering over the precipice of scepticism. What Newman may have in mind is a distinction between a principle that is explicitly before us or present as a major premise and a principle that is not a basis of the particular subject matter and not a premise in the argument but presupposed as a condition for starting at all. In this sense reasoning and the self are not taken in trust because we could not begin to trust without them; we have, as Newman says, no option; we can but misuse or mar the functions of the self. If this is his meaning, there is room for some such distinction, but it is highly dangerous when it is used, as it seems to be used in this section, to suggest a distinction in degrees of certainty.

The reason why Newman adopts the word *presumption* is suggested by the word *trust* in the above account, and it is made clear in what he goes on to say. He calls the proposition that "there are things existing outside us" a first principle, and one of universal reception. But— and this is noteworthy—this principle is founded on an instinct. Instinct is a force that spontaneously impels us not only to bodily movements but to mental acts. Now animals perceive in the phenomena of sense a something distinct from and beyond them, and as animals do not use general notions we are bound to conclude that animals, and men as well, act here by instinct, and that the general notion of an external world is not a condition of our accepting it, but an induction that goes far beyond our experience and represents a notional assent. He compares this process of arriving at the proposition with that induction whereby from particular experiences of conscience we reach the idea of the Ubiquitous Presence of One Supreme Master and give a notional assent to it. So again, "as regards the first principles expressed in such propositions as 'there is a right and a wrong,' 'a true and a false,' 'a just and an unjust,' 'a beautiful and a deformed': they are abstractions to which we give a notional assent in consequence of our particular experiences of qualities in the concrete, to which we give a real assent." To illustrate his meaning he takes the belief in causation and submits it to an interesting analysis. He will not allow that we have any so-called intuitive apprehension of a cause; it is rather an induction from a number of our own acts. From the experience of them we come to the notion of power combined with a purpose and an end, and so far as experience is concerned it is limited to agents possessed of intelligence and will. Our belief, therefore, in a world of physical causes and in the uniformity of nature is not so immediate or obvious as we are accustomed to believe in adult life. The fact, however, that our propositions about causality or the external world or the moral law are abstracts does not invalidate them, but it does show that they represent an act of inference, and that they are received by the mind with a notional and not a real assent.

This explanation of Presumption has, I think, been greatly influenced by Newman's reading of Locke, Berkeley and Butler, and contains a number of disputable statements. It is easier to follow him in his last division, which he calls Speculation. He uses it not in the sense of a conjecture or a venture on chances, but as the contemplation of mental operations and their results as opposed to experience. It includes, therefore, those notional assents which are the most direct, explicit and perfect of their kind, viz., those which are the firm, conscious acceptance of propositions as true. "This kind of assent includes the assent to all reasoning and its conclusions, to all general propositions, to all rules of conduct, to all proverbs, aphorisms, sayings and reflections on men and society. Of course, mathematical investigations and truths are the subjects of this speculative assent. So are legal judgments and constitutional maxims, as far as they appeal to us for assent. So are the determinations of science; so are the principles, disputations, and doctrines of theology." "As far as these particular subjects can be viewed in the concrete and represent experiences, they can be received with real assent also; but as expressed in general propositions they belong to notional apprehension and assent."

Such then is notional assent, distinct from inference by being unconditional and from real assent by the absence of that directness and force of apprehension which goes with the knowledge of particular things and images. In daily life the notional is constantly passing into the real. Certain boys at school acquit themselves poorly in class, but when they take up a profession they discover suddenly what is called an eye for their work, and become highly successful. "These are the reformers, systematisers, inventors in various departments of thought, speculative and practical; in education, in administration, in social and political matters, in science." There are also a number of truths, practical or ethical, which float on the surface of society. They are admitted by all, but need some incident to bring them home to individuals. Thus the slave trade persisted for a long time against the conscience of Europe, and needed the efforts of a Wilberforce before active efforts were taken to stamp it out; thus passages from some book which are read or learnt by heart as rhetorical commonplaces after long years come home and pierce the heart with their poignant beauty; thus to the devout the Divine Word speaks to the heart of the disconsolate, the perplexed, the tempted and the suffering.

Real assent is therefore far different from notional, but it should be noted that the distinctness of the images required for it are no warrant for the existence of the objects that those images represent. Too often the scientist, carried away with the vividness of his apparent findings, lets his imagination usurp the function of reason and will not listen to evidence contrary to the clear impression which is his. Nor again is real assent necessarily practical, for it is not imagination which causes action, but hope and fear and the other emotions. Lastly, real assents vary with persons whereas notions do not, and therefore they thwart rather than promote intercourse between man and man. Notional assent is of itself an ordinary act of our common human nature, and by means of these common ideas we can have mutual understanding, whereas it is impossible for me to share with another the peculiar joy that the presence of certain friends causes, or the insight into character or situations that comes by personal gift or familiarity. The perfect course is when what is notional turns into real. Notional beliefs, convictions, certitudes are necessary, but it belongs to real assents "to form the mind out of which they grow, and impart to it a seriousness and manliness which inspires in other minds a confidence in its views, and is one secret of its persuasion and influence in the public stage of the world. They create, as the case may be, heroes and saints, great leaders, statesmen, preachers and reformers, the pioneers in discovery in science, visionaries, fanatics, knight-errants, demagogues, and adventurers."

Newman completes his account of the relation of assent to apprehension by exemplifying their connection in the matter of religion. When that is finished he begins the second part of his task, which is the relation of assent to inference. His view of this relation must be considered a most remarkable attempt to answer a somewhat neglected problem, and whether his solution is to be regarded as satisfactory or not, he has at any rate made that problem stand out so clearly and provokingly that it cries for an answer. We are so accustomed to think of ourselves as rational beings who base all our beliefs and assents on proof or evidence that we may be taken by surprise when Newman distinguishes a conclusion from an assent, and most of us will be a little shocked and slow to admit his assertion that assent is always unconditional while inference is always made conditional by having premises. Our credulity must, however, be lessened after listening to Newman and pondering over the examples he gives. At the very beginning he throws out the proposition "I shall die" for us to chew. Do we or do we not unconditionally assent to those words? And if we do, he will politely ask us to demonstrate it, and if we look around for some arguments, press us to answer frankly whether our certainty is no stronger than the arguments we have been endeavouring to propose. The fact surely is that we are in the presence of a problem that is not nearly so easy to answer as we at first thought, and we must consider whether Newman's own solution is satisfactory, or whether a better one can be suggested.

The ordinarily accepted view common to scientist and philosopher is that absolute assent has no legitimate exercise except as ratifying acts of intuition and demonstration. Thus, as Newman exclaims, "assent becomes a sort of necessary shadow, following upon inference which is the substance; and is never without some alloy of doubt, because inference in the concrete never reaches more than probability." The argument in favour of the view is that an assent cannot rise higher than its source, that our proof cannot be stronger than the reasons we give for it. As a protagonist of this view Newman takes Locke and maintains that he is inconsistent in asserting that it is illogical and immoral to "carry our assent above the evidence that a proposition is true" and in owning, nevertheless, that we are rational in permitting strong probabilities to rise to assurance. Newman dislikes intensely Locke's *a priori* method, which condemns men as irrational because "they take to the water, instead of remaining under the narrow wings of his own arbitrary theory." Facts are stubborn things and to Newman it is an evident fact that assent is a distinct act of the mind which cannot be identified with inference. For proof of this he appeals first to experience. It is a common matter of experience that assents endure without the presence of the inferential acts upon which they were originally elicited. We have forgotten the warrant for them, but we are still as decided as we were years ago. Again the assent may fail, though the reasons for it and the inferential act which is the recognition of those reasons remain, and this happens not because we have come to doubt the reasons but by an unaccountable change of mind, which may possibly be due to moral causes, arising out of our condition, age, occupations or fortunes. Once more, assent may be withheld, though strong and cogent reasons are present. We may demonstrate a proposition to a friend to his and our own satisfaction; he admires the argument, acknowledges its validity, and remains a protestant all the while; and so it happens that men can see the ultimate result of a complicated problem in a moment and yet take years before they embrace it and see its bearing on their own assents. The truth is that in ordinary human intercourse argument and assent do not go invariably hand in hand; a probable argument leaves our neighbour entirely unconvinced, whereas his assent ought to oscillate according as the proof slackened or grew in intensity; and if he is of an obstinate turn of mind he will never be persuaded against his will. Even in mathematics the contrast between inference and assent is exemplified, not indeed in the simple plain propositions which all are forced to accept, but where the reasoning is long and intricate, and the attention has to be sustained. It has happened before now that party spirit or national feeling or religious prepossession has retarded the reception of truths of a mathematical character.

In arguing that inference and assent are distinct acts of the mind Newman is not denying that the two are connected, that assent may always imply grounds in reason, implicit if not explicit. Nevertheless, however closely connected, a difference remains, and it consists in this, that inference is conditional and assent is unconditional. There are no degrees in the latter. When "we read the newspapers . . . look through debates in Parliament, pleadings in the law-courts, leading articles, letters of correspondents, reviews of books, criticisms in the fine arts . . . we form no opinions at all upon the subjects discussed, as lying out of our line, or at most we have only an opinion about them." "We might as well talk of degrees of truth as of degrees of assent," and when we talk of a half-assent we mean assent as little as we mean truth when we talk of a half-truth.

The truth of this distinction can be proved by an appeal, not to *a priori* theory, but to facts. There are many assents that men give on evidence short of intuition and demonstration, which are as unconditional as if they had the highest evidence. The list that follows is so crucial for an appreciation of the problem under discussion that I must quote it in full. "First of all, starting from intuition, of course we all believe, without any doubt, that we exist; that we have an individuality and identity all our own; that we think, feel and act, in the home of our own minds; that we have a present sense of good and evil, of a right and wrong, of a true and a false, of a beautiful and a hideous, however we analyse our ideas of them. We have an absolute vision before us of what happened yesterday or last year, so as to be able without any chance of mistake to give evidence upon it in a court of justice, let the consequences be ever so serious. We are sure that of many things we are in doubt, and that of many things we are not in doubt.

"Nor is the assent which we give to facts limited to the range of self consciousness. We are sure beyond all hazard of a mistake, that our own self is not the only being existing; that there is an external world; that it is a system with parts and a whole, a universe carried on by laws; and that the future is affected by the past. We accept and hold with an unqualified assent, that the earth, considered as a phenomenon, is a globe; that all its regions see the sun by turns; that there are vast tracts on it of land and water; that there are really existing cities on definite sites, which go by the names of London, Paris, Florence, and Madrid. We are sure that Paris or London, unless suddenly swallowed up by an earthquake or burned to the ground, is to-day just what it was yesterday, when we left it.

"We laugh to scorn the idea that we had no parents though we have no memory of our birth; that we shall never depart this life, though we can have no experience of the future; that we are able to live without food, though we have never tried; that a world of men did not live before our time, or that the world has had no history; that there has been no rise and fall of states, no great men, no wars, no revolutions, no art, no science, no literature, no religion.

"We should be either indignant or amused at the report of our intimate friend being false to us; and we are able sometimes without any hesitation to accuse certain parties of hostility and injustice to us. We may have a deep consciousness, which we can never lose, that we on our part have been cruel to others, and that they have felt us to be so, or that we have been, and have been felt to be, ungenerous to those who love us. We may have an overpowering sense of our moral weakness, of the precariousness of our life, health, wealth, position and good fortune. We may have a clear view of the weak points of our physical constitution, of what food or medicine is good for us, and what does us harm. We may be able to master, at least in part, the course of our past history; its turning points, our hits and our great mistakes. We may have the sense of the presence of a Supreme Being, which never has been dimmed by even a passing shadow, which has inhabited us ever since we can recollect anything, and which we cannot imagine our losing. We may be able—for others have been able—so to realize the precepts and truths of Christianity as deliberately to surrender our life rather than transgress the one or deny the other."

Now these truths are not reached by demonstration, and nevertheless they are sovereign, and it is impossible to reject them because they lie outside the narrow range of conclusions to which logic, formal or virtual, is tethered. The philosophers confuse two things, a mental act or state and a scientific rule, an interior assent and a set of logical formulas. Their interest is to contemplate how representative symbols work, not how the intellect is affected towards the thing which those symbols represent; and there is as much and as little connexion between a logical conclusion and an assent as there is between the variation of the mercury and our sensations. In thus contrasting the two Newman has, I think, in mind a fact that has perhaps never received sufficient attention from the philosophers. That fact is that as often as not, previous to a scientific investigation of some truth we are already aware and certain of it, and our arguments do not affect that certainty. The man who starts out to prove that England is an island is already happily aware of the fact; the same is true of many moral, aesthetic and religious beliefs, and I suppose that there are not a few who after examining any one of the classical arguments for the existence of God would be prepared to hold its validity in suspense without any concomitant misgiving about the fact of God's existence. And even the philosophers confirm unawares their conclusions by common-sense.

So far Newman has been mainly occupied with contrasting assent and inference. He now approaches more closely the nature of their relation, that is, the problem that most deeply concerns us. To clear the way he distinguishes between simple and complex assent.

The first describes those innumerable assents which are exercised unconsciously. They are expressions of our likes and dislikes, our principles and our habits, or are due to credulousness and ignorance. A complex assent, on the other hand, is exercised consciously and deliberately. The question therefore must be settled, what is the connection of reasoning with this deliberate assent. In experience we find that inference can be both the antecedent of assent and also its accompaniment. I may be asked why I believe that India exists, or I may have forgotten the reasons why I believe a certain proposition. It may be that the revision of my reasons leads to a revision of my assent, but there is no reason why such an investigation should do so, no reason why it should imply any failure in my assent. To investigate the grounds for calling England an island is in fact compatible with an unconditional assent. "We do not deny our own faith, because we become controversialists; and in like manner we may employ ourselves in proving what we already believe to be true, simply in order to ascertain the producible evidence in its favour, and in order to fulfil what is due to ourselves and to the claims and responsibilities of our education and social position." No doubt inquiry is incompatible with assent, but inquiry is quite distinct from investigation. It is true also that there are certain minds which fancy they doubt as soon as they begin an investigation, and there are others who possess beliefs so delicate and sacred "that they will not wash without shrinking and losing colour." Moreover, it is a fact of experience that those who have begun with a prejudice may find that in the course of their investigation they are forced to abandon it, or at least revise it. But this does not mean that they started with doubt. "What belief, as such, does imply is, not an intention never to change, but the utter absence of all thought or expectation or fear of changing." "It is possible then, without disloyalty to our convictions, to examine their grounds, even though in the event they are to fail under the examination, for we have no suspicion of this failure." That change may take place slowly or suddenly, noticeably or imperceptibly; the objections themselves have no direct force to weaken the assent. What we do realize at the end is that our new assent has the strength of deliberateness and deliberation; we know now not only some given proposition but also that it is true; we assent to an assent and are, as we say, convinced.

Such a conviction Newman calls a certitude, and the proposition a certainty or thing known or matter of knowledge. Whether all certitude is also certainty or truth he leaves over for the time with the remark that among fairly prudent men there are far fewer cases of false certitude than might at first sight be supposed. Many may talk confidently, but when brought to book they will express themselves quite differently. For light upon certitude itself two conditions can be mentioned. The first is that no man can be called certain of a truth who can endure the thought of the fact of its contradictory existing or occurring. No matter how many arguments are brought against it they fade out of the mind as fast as they enter it. Such, for instance, is the attitude of our minds towards the fancy that "Great Britain is in shape an exact square," that "Napoleon really had a star," that "I shall escape dying." So, too, "did a man try to persuade me that treachery, cruelty or ingratitude were as praiseworthy as honesty and temperance, and that a man who lived the life of a knave and died the death of a brute had nothing to fear from future retribution, I should think that there was no call on me to listen to his arguments, except with the hope of converting him, though he called me a bigot and a coward for refusing to inquire into his speculations."

The second condition or token of certitude "is a feeling of satisfaction and self-congratulation, of intellectual security, arising out of a sense of success, attainment, possession, finality, as regards the matter which has been in question." When we have done right we are normally filled with a feeling as of religious peace, and analogously to this is that feeling of intellectual security on the attainment of truth. Now this state does not attend on processes of inference, still less on doubt. There are indeed pleasures attached to knowledge and to the pursuit of knowledge, but the pleasure of perceiving truth without reflecting upon it is not very different from that which we enjoy when we are reading a romance or novel. In no way is it the same as that which comes when we recognize that what we are perceiving is true, that we possess certitude. Again the pleasure in the search or hunt, in overcoming obstacles or adventuring against them, in the revelation of our own ingenuity, is well-known, but so far from being that of certitude it ceases when the latter comes upon the stage. The sense of finality has no peer. Even the joy of the philosopher reducing to order the maze of phenomena, passing by sure inference from point to point, exhibiting and analysing the inconsistencies of a rival system and the close-knit texture of his own, has a character of its own almost poetical, "as twilight has more poetry in it than noonday."

If, then, we readily acknowledge the existence of various conditions of the intellect with their accompanying pleasurable affections, we ought also without cavilling to accept this normal condition of the mind called certitude, with its specific, distinct affection. It reasoning with an act of assent, those who come after me, being mounted upon my shoulders, will be able to supply the correction. The point is that it is congenial to our nature to reach towards and to establish ourselves in certitude, and our ability to correct the past is a witness to this and to the justice of our assurance. Errors are warnings, not signs of the bankruptcy of the intellect. We do not dispense with clocks because sometimes they tell the time wrongly. "The sense of certitude may be called the bell of the intellect; and that it strikes when it should not is a proof that the clock is out of order, no proof that the bell will be untrustworthy and useless when it comes to us adjusted and regulated from the hands of the clockmaker."

Newman then is prepared to accept the saying that probability is the guide of life, if it is not exaggerated. There are genuine certitudes even though we at times mistake them and have to restrict them to a relatively small number. "We are certain of the elements of knowledge, whether general, scientific, historical, or such as bear on our daily needs and habits, and relate to ourselves, our homes and families, our friends, neighbourhood, country and civil state." "In human matters we are guided by probabilities, but they are probabilities founded on certainties. It is on no probability that we receive the information of sense and memory, of our intellectual instincts, of the moral sense, and of the logical faculty." But can any measure of such certitude be attributed to religious truth? Has not religion shown such variations in the course of time, hypothesis succeeding hypothesis and certitude going down before new knowledge, that it is impossible to call religious truth and certitude indefectible? Newman faces this difficulty and points out how the assent in religion is not to any one proposition but to a system, and in the acceptance of a code of life there are many assents. When, then, a man changes his religion he does not change all his certitudes. The first question to ask in his regard is whether there be no common doctrine in the two creeds, and if so, whether he has not changed a portion and not the whole of his beliefs; and the second question is, "has he abandoned those doctrines which are common to his new creed and his old? And then again, was he certain of the old, or is he certain of the new?" Those who join the Catholic Church "come not to lose what they have, but to gain what they have not; and in order that, by means of what they have, more may be given to them. St. Augustine tells us that there is no false teaching without an admixture of truth; and it is by the light of these particular truths, contained respectively in the various religions of men, and by our certitudes about them, which are possible wherever those truths are found, that we pick our way, slowly perhaps, but surely, into the one Religion which God has given, taking our certitudes with us, not to lose, but to keep them more securely, and to understand and love their objects more perfectly."

The conclusion on certitude is short and explicit enough to be put in Newman's own words. "It seems, then, that on the whole there are three conditions of certitude: that it follows on investigation and proof, that it is accompanied by a specific sense of intellectual satisfaction and relief, and that it is irreversible. If the assent is made without rational grounds, it is a rash judgment, a fancy, or a prejudice; if without the sense of finality, it is scarcely more than an inference; if without permanence, it is a mere conviction."

We now come close to the crucial problem of assent, its relation to inference. Assent is unconditional, inference is conditional; how then does one pass from the latter to the former? Newman begins with an analysis of formal inference. By means of sense we gain knowledge directly, and as we have reason to suppose that the universe is connected we proceed to infer from the facts we observe other facts which we do not see. Now, in order to do this we must set out about it systematically and find some instrument of reasoning which may be less vague and arbitrary than the talent and experience of the few or the commonsense of the many. As writing is a corrective of the defective memories of man, so, too, we establish a means of correcting the differences of mind from mind, a method which may act as a common measure and intellectual standard. Thus geometry and algebraic science have served a purpose, and in the same way, except that it is far more ambitious and comprehensive, we have the method of logical inference. By use of its symbols we are enabled to advance with precision and effect. "Let every prompting of the intellect be ignored, every momentum of argument be disowned, which is unprovided with an equivalent wording, as its ticket for sharing in the common search for truth. Let the authority of nature, commonsense, experience, genius, go for nothing. Ratiocination, thus restricted, and put into grooves, is what I have called Inference, and the science, which is its regulating principle, Logic."

Having thus as a preliminary damned inference with faint praise, it is no wonder that he distinguishes its conclusions from real assent. It is far more concerned with comparison of propositions than with the propositions themselves, and its aim is to make the propositions as abstract as possible. Hence it prefers symbols, and having stripped words of all their connatural senses, having drained them of that depth and breadth of associations which constitute their poetry, their

rhetoric and their historical life, having starved each
term down till it has become the ghost of itself, and
everywhere one and the same ghost, *omnibus umbra locis*,
it can make the word or term stand for just one unreal
aspect of the concrete thing to which it properly belongs,
for a relation, a generalisation, or other abstraction,
for a notion neatly turned out in the laboratory of the
mind, and sufficiently tamed and subdued because
existing only in a definition. Thus the rivers of reality,
full, winding and beautiful, are turned into navigable
canals, and the abstract term so obtained can lead only
to the abstract, a shadow of the probable unless we
reintroduce the concrete. "Thus since inference starts
with conditions, as starting with premises, here are two
reasons why, when employed on matters of fact, it can
only conclude probabilities; first because its premises
are assumed, not proved; and secondly because its
conclusions are abstract and not concrete." "As to
Logic, its chain of conclusion hangs loose at both ends;
both the point from which the proof should start and
the points at which it should arrive are beyond its
reach; it comes short both of first principles and of
concrete issues."

Newman does not overestimate logic or inference.
Nevertheless, in a fine passage, he insists on the indis-
pensable part which logic must play in life. This *amende*
need not detain us. Two passages, however, merit
attention, the one because it betrays the philosophic
and, as I think, unsound basis of his view of the abstract
or the notional, the second because it bears on what he
has to say later. The first is as follows: "We call rationality the distinction of man, when compared with other
animals. This is true in logic; but in fact a man differs
from a brute, not in rationality alone, but in all that he
is, even in those respects in which he is most like a brute;

reason, moral feeling, immortality, and all that he is besides— is his real differentia, in contrast to a horse or a dog. And in like manner as regards John and Richard, when compared with one another; each is himself, and nothing else, and, though, regarded abstractedly, the two may fairly be said to have something in common, viz., that abstract sameness which does not exist in all, yet, strictly speaking, they have nothing in common, for they have a vested interest in all that they respectively are; and, moreover, what seems to be common in the two, becomes in fact so uncommon, so *sui simile*, in their respective individualities—the bodily frame of each is so singled out from all other bodies by its special constitution, sound or weak, by its vitality, activity, pathological history and changes, and, again, the mind of each is so distinct from all other minds, in disposition, powers, and habits—that, instead of saying, as logicians say, that the two men differ only in number, we ought, I repeat, rather to say that they differ from each other in all that they are, in identity, in incommunicability, in personality."

The conclusion of the *Grammar of Assent* is adumbrated in the second passage. "Philosophers, experimentalists, lawyers, in their several ways, have commonly the reputation of being, at least on moral and religious subjects, hard of belief; because, proceeding in the necessary investigation by the analytical method of verbal inference, they find within its limits no sufficient resources for attaining a conclusion. Nay, they do not always find it possible in their own province of thought; for even when in their hearts they have no doubt about a conclusion, still often, from the habits of their minds, they are reluctant to own it, and dwell upon the deficiencies of the evidence, or the possibility of error, because they speak by rule and by book, though they judge and determine by common sense."

The suggestion contained in this passage is developed in the next section on Informal Inference, where the final answer of Newman to the problem of certitude and assent begins to take shape. It is clear, he says, from his previous arguments that our certainties in matters of concrete fact cannot be obtained by formal logical sequence. Everything goes to show that the true method is by "the accumulation of probabilities, independent of each other, arising out of the nature and circumstances of the particular case, which is under review; probabilities too fine to avail separately, too subtle and circuitous to be convertible into syllogisms, too numerous and various for such conversion, even were they convertible"; the difference between this method and logic is as great as the difference between the outline of a man's face and the sketch of him with all the details worked in. This reasoning does not supersede the logical form of inference, but carries it into the realities of life, "its premises being instinct with the substance and the momentum of that mass of probabilities, which, acting upon each other in correction and confirmation, carry it home definitely to the individual case, which is its original scope." Clearly it is not necessary that all the evidence should be explicitly before the mind, in fact it is impossible that it should be. We recognise two brothers without being able to enumerate their points of likeness and dissimilarity, and we can tell the condition and characters of others by innumerable small signs which are too minute and intricate to allow explanation. It should be noted, however, that in delineating this method we have not shown how we have advanced beyond the conditional character of all inference. It may seem, indeed,

ance," others of the *judicium prudentis viri* where a conclusion is arrived at not *ex opere operato*, by a scientific
necessity independent of ourselves, but by the action of
our own minds. Another name, which Newman prefers
to pass over because of its vagueness, is "moral certitude," a name given to judgments not only in the spheres
of ethics and religion, but also in that of physical science.
Are we to be content with just a name? No, it is possible
to hazard the suggestion that the principle of concrete
reasoning is parallel to the method of proof which is
the foundation of modern mathematical science, as
contained in the celebrated lemma with which Newton
opens his *Principia*. "We know that a regular polygon,
inscribed in a circle, its sides being continually dimin-
ished, tends to become that circle, as its limit; but it
vanishes before it has coincided with the circle, so that
its tendency to be the circle, though ever nearer fulfilment, never in fact gets beyond a tendency. In like
manner, the conclusion in a real or concrete proposition
is foreseen and predicted rather than actually attained;
foreseen in the number and direction of accumulated
premises, which all converge to it, and approach it, as
the result of their combination, more nearly than any
assignable difference, yet do not touch it logically
(though only not touching it) on account of the nature
of its subject matter, and the delicate and implicit
character of at least part of the reasoning on which it
depends. It is by the strength, variety, or multiplicity
of premises, which are only probable, not by well-
connected syllogisms—by objections overcome, by adverse
theories neutralised, by difficulties gradually clearing up,
by exceptions proving the rule, by unlooked-for correla-
tions found for received truths, by suspense and delay
in the process issuing in triumphant re-actions—by all
these ways, and many others, the practised and experi-

enced mind is able to make a sure divination that a conclusion is inevitable, of which his lines of reasoning do not actually put him in possession. This is what is meant by a proposition being 'as good as proved,' a conclusion as undeniable 'as if it were proved,' and the reasons for it 'amounting to a proof,' for a proof is the limit of probabilities."

To complete this account a short analysis must be given of that natural mode of reasoning whereby we move not from proposition to proposition but from concrete to concrete, from wholes to wholes. As already mentioned, we are not usually aware that we are using rules of logic; it is rather by a kind of instinct that we pass from evidence to a conclusion. This instinct, which is a kind of divination, belongs to rude as well as to gifted minds. The peasant looks at the sky and promises fine weather; the physician diagnoses a complaint swiftly and without much ado; the judge may be able to tell before the evidence is heard whether the prisoner is guilty. A similar power of intuition is to be found in some persons' judgment of music or character or again in the perception of a Newton when proof is absent. Newman gathers under the same gift the genius of a Napoleon in war, the calculations of mathematical geniuses, presence of mind, fathoming of motives, the feeling that something is wrong, especially in religion. Hence, too, "it is in our intercourse with others, in business and family matters, social and political transactions, a word or an act on the part of another is sometimes a sudden revelation; light breaks in upon us, and our whole judgment of a course of events, or of an undertaking, is changed." A peculiarity of this instinct must be added, that it is departmental; that is to say, that a genius at war may be a dunce in politics or business and a man wise in science may be as one blind in religion. *Cuique in arte sua credendum est,* and if we wish to know we must trust those of the best judgment in their special departments. Judgment, as Newman concludes, "in all concrete matter is the architectonic faculty; and what may be called the Illative Sense, of judgment in ratiocination, is one branch of it."

This Illative Sense is Newman's answer to the problem that he set out to solve. That certainty is a state which all of us can verify he assumes; he has argued also that certitude is not a passive impression made upon the mind, but in all concrete questions an active recognition of propositions as true. Now reason never bids us be certain except on absolute proof, and, nevertheless, formal inference cannot be more than conditional, cannot produce more than the probable. What criterion then can there be which will warrant our certitude? The answer is that the sole and final judgment on the validity of an inference in concrete matter is committed to a mental faculty, the Illative Sense. All that remains then is to explain the sanction, the nature and the range of the Illative Sense.

Of the sanction of this sense Newman says very little. He insists that the first elementary lesson of duty is that of resignation to the laws of our nature, whatever they are. Every being has a function, and that function is suitable to it and subserves its existence. Man, like all other creatures, has a nature with an aim and a specific perfection, and what is peculiar to him is that he is a being of progress with relation to his perfection. Man begins with nothing realised, and he has to make capital for himself by the exercise of those faculties which are his natural inheritance. This law of progress is carried out by means of the acquisition of knowledge, of which inference and assent are the immediate instruments. Now we cannot look at man and decide offhand how this law of progress will work; we must appeal to facts and see how these two instruments of inference and assent actually operate. If then we find that in fact the course of inference is ever more or less obscure while assent is ever distinct and definite, we must take things as they are, and instead of devising some sufficient science of reasoning, confess that there is no ultimate test of truth besides the testimony borne to truth by the mind itself, and that this phenomenon, perplexing as we may find it, is a normal and inevitable characteristic of the mental constitution of a being like man on a stage such as that of the world.

To explain the nature of the sense he appeals to what Aristotle calls *phronesis*, good judgment or prudence in conduct. No code or rule can supply us with the right answer to a particular problem of right action; we have either to use our own good judgment or rely on that of trustworthy wise men. Now the law of truth differs from the law of duty, in that duties may change whereas truths do not change; nevertheless the reasonings which carry us to the truth are many and distinct and vary with the inquirer, and it is as the controlling principle in inference that the illative sense can be compared with *phronesis*. They are like in this too, that *phronesis* is no vague general faculty, but departmental. A man may be exemplary in family life and a scoundrel in business, a good man may make a bad king, a profligate prove a great statesman. So, too, in ratiocination, men will differ according to the subject matter, one showing a power of divination in science, another in religion or history. In short, then, as an exercise of the mind the illative sense is one and the same in all concrete matters, though employed in them in different measures. "We do not reason in one way in chemistry or law, in another in morals or religion; but in reasoning in any subject matter whatever which is concrete, we proceed, as far indeed as we can, by the logic of language; but we are obliged to supplement it by the logic of thought; for forms by themselves prove nothing. Secondly, it is in fact attached to definite subject matters, so that a given individual may possess it in one department of thought, for instance history, and not in another, for instance, philosophy. Thirdly, it proceeds in coming to its conclusion, always in the same way, by a method of reasoning, which I have considered as analogous to that mathematical calculus of modern times, which has so wonderfully extended the limits of abstract science. Fourthly, in no class of concrete reasonings, whether in experimental science, historical research, or theology, is there any ultimate test of truth and error in our inferences besides the trustworthiness of the Illative Sense that gives them its sanction . . ."

The Illative Sense is a personal gift, but this does not limit its range. Whatever the subject matter of thought, it will show itself in operation. It will be employed on reasonings from primary facts as well as directed on personal issues, and will serve as the instrument of induction from particulars, and determine what are general laws and what conclusions cannot reach beyond bare probability. Thus it is by the illative sense that we believe in an extended material world, that we hold to the uniformity of nature and regard its laws as invariable. Its range, therefore, is vast. To illustrate its function Newman gives under separate heads some of those elementary varieties of opinion on which the sense has to act. First, as to the statement of the case, the aspect under which we view a subject, the preference for example of Bacon for efficient causes to final causes, the presentations of a case in court, the attitudes of a Warburton and Gibbon to history. Secondly, in the assumption of first principles in a course of reasoning and the exclusion of propositions of whatever kind; thirdly, the arguments with which a question is to be decided. Newman gives illustrations under each of these headings, but we need not follow him as the main lines of his view stand out sufficiently. Nor is there need to reproduce the thought in the concluding chapters of the *Grammar of Assent*, where he applies all that he has said to religious belief and the Catholic belief. The theory is complete, and it is time that we should try to form an estimate of it.

CHAPTER V

THE BASIS OF BELIEF

WISDOM is the clear, calm, accurate vision and comprehension of the whole course, the whole work of God; and though there is none who has it in its fulness but He who "searcheth all things, yea, the deep things" of the Creator, yet "by that Spirit" they are in a measure "revealed unto us."

NEWMAN.

TRUTH can never be told so as to be understood, and not be believ'd.

BLAKE: *Marriage of Heaven and Hell.*

CHAPTER V

THE BASIS OF BELIEF

THE summary of the *Grammar of Assent* in the preceding chapter will have failed if the reader is not left with a profound respect for the theory and the penetration of its author. Far too little attention has been paid to it, and I make no excuse for adopting many of its suggestions in the pages to follow. It is always a pleasure to find one's own thought already adumbrated or forestalled in the pages of a great writer, and where criticism is required it will be found, I think, that that criticism is often more with the form of expression than with the thought itself.

The main points of the theory are these: the conclusions of inference and assent are distinct. The one is always conditional, the other unconditional. Where we have assent it may be either notional or real. The notional is always concerned with propositions which are general, whereas the real has to do with the concrete. Now, in the concrete especially we decide unhesitatingly, and we are sure that we are right; that is, we are certain. Nevertheless, when we examine the grounds of our certitude, we shall find that it is not demonstrable. We have relied on reason, and that reason has been reinforced by some factor which is not to all seeming contained in the premises. Newman gives innumerable examples of this in daily life, in art, in morals and in science. Some power of divination belongs to us, a power distributed in various degrees among people and in different subject matters. The name given to it is the Illative Sense, the sense which discerns the unity and meaning in an apparently disordered mass of detail or evidence and grasps the point of an argument or a moral problem or a religious issue.

That Newman is appealing to facts, and facts of great importance, cannot be denied. We have to consider whether his interpretation and explanation of them are right. In his explanation he tries to eschew philosophic theories, but unfortunately in inhaling the ideas of his time he did not escape the meaning attached to them by a bad philosophic tradition. His tendency to use words like "instinct" and "sense," as, for instance, in "the illative sense," will make the philosophic purist wince, and it is only from his letters that we learn that the word "probable" was used by him in contrast with the demonstrable and not with the certain. More serious is the habitual disparagement of the notional as compared with the real. It looks as if this came from the philosophy he knew best, the views of Locke and Hume and Butler. Many of their assumptions must have been current in the Oxford of his time, and they provided him with what is no better than a nominalist theory of knowledge. His emphasis on the concrete, on vivid experience, on the symbolical nature of notions, rings true to empiricist teaching, and the emphasis has for effect to throw doubt on the value of logic and metaphysics. There are places where Newman corrects this impression, and it is true that his thought rises above the language in which he expresses it. Nevertheless, his conclusions are, I think, weakened by the too sharp separation of assent from inference, certitude from proof. The illative sense is introduced as a newcomer without antecedents and without its proper title, and is made to do duty for all manner of acts and processes of thought because in the preceding chapters thought has been deprived of some of its functions.

Almost all that causes dissatisfaction in the analysis can be traced back to his theory of the notion or universal. It is, as I have suggested, affected by nominalism, and as this error is by no means dead and has in fact showed its head in a recent classification of knowledge by acquaintance and knowledge by description, it will be well to point out where its imperfection lies. Newman, in a passage already quoted, describes how, as he thinks, the general notion is built up. We start with particulars, and as they are manifold and chaotic we bind them together into unities and organise them by means of formulas; at the end we have little more than a set of labels. That this may happen on occasions is true, but even when at the beginning of some investigation in science we are bewildered by the variety of objects before us, we are not completely in the dark; we have some rough idea of the nature of the objects, and we organise on the minimum of knowledge that we possess. All the time we are searching for more knowledge of the actual constitution of these data, and we control the investigation by our apprehension in particular cases of the true nature of some of them. This is the process followed in extreme cases of ignorance, and it is unjust to stretch the method to cover all knowledge. The truth is that in more obvious cases the unity which characterises certain objects is manifest at a glance, for the simple reason that we have no knowledge of particulars as such; we know them only as particulars of a universal.

This fact is ignored by the empiricists. Having relegated the function of the intellect to a lumber room, they are left with nothing but the senses and the memory and imagination. They suppose, therefore, that at the beginning there are present only a multitude of sensible phenomena or perhaps sensations, and they set about trying to explain how out of these ever-changing series without a name it is possible to construct the notions of the universal, substance, cause, the necessary, and give us a plausible account of the significant world in which we move and have our being. Their efforts are vain and must remain for ever ineffective, because they are trying to build without straw and make a dummy into a living man. There are no bare phenomena, there are no sensibles which are not sensible objects, no sensations which are not the sensations of somebody. I do not perceive first a sense datum and infer that it is something; I cannot think of a sense datum except as something, and the thing is not perceived by the senses, but apprehended by the mind; it is a universal and a notion. It would be easy to show that this holds true not only for a thing but for innumerable other more definite objects. I hope, however, that that is not necessary, and that it is clear to all that the universal is given concurrently with the particular, and that thought is not an after event doing its best with a world exclusively sensible.

The consequences of the mistake pointed out in the preceding paragraph have been very serious in philosophy. It does not, however, affect vitally the major part of Newman's work; in fact, the correction sets his answer on a much firmer foundation, and may enable us to bring together what have been unduly separated by him, namely, the illative sense and thought and proof. To achieve this I must return to some of the other questionable positions taken up by Newman.

The ground of his distaste for philosophy and metaphysics has, I think, been found. The brand of philosophy he had in mind was empiricist, and he was justified in suspecting it. His suspicion led him to talk of "sense" where he should have said "intellect," and to refer to instinct what is very far from being instinctive. Thus, for example, in several places he tends to regard the first principles which are at the back of all investigations and arguments as themselves either assumptions or instinctive. Our knowledge of the external world, of other persons, of causality, cannot be made evident by thought, but is based on some instinct which it is waste of time to try to criticise. For the same reason he holds that even the most severe deductive proofs end only in the probable; and so he claims that reasoning must always be completed by a new factor if it is to pass from the probable to the certain. It is clear that a great strain is put upon this illative sense if it has to do so much.

To make the valuable contribution contained in all this acceptable it is necessary first of all to restore the primacy of the intellect and so eliminate a natural criticism, that Newman completes his story by the introduction of a *deus ex machina*, a strange faculty which is as authoritative and as unreal as Mrs. Harris. When that is done it becomes possible to advance from the positions argued in preceding chapters and to inquire whether the problem of belief can or cannot receive a satisfactory answer without something like an illative sense; and if it cannot, what is the nature and range of what for the moment we may continue to call the illative sense. The intellect has the power of knowing the real world, and it is aware of the certainty of its knowledge in self-evident propositions or truths, in what can be deduced by necessity from these truths, in immediate experience, and perhaps in various other ways. The vital problem is concerned with these other ways, with what some are inclined to call beliefs.

The view stated in these last sentences differs from that of Newman in that it holds that notions can be

absolutely valid, that first principles are not assumptions
or instincts, and that therefore conclusions can be
unconditional. Is, then, his strongly held view, stated
over and over again, that an assent is distinct from the
conclusion of an inference to be rejected? This is a
very difficult question, and I shall try to keep the
discussion of it in line with the problem of belief. At
first sight it seems paradoxical to separate conclusions
and assents. I do not mean that in experience they
always go together; far from it! We are always finding
that our friends assent to views without any solid
reason, and will not pay any attention to our immaculate
arguments. Such waywardness, however, is not to the
point, for what we want to know is whether a separation
ought to exist, and Newman weakens his case by taking
examples which can be explained by credulity or
prejudice.

It is certainly true that many arguments in which we
can find no flaw leave us quite cold, while others touch
us to the quick. Newman used the distinction of the
notional and the real to fix this fact, and we have now
the word "realise" in constant use to verify it. "To
realise" has as a paraphrase "to come home to one,"
and this latter phrase offers a ready and easy explanation
of the distinction. It is not our mind which reasons;
it is we as human beings with tastes and emotions and
interests who reason or listen to arguments. It is not
surprising, being what we are, that we are inclined to
listen with more attention to evidence for earthquakes
in England than to news of similar disturbances in an
unknown tract in China. Many listen to arguments for
the existence of God, and, if unprejudiced, assent, but
remain indifferent until some day, please God, they
realise the value of God and the call to act on what
they know to be true. That is to say, many truths are

admitted listlessly and after a while are seen in their relation to practice or to what may happen to us or in some new context. I do not see that this is very different from the condition of, let us say, Rustum's mind with regard to Sorab. First, he knew him as a man and an enemy warrior, and later—too late—as his son. So, too, we know certain truths, and may later learn new relations which change our regard for them.

Another well-known fact is, that owing to a natural timidity of mind some cannot believe that their views and arguments are sound until they find an independent witness or hear another supporting the same point of view. Then, as it has been said, the strength of their assent is not doubled but multiplied to infinity. Here again the distinction of assent from inferred conclusion is due to the fact that it is man, not thought, that reasons.

So far, then, we have been able to find no justification for Newman's assertion, and if we turn to the methods we employ in trying to convince another and win his assent we shall find that apparently we do not consider the distinction at all. We appeal to demonstration, and are not happy if the listener assents on any other ground than the reasoning itself. If it is said that we try to be persuasive and avoid bare syllogisms, the answer is simple. In most arguments we take for granted or are aware that our opponent clings to his position because of sentiment or emotion, and persuasion has for its end to transfer the emotion to the view we think to be right, or to stir up a counterbalancing emotion. That we have so often to do this is a reflection not on reasoning but on our poor human nature!

Nevertheless, the case cannot be decided against Newman's distinction on what has been written above. There are many writers who support him, and their authority is not to be despised. They are concerned more with the problem of judgment than with that of inference, but as the conclusion of an inference is only one form of judgment, what they have to say has a direct bearing on the present problem. Before turning to their arguments it may be well to keep in mind an example of inference that seems to favour Newman. In formal logic we give abstract cases of inference where the whole strength and truth of the concluding premise depend just on its being a conclusion from the preceding premises. Now we listen to this, and we affirm the conclusion, but in fact we may question whether we give what Newman calls an assent to it. We prefer to say that the conclusion is true in so far as it follows from the premises; we regard it and say that it is correct; but do we pronounce on it unconditionally?

The same doubt can be raised in the case of all judgments, and with a still better reason. Assent, as all will admit, is the formal constituent of judgment. When, therefore, we are presented with a proposition that "S is P," is the assent identical with the inspection of the two terms and their perceived connection? Some philosophers answer in the affirmative, so that assent for them is what has been called comparative apprehension. This view looks straightforward; but the appearance is deceptive, and I believe that it is closely connected with very dubious presuppositions, for instance, that all judgments are analytical and that Descartes's ideal of clear and distinct ideas is right. Even without entering into a discussion of these latter we do not need much reflection to foresee certain difficulties. We have to suppose, for instance, that S and P are both understood in themselves and in their relation before we judge. If so, then the truth must be already known at least dimly before we juhge. More serious still: a comparative apprehension can vary only in degrees of clearness and obscurity, whereas assent may be judicious or foolish, possible and certain. As Newman remarks, assent is based on evidence, but it may vary not so much because of the motives as for other causes which he mentions. Furthermore, if assent is the same as comparative apprehension it is very difficult to explain how what is obviously true can be denied. 'I have said above that the oddity of some of our assents is due to prejudices, interests, likes and dislikes; but though this is true, it leaves a mystery which it does not attempt to solve—how it can happen that what is completely rational can be greeted by us sometimes as irrational. Grant that other factors interfere with the rationality of our judgments; there is the fact; but the fact cries for an explanation.

As I have seldom, if ever, seen this particular problem recognised and treated as it deserves, I shall make no apologies for dwelling on it. When I say that certain truths are self-evident, I know what I mean and I am certain that there are such truths. Now I cannot mean that this self-evidence is confined to myself, because it is the evidence of the object or the principle or the proposition which compels the mind to perceive it. Hence I have not the slightest doubt that my friends equally with myself are aware of the principle of contradiction, of sufficient reason; that they are conscious of sensation when they are sensing, of thinking when they are thinking, of the difference between thinking and sensing, thinking and body, their own identity as subject of thinking and their difference from other beings, of activity and passivity in experience, of choosing, and having violence done to them and a host of other experiences. Usually in conversation and writing we take for granted these truths and these experiences, and in fact the whole world of discourse hangs on some of them. Nevertheless, when a man begins to read learned books and sit at the feet of the scientist and philosophers, he not infrequently begins to doubt them. One may have to argue with a man who says that he does not exist and to tell him that it is self-evident that he does exist; or again to have to go to pains to show a man who denies the principle of contradiction that he cannot be meaning what he says, that it is as evident to him as it is to us and that therefore he is mistaken in thinking he can deny it. How is this extraordinary situation possible? If "self-evident" means anything, ought it not to mean that there is no possible room for a mistake? It looks as if we ought either to give up the assertion that there are self-evident truths, or hold that the denials of them cannot be sincere. But the latter must be ruled out, as it is against all the evidence; we must try, therefore, to escape the other horn of the dilemma.

Those who hold an extreme realist position in philosophy are surely in a desperate plight, though it must be owned that they have never appeared to be disturbed by the difficulty, and continue to maintain that we have a direct apprehension of reality, and that there are certain objects that reveal their necessary connection to us immediately. Those who cling to what has been called comparative apprehension are no better off, for if on inspection and comparison they behold the necessary relation of S and P, they cannot possibly be mistaken or entertain a reason for doubting it. The only solution is to re-examine the meaning of "self-evident" and find a distinction between the evidence and the assent, and this would bring us back to Newman.

The presupposition which has led to the *impasse* is

that self-evidence has for its counterpart a kind of intuition on our part, that we have only to look and cannot help seeing. Now this cannot be the whole truth. The assent must be more complicated than was thought, and what has already been said in the preceding chapters on the nature and ideal of knowledge should have prepared us for the true explanation. If knowledge were intuition, then the form we see it take would be most extraordinary. That form is that "S is P," no matter whether the content is a new discovery in experience or science or an obvious truth like the principles of identity or contradiction. We are bound to use the form of subject and predicate to express the truths that "a man is a man," that "he is a rational being," that "he cannot be a man and not a man at the same time." In others words, we do not simply absorb the nature of the object in one look or glance; to know by human knowledge is always to synthetize, to make a composition, as the old writers on philosophy described it. The world steps on the stage of the mind in motley; or it is like a boxer who taps us now here and now there. We have to reconstruct what is happening, to see it for ourselves as a whole; and the secret of our knowing is that we do this in accordance with the nature of the object. We join together what is in reality conjoined, but what by the complex character of our nature has been sundered at our contact with it. Hence we find it natural to say "that is so and so," "it is true that . . ."

To put this in a way still more reminiscent of what has already been explained, the ideal of knowledge is that we possess the object even as we possess ourselves, that it should become our own act, our very life and self-expression. Such a state belongs pre-eminently to God, who in knowing Himself knows all things and is undivided in his self-knowledge. We on a lower plane approximate to this, and for the present are struggling to gain our souls, being well assured that if only we could do this we should love both and enjoy most intimately all else as well. At present I say that we are struggling towards this consummation, and it is in the very act of knowledge that this struggle is seen. The intelligible world lies before us, but that it should be understood we have to make it our own, to make the material immaterial, to turn it into matter of thought, true and personal. This calls for an effort, not an effort that tampers with the natures of the real world—for that is not the function of thought—but one that records them and declares them. The ancient philosophers with great penetration grasped the significance of the Word, and Christian theology adopted their tenets. The Word is a self-expression and an assent; it is active and not passive; it is a synthesis and a truth.

If this account be true, the distinction of Newman can be maintained with certain modifications. In the first place the assent will be dogmatic and decisive, and the same in kind whatever the nature of the judgement, and to this extent it can be called in Newman's language "unconditional." Secondly, it leaves room for error and for the anomaly already discussed—that a proposition which is self-evident or a conclusion which is rational can be denied without insincerity. For because the proposition is a synthesis there is an interval, as it may be called, between the conjunction of the two terms, an interval not necessarily of time but of thought. A and A are really inseparable as being identical, and the proposition is therefore self-evident; but nevertheless, as conceived, they have to have an initial difference which has to be overcome; they are identical, but they have to be identified by us. This marginal distinction leaves time for distraction, for the interference of previously thought relationships, for darkness to descend upon the evidence. As, too, there is always some degree of abstraction in our thought, the interval permits of our thinking of some example which goes against the evidence, a mote in the eye which checks clear vision. It is worth noting that in practice when we find a friend resisting the evidence of a truth, we proceed to select illustrations of the same truth from another field, in the hope that with one of them this interference may be absent, and that then he will assent to the obvious—the evidence will catch him by surprise and be seen in its unity. Clearly what is said here of self-evident propositions will apply with still greater force to propositions which are the conclusions of an inference. The mind has more to swallow as a whole, the evidence has become more abstract, and there is a greater interval for distraction.

If instead of the word "distraction," we use "distortion," we shall find another reason for the anomaly, closely allied to the first. In the process of making the evidence one's own, the form or habit or disposition of the mind tends to play an important part. Modern psychology has coined the word "complex," and metaphysicians use "pattern" to cover this factor. Our knowledge grows by a kind of symbiosis; former meanings are enriched and perception is normally apperception. What we learn is systematised by us, and in this exercise we act not merely as thinking beings, but as human beings. That is to say, thought, will, and emotion all come into play and co-operate; what is conceived is taken over and fitted into some already existing point of view, and, thus installed, it becomes part of the pattern or complex. Hence it is that we speak of the value and necessity of experience, of the advantage of being familiar with the subject matter with which one may have to deal. Thus it is that a man who has no head for abstract calculations may show nevertheless financial genius; that an artist can see immediately what a fellow artist is at, whereas the amateur is completely at a loss; that the appreciations of one age may be a mystery to another; that gross misunderstandings can arise in the interpretation of art, literature, philosophy and religion; that we may miss the points of remarks, of jokes, of plans and policies; that our minds fail to perceive what to others is almost self-evident.

It is because of the existence of this pattern which is active in our thinking that distortion can so easily take place. But it must be noted that in an open-minded man the pattern does not interfere with truth; on the contrary, it is of the greatest service, since it enables him to perceive the proper relations of object with object, the intricate connections that like a delicate spider's web are invisible to the untrained mind and, one might add, to the dry-as-dust as well. A pattern or complex reinforces the native power of the intellect, and it is not until the affective or desirous constituent of the complex usurps the authority of the main constituent, the mind, that distortion comes about.

One other remark before passing on. Beside the smaller patterns there is to be found in most people a general pattern or dominant monad, which determines the whole outlook and unifies the minor patterns. It shows itself in the tone of mind which we describe as optimistic or sceptical or agnostic or hard and matter-of-fact. It explains why a Harnack could say that he would rather reject all the evidence for Christianity than admit the supernatural; why a St. Augustine, on the other hand, could declare that he would not believe the Scriptures were it not for the authority of the Church, and that there was no purpose in thinking out a philosophy save to attain the life which gives blessedness. Each and everyone has a vague or clear, narrow or wide, inarticulate or articulate philosophy of life to which they bring their new experiences and information.

The importance of this consideration will be more evident when we come to the subject of faith. At present, what stands out is the influence of these patterns on assent and belief, and it should be remarked that falsehood and disaster attend much more easily on a large pattern than on a small. The judgments we pass on the trivial and incidental, on what can be focused within short range, can be corrected without much difficulty if they are wrong. The man of one idea is a force—*timeo hominem unius libri*—but the idea may much more easily be distorted or inadequate, because there is so much evidence which it has to cover; it is also very difficult to eradicate, because the roots and tendrils of it are most closely intertwined; and it is lastly, most disastrous if wrong, because it affects the whole of life.

L

CHAPTER VI

THE ILLATIVE SENSE OR INTERPRETATION

Maintenant il faut que je me débrouille tout seul au travers de ce pays inconnu.

Inconnu? pas autant que mes yeux voudraient me le faire croire, il y a quelque chose en moi qui sait qui le paysage a un sens.

Un invisible courant peu à peu me rend les repères et les distances.

Quelque chose guide mes pieds et je sens que de ce sol à mes semelles il y a une ancienne habitude.

Et voici soudain le dallage que je heurte sous l'herbe rude.

Mon pas pour quelques mesures se lie à ce mouvement tout préparé qu'on lui offre.

PAUL CLAUDEL: *La Route Interrompue.*

CHAPTER VI

THE ILLATIVE SENSE OR INTERPRETATION

OF the points in the *Grammar of Assent* that we have
raised for discussion there remains the Illative
Sense. Newman used it to explain a great variety of
judgments. I propose here to make use of it only in
order to throw light on beliefs, and especially to see if
by its aid certain beliefs can be called certitudes. According to the common doctrine truth is either self-evident or
demonstrable. That is to say, we can be certain where
there is direct experience, as for instance of colour or feeling or desire; when we apprehend primary truths; and
when we can infer that certain other conclusions follow
necessarily from the experience or the primary truth.
If this is a true account, then the possibility of attaining
certainty by other ways is ruled out. We have to
inquire, therefore, whether this doctrine is not too
exclusive.

Newman, with his eyes ever watching life as it is led,
gives a great number of examples of belief to which
most men would unhesitatingly apply the attribute
"certain." We are sure that England is an island, that
Napoleon existed, that we shall die. Let us begin with
the simplest example of all—our certitude about the
existence of the external world. English philosophers
have given great attention to this subject in recent
years; they approach it, however, somewhat unfortunately from the angle of sensation. They ask themselves

what it is they see when they look at a visible object such as a penny; what seems so obvious to the ordinary man has proved a sore problem to them, and some quite fantastic explanations have been offered. One such view is that all the sense-data that can be seen or sensed exist independently of our organism and sensitive faculties, these latter having nothing to do with relative size and shape or variation or colour except that they limit what we do see to what we actually see. Thus, if we watch a train coming into a station or a ship first seen on the horizon coming nearer to land, every variation in perspective is existent before as well as after we see it. When, on being struck in the eye, we see stars, when a solitary candle gives us the illusion, as we are accustomed to say, of many lights, what has happened is that we have been fortunate enough to see a multiplicity hitherto hidden from us. Another view is that colour, size, etc., are sense-data in the literal meaning of those words; that is, they are peculiar kinds of objects that we have in sensing, which by themselves tell us nothing about the real world. It may be that they are caused by real objects, or that they are in some sense of the term mental and as such replicas of the external world. These and many other theories take their rise from the fact that what we see, whether we call it an illusion or reality, is something and not nothing. The variations in size and shape and colour that we observe in a moving object or when we change our position have to be explained.

Were it the occasion I should try to show that it is possible to avoid the extreme kind of theory just mentioned, and to justify the belief that there is a standard shape which belongs to the external object, manifesting itself in the perspective and in the correction which we can make of illusions. But what concerns us now is the relation of the sense-data to the object to which they belong or with which they co-exist. The fact is that we never see sense-data by themselves; what we perceive is a coloured object. At the minimum what is coloured is something, but usually we go on to say much more than this. When we see certain groups of sense-data, without the slightest hesitation we give a character to the kind of object they manifest. To speak of a group of sense-data is not, it must be acknowledged, by any means to give a full account of the facts. The sense-data are grouped in a peculiar way, and there are other indications, such as of causal activities in the object, which give us the awareness of a determinate kind of unity. We have, then, always in our experience a sensible object to which we give a name.

So far, so good; indeed, some may wonder why what is so obvious should need a paragraph. But in the obvious there are sometimes clues to be found, and this is a case in point. Many, in looking at a sensible object, will suppose that they see all there is to be seen. But this is not so; we habitually assume what we do not see. We call a certain shape a cube, and we do not see it as a cube; we come up to a door, and we take for granted that it has another side to it; on entering a room we turn round, and assume that we are looking at one room. These are simple examples, and they could be multiplied indefinitely, but they suffice to prove that in perception we pass continually beyond immediate experience, that we have discerned unity in a group of phenomena, and that we can dispense with a certain number within the group and nevertheless retain our assurance of the existence and permanence of the determinate object. Now the process of thought involved here and the state of mind concomitant with it or resulting from it demand attention. The state of mind

verges on certainty or definitely is certainty, and the
process is one which cannot by any stretching of the
term be called "inference"—if a word be sought,
"interpretation" might suit. We always, as has been
said above, behold an object, and an object which is
more or less determinate. The detail may have ragged
edges, but it never lacks some kind of unity; and this
unity is reached not by inference, but by some interpretation, of the manifold in terms of its unity or a unity.
We may be wrong in our interpretation, and in fact this
often happens, so that it is best to call the first stages
the apprehension of a *prima facie* object, a gift horse that
we must look in the mouth.

This distinction between the *prima facie* object and the
real object has for its counterpart one between credulity
and commonsense, commonsense and certitude. The
credulous believe everything they are told, and since
our mental life begins with instruction, they take for
granted in experience what is hearsay, and never seem to
criticise it. Quite different is the condition of mind
called commonsense. It is the general attitude of most
men; it accepts without question from testimony the
existence of a past, and a past in which many historical
events have occurred, and it takes for granted the *prima
facie* object until some doubt is instilled into the mind
by reading or argument. This state is very close to
certitude proper, in that it is free from doubt; it is distinct, because certitude is positive and incompatible
with doubt, either because possessing it we possess also
the reasons why we are certain, or for a reason to be
unfolded later. An excellent example of this belief is
that the sky is blue. Here is a *prima facie* object: we see
blue and we see something which resembles a vault
in shape, and, as we never perceive without perceiving
something, we take the apparent object for a real object

without any hesitation. Now it must not be thought that this is an isolated case; the same happens continually in our life, and from childhood onwards we have been interpreting. The proof of this is that we talk without check of tables and chairs and cakes and food and drinks, of stones and flowers and hills and streams and seas, of all the manifold objects that come into our everyday experience. Now that we are grown up and have learnt to be critical we should be prepared to say, if asked, that we probably do not know the real natures of a large number of these familiar objects, and—somewhat unwisely, perhaps—we might refer our questioner to the man of science for fuller information. Unwisely, for the genuine man of science on being consulted would probably answer that he possesses only a *docta ignoratio;* he will be able to correct some of our most naïve assumptions by means of microscope and telescope, but he is just as dependent as we are on the objects of perception, both for a starting-point and as a court of appeal. It should strike us as odd that we, who have almost all the cards in our hand, should call in to our aid one who has discarded all the court cards, and even after that fixes his attention on one suit.

That is not to say that we can succeed always without verifying our knowledge of *prima facie* objects. We do this, and in many ways, one of which is, without a doubt, by keeping in touch with scientific experiment. Conscious of the depths of nature which are still unprobed, we should be foolish and arrogant to assume that our small stock exhausts the possibilities of knowledge. We live and learn, but it is one thing to expect a form of knowledge that will transcend and transform what we have, and another to hope humbly that in this life it may be increased and deepened. The first expectation is, I believe, a will o' the wisp, the second a fact of experience, and it does not entail that what we already know by perception is erroneous. I must now try and show that in certain cases it may be certain.

The gist of the argument so far is that much of our knowledge is gained by the interpretation of a group of sense-data or phenomena in terms of a determinate unity, and that this procedure cannot be called inference. Is such knowledge ever certain? To some the question must seem trifling. A spade is a spade for a' that; there are many objects and distinctions as familiar to us as a spade is, and if once we start questioning their truth, we shall never come to an end. Those, therefore, who are already satisfied with this answer can follow what is to come light-heartedly. It will be well, however, to carry on with the problem, because the certitude which is our quarry is concerned not so much with perception as with those general beliefs which touch life and lead on to religious faith. Let us take for a start a set of experiences (in a general sense of that term) which are like our perceptions of chairs and tables but are more clearly an interpretation. We pick up a novel and read it through at one sitting. A short time after, an inquisitive friend cross-examines us on our reading, and we fail lamentably. We cannot remember at all that clever saying at the end of chapter three; we have missed the point of the heroine's remark at her third crisis; there are several sentences cited by our inquisitor whose meaning we are unable to unravel. At the end he says, "I suppose you read the book, but you don't seem to have understood a word of it." His criticism is both infuriating and unjust. We can quite well understand the author's complaining that readers should be more careful and not rush through paragraphs which he has spent hours in composing and has packed with meaning. But we can nevertheless claim that while we have scamped the detail, we have understood the book, because we have understood the story as a whole and seen it in its unity. Apart from the classical authors which we have been forced to study at school and university, our bedside books which we read over and over again, and one or two loved authors whose works are seldom out of our hands, there are few books that we know thoroughly. Nevertheless the great world of book-readers would rise in its wrath if it were calmly told that in ninety cases out of a hundred it had missed the meaning of what it was reading.

We seem, therefore, to have a faculty for interpreting the general sense or meaning of what we read and see without full knowledge of the details. If we have made a tour of the east of England and visited the cathedrals, we come away with impressions which can be very decided though very general: even if verger and dean were spirited away and the interiors used for marketing, they would still clearly be buildings constructed for religious purposes; and only after a length of time when memory grows indistinct could we confuse York with Ely. Again, a traveller abroad must be exceedingly unobservant if he does not gather an impression that the inhabitants of different countries differ in looks and manners. The usual habit is to exaggerate these marks, and to classify men and women by nationality in an inordinate way. But the exaggeration bears witness to the fact that all integrate their experiences into some kind of wholes or unities. I am not claiming at present that these impressions are necessarily true; it is clear that they are quite confused, and generally contain as much falsehood as truth. But they are evidence of what I may call "global" impressions, and bear a certain likeness to that apprehension we have described in discussing our knowledge of sensible objects.

Simpler and clearer cases can be drawn from our

experience and judgments in art and literature. In reading there are many acts that we perform, which, were they not so easily and subconsciously carried out, would fill us with astonishment. A word is composed of a varying number of the letters of the alphabet. Each of these letters is in itself unmeaning, is in fact nothing more than a dark shape. Nevertheless, we read into them when combined various meanings; and not only that, but we interpret a series of these combined letters or words as a whole. Even that is not all; the sentence as read takes time, appreciable or not appreciable. Each sensation, therefore, instead of remaining separate, joins itself to the next and fuses with it. The last words of the sentence are unintelligible without the first, and, be it noted, the first words anticipate the last and derive their meaning from them. So it is that the last shall be first and the first shall be last! Those, therefore, who in words profess a doctrine of sensationalism should eat their own words. Every word and every sentence that they utter is a denial of their faith. Language is incompatible with a matter-of-fact attitude, the attitude which regards philosophy and religion as a venture beyond the facts.

An illustration very similar in kind could be drawn from music with its chords and harmonies; but in order to vary instances let us turn to cases where interpretation is acknowledged by everybody. A difficult passage in a foreign language is set before students for translation. Some may have to send in a blank sheet. Others can make out the meaning of some of the sentences, but cannot catch the general meaning; if finally they do succeed, then it is because of certain clues which suddenly or gradually fit together. Instead of a disconnected series of sentences the student sees the connection of the whole, and that whole of meaning appears now as simple and inevitable. The state of mind is like that of the solver of one of those puzzles which used to be put into magazines. A full-page scene was drawn and one was asked to find five faces, or the heroine and the villain. Once seen, the faces stood out as obvious. (In passing one might point out that camouflage is a trick which rests on the principle here being asserted, namely that human beings *jump* to conclusions and interpret *prima facie* objects as wholes of a determinate kind.) The genius is always seeing the obvious, whether his flair be in solving puzzles, picking up clues to detect the criminal, real or fictional, seizing on the significant among historical facts or catching the sense of an obscure painter, musician, or philosopher. We are all being put to the test by modern works of art. They are for the most part organised, but it is with difficulty that some see the organisation, partly because they are looking for a story which is not there, and partly because in our everyday perceptions there is no transition between our apprehension of the sense-data and the sensible object, whereas in this style of art the form is separated as far as possible from the content.

In the examples so far given I have tried to show the working of an activity which synthesises the data, integrating experience into determinate wholes; but it is to be hoped that in some of these illustrations the attitude of the mind will have appeared to the reader to be very like certitude. The data take shape before the mind and are finally so disposed that their unity cannot but be the nature of the object. There is a likeness here to what is called a first impression, but there is also a striking difference. However strong the impression is, it does not commit us; we are aware that it is just an impression, that is to say, a glance which may not have taken in all the essential facts or elements. I do not deny that global apprehension, or interpretation as I have called it, may approximate to an impression, and at the limiting point be indistinguishable from it. There seems to be a certain progression from an impression to a bull's-eye shot of the mind, which has, we are sure, hit the mark, and that is the nature. Or we can if we like plot out degrees of apprehension or belief in this way. At the bottom of the scale come impressions, superficial and deep, for the truth of which we find it very difficult to register the evidence. Next on the scale comes reasoned belief, when we state our evidence as convincing or highly probable. Highest of all comes a certitude for which we cannot set down the evidence, for the reason that the evidence is too vast, too infinite to be itemised. I have not yet said anything explicitly about this last; I have kept it as the *pièce de résistance*. But what is to follow will lead on immediately to it.

We have now to give some instances of certitude of a kind which can be said to fall under belief (where belief is contrasted with knowledge by inference and first principles). As a preface to this task it should be noticed that it does not matter if no general criterion can be given for distinguishing certitude from probability. As Newman remarked, it is quite sufficient if in definite cases we can be sure from the act itself that we are certain. In books of logic a general criterion is usually set down, such as objective evidence. But clearly such a criterion cannot serve as a norm already known which we can conveniently apply to the particular act, like a foot-rule. A true judgment is known to be true in the very act of judging, and does not wait on some general rule for its justification. So, too, in acts of interpretation, what we have to do is to examine instances and find out whether any of them bear the hall-mark of truth.

Now that such instances do exist we have already

had from the *Grammar of Assent* compelling evidence. Is there anyone who is prepared to deny that England is an island, that there is no war going on at this present moment in the country——? "We accept and hold with an unqualified assent that the earth, considered as a phenomenon, is a globe; that all its regions see the sun by turns; that there are vast tracts on it of land and water; that there are really existing cities on definite sites, which go by the names of London, Paris, Florence and Madrid." Whether we have travelled and seen places with our own eyes or stayed at home and relied on the word of others, makes no difference to our assent to the existence of Paris and the other facts and places mentioned by Newman. If this be so, then knowledge by interpretation is operative not only in the presence of objects which fall under direct experience but also with evidence which comes to us by word, by the testimony of others. We are accustomed to rate testimony lower than direct evidence, and with reason; nevertheless we have only to consult such examples as have been quoted from Newman, to examine our judgments of history, and to remind ourselves that far the greater part of our knowledge is dependent on information from others, to realise that there must be some intrinsic worth in testimony.

It will be well to arrange under definite headings the cases where interpretation is accompanied by certitude. The first is covered by what in books of logic is called induction. Unfortunately the explanation of this induction has been hindered by two prejudices. The first came from admiration for the Aristotelian logic. Now the glory of that logic is the discovery of the syllogism and the presentation of it with its various types and formulas. So perfect did it appear as the instrument of correct thinking that succeeding philosophers succumbed to the temptation of reducing all other forms of knowledge to it, with the exception of first principles. In the reaction to this tendency which followed the Renaissance and the abortive *Novum Organum* of Bacon, philosophers proclaimed a new method, the method of induction. This method proved highly successful in certain provinces of science. The explanation, however, was less successful. A general distrust of metaphysics and the work of the intellect pervaded Europe at the time. Knowledge had made no advance in the physical order by means of metaphysics, so it was thought; far wiser, therefore, to relinquish abstractions and rely on the data of sense; sensible fact was all that was needed. The result of this choice was to provide the world with some excellent methods, and at the same time with some thoroughly unsatisfactory explanations of them. A power stood behind the throne which was doing all the work, and its presence was ignored. This power was the intellect, busy all the time detecting the intelligible unity underlying the multiple phenomena of sense.

Scientific thinkers are at last taking note of this omission and trying to make up for it. They have been led out of Egypt by Mr. Whitehead, who has pointed out that their rash acceptance of the assumptions of Hume must prove as fatal to the claims of science as to the claims of religion. In emptying belief out of the bath they emptied themselves as well. The strange thing is that this was not obvious from the beginning. If "all our perceptions are distinct existences," and "our impressions loose and separate"; if the objects of sense are nothing but disconnected data, then I have no right to go beyond the present and to predict the future, no right to rely on the past, no right to suppose any uniformity or permanence of pattern whatsoever. Now science has never observed such ruling, and therefore it is guilty according to its own estimate of acting irrationally, of believing, as the divines do, without any foundation. It has had, therefore, to retrace its steps, and though it is still a little grudging in its acknowledgement of religious belief—for prejudices die hard—it is ready to accept a belief in what may be called the noumenal as opposed to the phenomenal. This concession prepares the way for a reconsideration of the process of induction.

Induction is neither by syllogistic inference nor by exhaustive enumeration, but a type of what I have named interpretation. The multiplication of experiments, the refinement of data, serve to eliminate the irrelevant and leave the way open for the mind to detect the essential; once that has been discovered the rest slide into their place. No doubt this is an ideal which the man of science dealing with very refractory material does not find realised; in its place he talks of the uniformity of consequent and antecedent. He forgets, in doing this, that the language of uniformity, to have its full effect, must insinuate the presence of real causes, that invariability is a sign of a connection founded on nature, and that it is precisely because this is so that interpretation has the first and the last word in induction. Just as one may show charts and statistics of an obscure disease without end and without result to a quack doctor, so to an unintelligent scientist the records of the data and the experiments are so many black dots. It is the genius who leaps to the proper cause, the man with a power of interpretation who sees the hang of a thing, who looks within and grasps the cause.

That this success is not due to a mere enumeration is obvious. Enumeration in many cases could not be exhaustive, and the difference between ten and ten

M

thousand is negligible when the condition for certitude is infinity. Besides, the more intelligent the interpreter the smaller the number of instances required. That the process is not syllogistic is equally obvious, though it has been disputed. Those who argue for the syllogism arrange the premises so that the principle of sufficient reason or the uniformity of nature or some such general principle figures in the major premiss. But such a syllogism may do for a museum of exhibits; it is certainly not the process of induction. I do not discover the cause of a series of headaches by an appeal to the principle of sufficient reason; I presuppose it, as happens in all thinking. The trouble is with the minor premise, to wit, "the principle of reason demands that the connection observed must be a connection of nature." For that to be true the principle which figures in the major must be already presupposed; hence there is no need to make a fresh appeal to it. What the scientist is concerned with is precisely the discovery of this minor, and when he shouts "Eureka" he knows that he has interpreted the data aright and lit upon a cause. I do not say that he has comprehended the cause in its totality; that rarely, if ever, happens. The most he can achieve is to make reason out of the phenomena presented to him. He is like the husbandman who reads the signs in the sky and says "There will be a storm to-night"; but whether that storm will be like the storm of a few days ago, what new powers it will show, he knows not. When Crusoe saw the sign upon the sand, he saw the evidence of a man, but he did not as yet know Friday.

The reference to Friday suggests a second type of interpretation, our knowledge of individual men. There is first the fact to be explained that we know that there are beings outside ourselves who are not only living, but similar to ourselves in being human. Psychologists and philosophers have worried over this simple fact and offered various explanations. The more common one is that we infer it. I will not stop over this problem except to suggest that it is a case of interpretation. We come *pari passu* to a knowledge of ourselves and others. We do not first examine what we are and by an act of precocious philosophising infer the existence of fellow beings outside us. Even if this were true, it would not explain how we seized on certain data and decided to call them human. It is more likely that the child comes to know itself by its discoveries of human nature in others. This, too, would be an exaggeration if it suggested that a child started with itself as a complete stranger—and there are psychologists who tend to make this mistake. A child *is* and is active before it comes to articulate self-knowledge, but all the while, since it is itself the subject of its own sensations, desires and perceptions, there is an implicit awareness which is being developed concomitantly with its voyage into the strange world which is not itself. That strange world takes shape, however, without any mental labour, in faces and in the voices of other beings, and these others articulate its own consciousness of self, and its own self interprets these others as human, as friendly and kind, or frightening and forceful, or protective and responsive, both in one inseparable process.

Whatever be the means whereby we come to know other human beings, our discernment of them as individuals must be put down to interpretation. The child comes to know its mother as distinct from all other people on the earth, and to recognise her presence and her thought and work from all manner of tiny indications. One note of her voice, one gesture in a dim light, one movement of the body, the sound of her footsteps afar off, may be sufficient. A like quickness, though in a less degree, in detecting our acquaintances belongs to all of us. I do not suppose that we have to make up our mind that the people we are living with, at home, in business, at clubs, are the same when having left the room they return after a minute or within a short or long while. It would considerably interfere with our comfort and our occupations if this were so. Imagine at the theatre having to infer that the chief characters were the same each time that they made their entry after an exit, that there were good reasons for supposing, if we were to argue it out, that this must really be the Hamlet that we had lately seen! Imagine, too, the annoyance and embarrassment of the poet or novelist should the thread of his discourse be interrupted by uncertainty whether his typist is the same person that she was a few moments before!

The formalist may maintain that what has happened is a rapid and condensed inference. His wish must, however, be father to his thought, because he will never be able to write out a syllogism which is in the least like the experience. No person is completely identical in appearance from one moment to another. So far as the data presented to the sense are concerned there is nothing but similarity, and yet we have not the slightest difficulty in reading through the two similar presentations an identity of content, of person. What this must mean is that given sufficient detail the mind has the power of interpreting what that detail signifies. The signs or evidence having reached an indefinable limit of abundance, we are certain of the true interpretation, despite change and variation in the data which make up the evidence. I shall return to the question of the amount of evidence required later. What we can say at present is that it is just what we mean when we use the word "obvious" or say that a fact strikes or leaps to the eye.

What has here been written of the recognition of individuals holds, too, for other animate objects, such as cats and dogs, canaries and parrots; for inanimate objects such as decorate our room, for places we visit, the street we live in, the villages and towns we pass through often in the train, for sounds we hear, which despite the variance in accent and inflexion convey to us the same meaning, and for countless other facts which we take for granted.   I have already taken the examples of a text, of a passage for translation, of the story in a book.   I will therefore pass on to a third type which is based on testimony.   This type is of special interest because, if it can be shown to reach in certain cases to certitude, we shall have cleared the way for certitude in faith, faith in the word of another, faith in the revelation of God.   So closely associated is the word belief with this type that it is in current usage often identified with it, and almost invariably it is supposed to be inferior somehow to direct experience and knowledge.   Once again the examples quoted by Newman prove a stumbling-block to any such contrast.   Are we really less certain of the existence of America because we have not crossed the Atlantic, less certain of the reign of Queen Victoria than that of George the Fifth?   It is possible that many of us have never seen our present King, so that we ought on our principles to relinquish certitude even of his existence.   Does it not seem, then, that in the face of testimony we also exercise what I have described as our faculty of interpretation?

Belief in testimony means belief in the word of another.   The word of another may be either spoken or written, and we can distinguish at least two types: one where the writer or speaker is accepted purely on his authority, the second where we ask him to produce his evidence. To take an example: a short while ago I was informed that, when a preacher was broadcasting in a church, listeners at Amsterdam or Vienna or New York could hear what he was saying before those who sat at the back of the church. My informant went on to give the reason, namely that the words were broadcast by the beam system, whereas in the church the words were heard by sound waves, and sound waves travel much more slowly than light waves. Now I might have relied on the authority of my friend and believed him simply on that, but in fact he also supplied the evidence for his statement. These two types of testimony are clearly different, though not so much as one might suppose. The reasons my informant gave rested also on testimony and authority which he himself had already accepted; neither he nor I had experimented with waves of light and sound, and we were far too ignorant to argue out for ourselves the truth of the theory and its application. Again, a large building stands near to where we lived as children; we had always been told that it was the remains of a medieval castle. We are certain now that this information was correct. We have learnt something about medieval history, its life and art and manners; we know the style of architecture used during its phases, we know, too, of the family which lived in the neighbour-hood. As a result we have not the slightest doubt what the building is. It will be seen in this second example that at the beginning authority was the sole source of our knowledge, but that as we grew up that knowledge was confirmed in all manner of ways, many of which, if not all, depended on testimony of some kind. After a period, long or short, the data presented themselves to us in a way which admitted of no mistake, and were integrated into a unity which admitted of only one interpretation.

From the preceding paragraph it will be plain that there are different kinds of testimony, and therefore different motives for assent. If I am very credulous, it is enough for someone to tell me a piece of news for me to believe it, but if I have profited by experience I am cautious in believing the word of another. When, for instance, a doctor is recommended, I make a number of inquiries to confirm the first testimony in his favour; I ask other persons' experience, and go still further by examining the effect of his prescriptions on others' health; in doing this I supplement testimony so far as I can by observed fact, and only then do I trust his judgment; when, then, he speaks with authority and insists on my taking some cure of which I know nothing, I believe in his word, but only because I have already verified beforehand his credibility.

An interesting question here arises: can my motive of assent be called in any true sense belief in his word? To this we hope to return again. At least we can say that it may happen that I grow so confident in his skill that I assent to everything he says solely because he says it; and the proof of this is that I will not hear anything against him, that I dismiss all the objections brought against his reputation, taking his word against the whole world. This attitude of mind is close to that given by Newman when he says that he would reject as intolerable any evidence that his most trusted friend was unreliable or treacherous. We know how in fairy tale and novel the supreme trial for the lover occurs when all appearances are against the fidelity of the beloved, and she asks him nevertheless to take her word.

For the moment let us leave this form of belief and return to the question of certitude. I have brought forward as instances of unhesitating assent the existence of Queen Victoria and the medieval castle. Both depend on information received, which is supported by an abundance of indirect evidence. These are clearly not two exceptional facts; there are a host of others to be found in every history book. Figures and characters of the long dead peer out at us, and they are as real to us as the living—the uniformed Napoleon with his pale face; the grandiloquent Chatham; the thick-nosed Cromwell with the warts; snuff-taking, punctual little Kant; spidery Richelieu; the ill-fated Stuarts; the Plantagenets; and not only men, but places and times and epochs—Florence and Geneva, Genoa and Venice, England under Puritanism, the Spain of Charles the Fifth and Philip the Second, the court of the Renaissance Popes, the thirteenth century, the Rome of Augustus, fifth century Athens, Judea under the prophets and kings. The longer we pore over the past the more clearly do persons and periods and peoples take on a colour and shape and atmosphere which cannot but be authentic. We may be wrong in details, but the contours are correct, and we could never confuse one with another, any more than we could mistake Manchester and Verona. Now if this be so, then once more we must call upon the factor of interpretation. A vast array of data are before us; shapes which are similar come before the eye, and nevertheless we give them individual names and pick them out from the mass without any difficulty or hesitation. We have synthetised, integrated these data in accordance with the real nature which they reveal; we have seen how they are connected, their unity and determinate character. Hence it is that the philosophers —and such exist—who deny that a certitude can be obtained in history do so because they approach the question with an inadequate equipment. Convinced as they are that shy truth cannot be won save by immediate experience or by the immediate apprehension of first principles and deductions from them, they have deprived themselves of the possibility of explaining and justifying the many truths we all of us enjoy by other means.

The argument in favour of interpretation will, I hope, have carried conviction, but the reader may well be asking for some standard by which to know when the interpretation is certain. Obviously there are grave dangers in allowing such certitude. We shall have error rampant, disguised as truth under the name of impressions, taste, "feeling for things," relative and subjective points of view and certitude. I have already anticipated this difficulty. No amount of warning and teaching can save us from the danger of error. That we go wrong in judging is no argument against judgment itself, and similarly the mistakes made in interpretation cannot be turned into witnesses against the claims of interpretation. The fact that I mistook a stranger in the street for my best friend cannot be used to prove that I do not know my best friend when I actually meet him—and, as we have seen, this knowledge is one type of interpretation. The fact is that we are sure at times to confuse states of mind which closely resemble one another, but are really different. When our friend tells us that he remembers some fact, we may be certain that he does not, but he will have to find out the truth for himself afterwards; and when the young girl at a revivalist meeting assures the world that she is converted and has faith, there is no means of convincing her at the time that she may be under an illusion. We might be content, therefore, with the general position that there are cases of interpretation in which certitude can be found, and there are cases in which it is not, and that no general criterion can serve in practice to mark them off from one another.

A suggestion,* however, can be offered, not as a criterion but as an explanation of why it is that certain beliefs seem to be so well founded. All knowledge is based on evidence, and our normal procedure when a statement has to be proved is to state the evidence. The trouble is that we are constantly unable to give the evidence required. This may show that we ought not to be so cocksure in what we are saying, and indeed it is a duty where possible to make our statements according to the evidence. But at times it is, if not impossible, inconceivably hard. How can the connoisseur point out the difference between a masterpiece and its copy to one who has no eyes to see? How difficult it is for the Catholic historian to prove that the picture Gibbon gives in the *Decline and Fall* is one long distortion, for an Englishman to show a foreigner that cricket is a game worth playing! So often it happens that a custom in a family or group or nation looks quite ridiculous to a stranger. I have known a German book about an institution with which I am familiar, in which, despite a vast store of learning and accumulation of evidence, the life and purposes of that institution were time and again unconsciously caricatured. The possession of evidence does not, therefore, always save a man from error, and the inability to give the evidence does not always mean that we lack certitude. Let us, however, admit that as a general rule knowledge of a fact goes with knowledge of the evidence for that fact. The admission may help us to understand why in certain notorious instances that evidence appears to be wanting but is really there.

As what is now to come may prove difficult, I had better begin by giving a clue to the argument and

* For the theory in the following pages, I am indebted to the late H. S. V. Bickford.

conclusion. There are a number of truths of everyday life of which we are certain. When asked to give the evidence for them we are unable to do so. The reason for this is not the paucity of evidence but the abundance. So abundant, indeed, is the evidence that it approaches to the infinite. All that we know supports it, so that if it proved to be untrue an abyss would open at our feet; we should find ourselves in a world far more fantastic than that in which the cow jumped over the moon. Now this infinite evidence does not come to us as infinite—that is clearly impossible—but as a unity and whole of internal consistent parts, and it is this massed unity of concordant experiences which gives the mind its security and certitude. Just as the mystic saint sees everything revolving round God, so the ordinary man moves happily and confidently forward because of the unity of his universe. As can be seen, this explanation fits in with what has already been said about global apprehension, integration and interpretation.

And now to prove this. In any investigation the more items that we find which point to a fact, the more likely, so we believe, is that fact to be right. This belief is seen vigorously at work in books which try to prove that Bacon wrote the plays of Shakespeare, in discussions of the rectitude of Mary Queen of Scots, and every day in the law courts. The more abundant the evidence and the more it converges, the higher the degree of probability. What degree is necessary for certainty? As I have argued, there comes a point when the truth shines out, when the fact or object or meaning is manifested in its unity through the signs. But it is by a different path that we now want to reach an answer, by a closer inspection of that evidence which in certain cases of certitude is present. The mathematician and the scientifically inclined critic would say that for certitude proper the number of pieces of evidence must be infinite. He is thinking, no doubt, of external evidence, but he would apply the same test to internal agreement where a vast number of parts cohere together without contradiction. At first such a condition of certitude seems impossible of fulfilment; but let it be used as a working hypothesis. Suppose an infinite number of pieces of evidence joined in a pattern. Now it could conceivably happen that like a gauze or web or robe the pieces which make the pattern might present themselves to the eye as a whole unified pattern and remain themselves indistinguishable. Let us see whether truths which we would call evident answer to this description. It is certain, we say, that England is an island. How do we know this? The reader, if he puts this question to himself may be inclined to laugh at its simplicity and answer "by maps, of course!" But let him beware. Is he as certain of the features of the territories in Africa and South America? If he answers in the negative, then it is clear that maps are not his sole evidence, seeing that these places are also on maps. It is not maps alone, but maps supported by other evidence. That evidence, it may be said, is covered by the fact that everyone says that England is an island. Neither will this, however, suffice; for a second's thought will show that the fact is very rarely indeed mentioned explicitly, and even if it were the opening gambit of conversation, nevertheless there are a number of things which are constantly being said of which we are not at all certain. Exasperated, the reader may exclaim that he has sailed round England and knows by experience that it is an island. We have now his word and nothing else, and if we are mischievous we may challenge his experience by asking him how he is certain that he was not sailing round an inland sea. If he, feeling cornered, boasts an aeroplane, we had better desist and take another example.

As a convenient example the following may be chosen: how do I know that no Bolshevist revolution has broken out at the present moment in England? The answer, I think, would have to be something of this kind. It is impossible that in a country like England, where news travels so quickly, we should not have heard of it. The newsboys would be shouting it in the streets, and all the modern inventions for communication would somehow have transmitted the news. No one can deny that this answer contains a truth. But in itself it is not satisfactory. Error is still possible. A certain minister of religion with a sense of humour once startled England with bogus news of this kind over the wireless, and the prudent man does not publish as certain what he reads on posters. Besides, the reasons given are themselves dependent on a host of other assumptions, and these assumptions, if taken one by one, are possibly erroneous. I do not think, therefore, that it can be maintained that the answer which has been given is a full explanation of our certainty. What we really mean is that if England were in revolution the bottom would be knocked out of all our certainties. In stating the answer in the form given above only a few of these certainties were mentioned, and thus isolated they float in the air. In fact, like the hydra they draw their strength from the earth on which they rest, from the world of discourse to which they belong. They are guaranteed by an infinite number of other certainties or facts, all of which would have to be wrong if the statement made about the state of England were right. It is this massive content of inextricably interwoven beliefs which makes us reject certain alleged statements as obviously wrong. If I meet a man at a concert and take him for X, and then discover afterwards that X has been dead some time, I shall be a fool if I cling to the evidence of my senses. The overwhelming evidence connected with every department of my beliefs makes the fact of his death certain. So again, if England were not an island, or if a revolution had really occurred in the country, there would ensue such indescribable confusion in every connection of my world of thought that I reject these assertions forthwith.

It should be noted that there is no carefully worked out hierarchy in these certainties of mine. It may well be that there are propositions which are self-evident and that these condition all my beliefs, but I do not deduce from these in a descending scale a series of facts and truths. On the contrary, we shall find if we look into the matter that the truths we have learnt from the cradle and at school support one another mutually, that what is incongruous is dismissed while the rest coalesce into a body of beliefs which form a pattern or garment without seam. The truths that my mother is my mother, that famous persons mentioned in my early childhood actually existed then, that England is an island, that God exists and has revealed Himself, grow with the years like the snowball, gathering round them everyday new bits of evidence. In time they may be thought to clash with some other massive or vivid content of experience, and then we have those revolts from convention and traditional teaching which are so noticeable in adolescence, or else they become part and parcel of our outlook on life, our test and guarantee of information given to us. It should be noted secondly that the ground of this certainty is a consistency of evidence of an infinitely complex kind. Hence it is impossible to tabulate it, to give all the items which make it up. It is not surprising, therefore, that we are unable to treat such cases of certainty in the way in which we have been taught that proof should be given. The scientist lays it out on the table and asks for it to be examined, and then goes on to claim that all certainty should be able to follow this rule. But it is much more likely that with his finite evidence his conclusion is only probable, whereas those who have certainty of the kind I have described have infinite evidence and are therefore powerless to put it forth in separate items.

This fact, however, gives rise in turn to a new difficulty. If the evidence is of an infinite complexity, how is it that we are able to recognise it? To see this difficulty, compare the two situations where finite and infinite evidence are respectively involved. In the first we can examine that evidence, weigh its force and say to a critic, "here is the evidence which you can estimate for yourself; it is for these reasons that I believe what I am now telling you." In the second situation this cannot be done, and nevertheless there must be a ground for our certainty, there must be something to see. In other words, there must be some way in which we recognise what is infinitely complex and consistent without having to count each item in it. What has already been said about perception, integration and the interpretation of unity has prepared us for the answer. It has now to be developed in terms of what may be called the unity of indirect reference. This unity is of such cardinal importance and so easy to understand that I must beg the reader to pay special attention to it.

The function of this unity of indirect reference can be seen if we examine our knowledge of any object of common and everyday experience, for example, a tree. We learn in childhood to call a certain kind of object which has affected our various senses a tree, and experience teaches us that in all men the sensations similar to ours are associated with the word "tree." So it comes about that we behave as though the evidence of our senses and the experience of others were evidence sufficient for certainty, and we take it for granted that when we see a tree both that it is really a tree and not an hallucination, and also that all others who look at it will see a tree. The consequence of this is that when a number of men are in the presence of some such natural object, each of them takes it for granted that all the others regard it as a tree and not something else. This being so, they do not spend time telling each other about this banal fact; on the contrary they never allude to it directly at all, unless the wish to impart some new piece of interesting information to a friend or new comer leads them to do so, and if this happens the reference to the common certainty will be almost invariably indirect. For instance, if several men are near a tree, one may say, "The man near that tree is my father." By remarks such as this it will be easily seen that a common object of certainty, like a tree, is implied in an infinite number of contexts though it is very rarely mentioned. Therefore every natural object affecting sense, every existing condition of affairs, such as the form of government in a country or its main geographical features, every common experience of human nature, are present in our conversation and reading, not in direct statement but by indirect reference, so that our speech is composed of a tissue of such references bearing out each other. This tissue it is which supersedes evidence given point by point; we have instead a conspiracy of infinite evidence saying the same thing.

Our search is not, however, yet ended. Some may think that we have so far advanced only a hypothesis and may demand proof that this unity of indirect

reference gathers in infinite evidence and so reaches
to certainty, and again that this consistency has to do
with facts and not merely with thoughts. To take the
latter first. Observation of the development of any one
of these certainties which I have cited will show clearly
that it is in contact with fact all the time and that it
is controlled by facts. The simplest illustration would
be to trace the growth of the belief that England is
an island from the primitive stage, when, shall we say,
an early Christopher Columbus landed on our shore.
One of the first colonists or a descendant would make
a voyage and bring back news that the land they
dwelt on was an island. He might well be believed, but
as long as the interests of the colony were centred on
the district in which they lived, there would be little
occasion for them to refer indirectly to the circum-
navigation of their comrade and the newly discovered
character of the country. Hence they would not take
it for granted and use it in the context of their speech,
until the fact came into contact with their everyday
life, until, for instance, trading stations had grown up
all round the coast with maritime communications and
land routes. If this is so it proves that indirect reference
takes place only when men are in contact with facts,
and that, therefore, the certainty is one about the actual
nature of things.

The next task is to show that this indirect reference
has for its effect unity and certainty. The scientist,
as I have said, will grant that it gives certainty if there
is infinite evidence. Now this latter may be impossible
to prove, but we have only to take the example, that
England is an island, to see that we have something
which is practically indistinguishable from it. Consider
the number of indirect references to it in our conversations about travelling, correspondence, defence, educa-

N

tion, commerce, politics, in every concern of life; remember, too, that there is every possible variety and shade of meaning in such references—and it will be very difficult to escape the conclusion that we have a texture of infinite fineness, a unity, that is, of infinite complexity which explains our certitude. If we are still unconvinced by this the reason may be that we are not sufficiently aware that every idea we express has with it a train of attendant ideas, the multitude of which no man can number. I cannot, for instance, speak of a journey from England to America without the aid of the ideas of sea and railways and crowds and shipping and harbour and winds in the background. Furthermore, there are a vast number of cross references; the lines of one thought may go in different directions and nevertheless meet, because of intersecting lines. As an illustration take three parties of men looking at the same stretch of fields. 'Field' is the common notion, but one has attendant on it thoughts of hunting or shooting with all the ideas that are subsidiary to such a pursuit; another group are farmers or farm hands, and think of the produce of those fields; the third party contains an artist who looks at the land as a possible scene for a picture. Here is an identical idea with different indirect references, according to the thought of each group. If now they meet and converse, the far-stretching lines of reference intersect and without interference with their unity. This is what I mean by saying that all conversation is based on the unity of indirect reference and that this unity is an indication of an infinitely rich complexity and therefore of truth.

How much of our knowledge is built up by indirect allusion I leave aside as not belonging to this discussion, but clearly the extent is larger than we might at first suppose. We rarely talk directly of things which we believe to be as obvious to others as to ourselves. It is the novel and the unexpected which interest us, and we try to communicate the news to our neighbours. This news has, however, all round it what is established and certain, like a circumambient atmosphere in an Italian landscape which delineates details with a pure and brilliant clarity. The wider the horizon the more wonderful is the unity of the detail, and it is this unity which is the sign and assurance of truth. Until it reaches a certain complexity there is always the chance that our thought is mistaken. Thus a child having little experience is unaware that what it thinks may clash with unknown facts, and its dogmatism is not taken seriously. But when adults converse a vast region of indirect reference is common to both, and no contradiction comes to light. Sometimes, indeed—perhaps many times— an uncomfortable sensation is felt that all is not right. The words our friend uses have nothing wrong with them, but a far-off discrepancy is signalling to us. There is a crack deep down in the foundations of the building which we are first aware of by a feeling of malaise in looking at the central arches. How often it happens, for instance, that in conversation with another we begin well; then after a time there creeps over us a foreboding of error somewhere; suddenly the cause is realised, and we say: "Oh! you think that I am so and so, do you?" or, "You fancy that I am related to X, but I am not. Someone of the same name is, but I am not that person"; we all remember mistakes of this kind, mistakes as to place or occupation or reputation, and they are interesting as bearing out the unity of indirect reference. For a while the unity and concord of two minds remain complete; then a far-away reference contained in some remark disturbs the unity, and it may be a long time before it comes sufficiently near to direct reference to be recognised.

This discord or friction is the mark of error and the absence of it is the sign of truth. This latter does not mean, of course, that on the strength of its absence we can, on all occasions, and with every subject matter, declare that we are certain. With the advance of years and wisdom we are constantly correcting past beliefs or shaking them off. Forearmed we make hypotheses, hoping to see them verified. But in saying this we must not exaggerate. These hypotheses usually belong to a province of reality which lies apart from the ordinary world of discourse. Indirect references to it are not constantly being made. And if we find that our common beliefs suffer correction with time, that is because they were confused at first and contained more than we supposed. We say that the sky is blue, that the sun sets, and these statements persist and will persist because they conflict with so few other elements of knowledge. We correct them on learning science, but the correction does not touch what we perceive. We still, as we think, see a blue sky and a sun descending below the horizon; it is the false inference which we have made from the perception which has to be modified. Nothing that has been said in these pages justifies the pretension that we know exhaustively the inner nature of reality. There are deeps within deeps, there are secrecies which the sense-bound mind of man cannot penetrate. The whole point of the argument from signs is that we are able to detect something of the realm of matter and spirit by means of the sensible signs, its appearance. When we say that we can read another's face we are not claiming a full knowledge, an intuition of his mind; but we have caught an expression of it. Similarly the mighty orchestration of the universe in experience gives us a certainty that what we are saying and perceiving is true. The unity perceived, however, will vary with different men in depth and clarity of penetration, and the greatest genius will be the first to acknowledge that he is a dunce and superficial in his interpretation.

Let us admit, therefore, that the absence of discord does not necessarily spell certitude, and again that certitude when it is attained does not imply exhaustive knowledge or intuition. We have, therefore, to ask when and where the unity is so complex and consistent as to bring with it this certitude, and a justifiable certitude. As already suggested the answer is, when the evidence is infinite and infinitely complex, and if it be objected that this answer involves a circular argument, we must fall back on a power of the mind to recognise when it is in the presence of such evidence. It is quite true that infinite evidence can be seized only in the form of unity; it is true, too, that we have tried to distinguish some unities from others by urging that some must be of only finite texture while others are of infinite. Such argument does, I admit, appear to move in a circle; but the difficulty is artificial, because we are trying to articulate certain facts of consciousness, and it surely is a fact that the difference between a child's beliefs that the English are the best fighters in the world and that England is an island has to be explained in some such way as I have set out. For a while the first statement may show no internal contradiction. The indirect references to it in a very patriotic family may all seem to bear it out, and so a great amount of evidence is seen in a unity which is not questioned. Time, however, will make the belief to crumble or lean heavily to one side. We can easily see that the evidence was not infinite, and we can easily distinguish between this belief and the certainty that England is an island. This latter is supplied daily with new evidence; if it proved false then no fact, no event, would be certain, and it is this rippling sea of evidence which makes the truth to us so obvious. We have, indeed, to twist our minds away from clear distinctions in consciousness if we deny that, on reflection, we ought not to say that we are certain that the English are incomparably brave while we are bound to hold that England is an island. These are facts which demand an explanation, and the explanation given above safeguards the distinction as well as explaining it.

There is good reason, therefore, for thinking that the mind has the power of recognising when the complexity has reached the requisite degree for certainty. No rule of thumb can be given which will tell us once and for all when and where on all possible occasions this requisite complexity is present. It would, no doubt, be advantageous to have such a criterion, but in fact we have always to fall back on some definite case and examine that without prepossessions or prejudice. At the best we can lay down certain necessary conditions. There must obviously be a great degree of complexity seen as a whole; next, there must be no ambiguity whatsoever in the terms or the thought, and thirdly the mind must have a quiet assurance free from all possible doubt. As a test of this latter the mind must be prepared to accept with serenity all possible logical conclusions, known or unknown, not only without forethought, but without even the consciousness that the chance of exercising forethought would be an advantage. For the rest we must trust the native strength and power of the mind. In knowledge we undergo an ever-changing experience, and it is one of the marvellous functions of the mind, that, despite its activity, it suffers the infinitely varied experience to take shape within it. If we may be allowed to speak of the external world making impressions on that mind, we can then picture the result as far more intricate than any work of bronze hammered by a Vulcan into a pattern. Every moment winged words strike us, sensations leave their effect, and in a variety of ways to cause bewilderment. Nevertheless, these hordes of impressions form into an order with a minute tracery like the facets of a fly's eye, nay, rather, a thousand spiders' webs worked into one pattern. Now, when we recall that error consists in believing a thing to be what it is not and so believing something which is inconsistent with other facts, are we not forced to conclude that the absence of any such inconsistency in the myriad interlacing content of experience I have described is a mark of truth and a pledge of certainty?

We can go further than this and claim that if there are degrees in belief and certainty, then this kind of certainty is the most sure of all, or if this sound paradoxical we can at least distinguish degrees within the strength of evidence. On the bottom rung of the ladder will be found proof which depends on external evidence taken piecemeal. This is the proof which science honours and is supposed to employ. As a matter of fact it uses almost always evidence of the next order in the series. This is what I have already discussed under the name of interpretation. It depends on internal consistency, on a unity which the mind descries. It sees the evidence as a whole and as determining only one object and pattern. As might be expected this covers what is most sure and what is most fallible, the flashes of insight of the genius and the plausible but mistaken guesses of the opportunist. The latter is frankly a guess, and nothing more need be said about it; on the other hand the flash-light of "interpretation" does really explore the determining constituents of the unity though it sees them as a whole. It has as its concomitant always a feeling of finality, an assurance of the inevitability of the interpretation. Lastly, and highest of all, comes the certainty based on infinite evidence and brought about by what has been called the unity of indirect reference. These everyday certainties are so strong that they are capable of overriding the assents given in the two former classes if any conflict arises between them.

The conclusion reached may seem to some extraordinary for the reason that they have been told so often that scientific certainty is the ideal, and perhaps the only legitimate form. This suggestion they have accepted on authority and without inquiry, but in accepting it they have done violence to their inner convictions, and in fact their acceptance is nearly always only theoretical, because in practice they still continue to observe a different estimate; and it is this universal estimate which I have set down in the preceding paragraph as the true one. The immemorial belief has been right and men have been led to depart from it by undue regard to scientific authorities. Their methods looked austere and, as they were used by learned men, the simple were too modest to claim a superior knowledge, especially as they were unable to offer a rational defence of the claim. They were slow, too, to see that the scientists in every advance they made broke their own rules by what some called inspired guessing, but was really fine interpretation, and that though they pretend to despise the ordinary objects of perception, such as chairs and stones and cats, they always control their investigations by means of this despised knowledge and in their conclusions hope to throw light upon them. The classification, therefore, which at first sight may seem extraordinary, is the one which every man in practice assumes to be true, and all that the arguments given in its favour have done is to attempt a long-overdue rational justification of it.

It is time now to gather up the conclusions reached. Newman showed that many of our assents sat loosely to the inferential process of which they were supposed to be the conclusions, and that they were held with a certainty far beyond the evidence given in the premises. He spoke of probabilities accumulating into certainty and of an illative sense which divined the meaning of evidence. This was his answer to the problem of belief and the possibility of certitude in beliefs. I have suggested that the admirable analysis which he gives is weakened by the habit of philosophic thinking in his period, and that the many good points he makes must be translated into a different idiom for their proper worth to be appreciated. I do not believe that the probabilities as such can ever make certitude, whereas there seems to be no doubt that evidence can so accumulate and cohere together as to reveal inevitably a certain pattern and meaning. Again, it is difficult to find a place for an illative sense or instinct in any convincing philosophical system, whereas there is a heap of evidence to be drawn from modern psychology, from observation of the methods employed in the sciences, in historical investigation, in the fine arts and from everyday experiences, which fits in with what I have called interpretation; and this fact of interpretation is in turn easily fitted into a sound philosophical theory of knowledge. I have, therefore, tried to analyse this power of interpretation, and to exhibit its working in perception, in recognition of individuals, the correct reading of texts, in our acceptance of testimony about places and persons and past historical facts and conditions. In our interpretations certainty is often present, but to prove this beyond all cavil for some experiences I have appealed to manifest examples such as that England is an island. From an analysis of the motives for believing such truths it came out that an infinitely complex and consistent evidence may be present under the form of unity, and that beliefs of this kind while unrecognised by the ordinary canons of logic are, nevertheless, the most potent of all our certainties, and far more firmly grounded than what goes by the name of certitude in many grave books of logic and science.

CHAPTER VII

AUTHORITY IN BELIEF

Moi, qui suis faible dans la vie, j'appuie sur ma sœur, qui s'appuie sur son confesseur un Jésuite (ces gens là sont trés forts) qui s'appuie sur Rome.

Cezanne.

The knowledge which can be made common to all is a foundation upon which a certain increasing school, finding popular "opinion" too sandy, is endeavouring to build up a new state of things, religious, moral, political, and social. This kind of "positivism," which claims for its sanction the common, that is to say the lowest, experiences of mankind, is and always has been the religion of the vulgar, to whatever class they belong. . . . The doctrines of liberty, fraternity and equality are known instinctively only by very bad children.

Coventry Patmore: Religio Poetae.

CHAPTER VII

AUTHORITY IN BELIEF

FROM belief through interpretation we can pass to another use of the term "belief," as something distinct from "vision"—this will be used from now onward, unless the context makes another sense clear: *fides ex auditu;* belief on another's word, on authority and written testimony. This implies that we have not the evidence directly before us, that we are not compelled by what we see. I do not say that this distinction is free from ambiguity—there are some who would maintain that an assertion about the future must be a belief, and that communicated information may, if the medium be pure, deserve the name "direct"—but it will serve. We shall never be in a position to see the correct solution to the problems involved, if we prejudge the matter and assume that belief is necessarily a form of knowledge inferior to vision. It has been the fashion for some time to extol experience and decry belief, and the result, as we shall see, has been unfortunate. To counteract the effect of this fashion it is necessary to begin with an apologia for belief.

In any community of men and women, large or small, both belief and experience are necessary for the continuation of life. The well-being of civilisation depends on a well-adjusted balance between these two; and therefore the plea for belief which follows must not be understood as an attack on experience as such. Obviously the end and consummation of human activity is vision and enjoyment, and Christianity with its promise of the Beatific Vision in the hereafter has no other purpose than to prepare men for that beatitude. It comes into conflict, indeed, with secular ambitions, but this conflict is caused not by any denial of experience, but in its teaching that, so far as the supreme ideal is concerned, we must live by faith in this present life. This faith is, of course, religious and supernatural, but what is said of the highest can be applied also to mundane beliefs. The majority of men have always lived under authority and taken their beliefs from others. It is their right and duty at times to question customs, laws, authority and beliefs, but it certainly is not normal or wholesome to question everything. There may be a few who in the full vigour of their extraordinary powers are capable of doing this, but the average man and woman have neither the capacity nor the time. The danger is that we may feed them with false hopes of so doing. Two results generally follow, conceit and cheap sophistry, with an aftermath of scepticism. The false hopes are encouraged by those in responsible positions, with the best of intentions and the vaguest of principles. Whereas, it is their part to have clear conceptions of the end in view, its possibilities and consequences, they trust to a good will and the shibboleths of the day. The policy and outlook of men who are otherwise level-headed have been weakened by a romantic conception of human nature, a conception dangerous in its consequences and apt to foster a spirit of unreality and even hypocrisy at meetings and conferences where the welfare and destiny of civilisation are discussed. I say "unreality," because the weaknesses of human nature are slurred over or ignored, and it is taken for granted that a modicum of education and freedom are a divinely discovered means of rescuing man from the temptation to do wrong, to pursue selfish ambitions and to judge intemperately and foolishly. The unreality of this cannot, however, be hidden altogether, and that is why hypocrisy enters in. The gibe intended for the church-going business-man, that he kept his piety for Sunday and his impiety for week-days, recoils on those who having excited undue expectations have to spend most of their time frustrating them.

The truth surely is that men are a compound of strength and weakness, and so various in character and talents that it is madness to demand of them all the same critical judgment on the questions which have troubled even the greatest intellects. We all start life with beliefs which we have learnt from others, and we all need a discipline to mould our character and our thought. Nor does this cease at some adult stage. We never cease to rely on community life and to lean on good friends, to give of the one talent which may be ours and to gain by the gifts and talents of others which we do not possess ourselves. We stand on the shoulders of the past and learn to the end of our lives from the accumulated experience of mankind. Socrates discovered wherein he was wise when he looked into himself and said that at least he knew that he was ignorant. Such wisdom is allied with modesty, and if he did question all it was in no spirit of self-assertion, no joy of eristics. The sophists, on the other hand, show a love of questioning for its own sake, and take a pride in their own astuteness. They represent an extreme, no doubt; but the constant encouragement to all members of a community to think for themselves, to regard personal opinion and not truth as the end of education, to consider their own right to judge as equal to that of no matter whom—this has for result the production of a type which is not far removed from that of the sophist.

When authority ceases to function, there vanish many of those virtues and habits of thought which are the unseen mainstay of society, such as reverence, loyalty and obedience, the distinction between status and person, and the desire to pay honour where honour is due. The ancients spoke of the ideal of *otium cum dignitate;* there is at least this of truth in the words, that the best work is done by minds which are at peace, in a tranquillity of order. Where all is a sign of interrogation, if not of contradiction, there can be nothing settled, and where there is nothing settled we have neither the time nor nerves nor disposition to create. Apart from the distraction which is the despair of those engaged in art, philosophy and contemplation, there is a wound in the spirit, a sensitive sore which prevents the mind from going about its proper business. This sensitiveness turns every man into a busybody and produces a disequilibrium in the body of the State. The Platonic ideal of the State has many obvious weaknesses, but at least it was built on justice, a justice that meant that everyone had a function in an ordered community, and that while all had opportunity offered to them the arrangement of affairs lay with a few wise men invested with authority.

So far I have been urging that democratic conceptions, if not carefully watched and controlled, can fall into the hands of a philosophy which is false to human nature, one which refuses to recognise under the absolute equality of human souls diversity of talent and capacity, and weakness which needs constant discipline and ordering. And whilst this is true it must also be recognised that there are weaknesses inherent in human authority. Those who are rich and in positions of authority are at least as likely as their subjects to seek their own ends. The abuse of authority is as notorious as the evil which follows on universal private judgment.

Let us look to the places where authority over belief now resides. Outside the Catholic Church there is hardly any authority to be found in religion. It has not, however, disappeared off the face of the earth, for the reason already explained, that belief is natural and essential to man. What has happened is that authority has changed its abode, and it is now the expert who is heard with deference and often with a credulity that puts into the shade the credulity that is supposed to disfigure past and primitive peoples. Let me repeat that it is right, that it is better that we should listen to masters in their own subjects than pretend to be omniscient critics ashamed to take the word of another. This general principle is not, however, of much avail for practical decisions, and as to-day the number of experts is legion and their authority of varying import and extent, a set of rules for the practical guidance of ordinary men is very much needed. It is not the fault of the scientists themselves so much as that of the middle-men who popularise their views that their sayings are received with the same respect as that given to the oracle of Delphi. The layman is too often cozened and cajoled by the publicist and dictated to by the expert for the situation to be a happy one. We are too close to the monstrosities of Victorian architecture which were recommended by the pundits of that day, too conscious of the evil effects of former economic dogmas, to be right in accepting contemporary scientific bulls without misgiving.

This subject of the authority of the expert is a vast one and for satisfactory treatment would require a book after the manner of Mr. Shand's *The Foundations of Character*, which I mention with a special purpose,

o

because the method employed in it of drawing up canons is one which could well be followed here for the practical guidance of the layman. In the present work only a a few indications can be given and some suggestions made. An inquiry ought, I think, to begin with a division into two parts, the first concerned with the subject-matter, the second with the character of the expert. Now the subject-matter ranges through all the provinces of knowledge, and as there are some provinces open to all, others closed except to a very few, some fields of knowledge evident to all without training, some evident but only after training, while others again are of their nature so indistinct or lost to sight as to render certainty impossible, we have to limit the authority of the expert accordingly. There is first of all a domain which is equally accessible to all, one which is sometimes called that of common sense, but, in accordance with what has been laid down in former chapters, may more fittingly be described as that of obvious interpretation and self-evident truths. As belonging to it may be cited the truths which are presupposed in every act and thought, the principles which, as Aristotle says, are assumed in the sciences because they lie outside their province. These truths form a commonwealth where no one stands on precedence. Like birth and death they belong to our very constitution, for we could not live at all were we not conscious of the meaning and difference of ourselves and others, of matter and mind, justice and injustice, truth and falsehood, freedom and necessity. No one in practice ignores these truths. I do not say that all explicitly admit them; it is enough if they implicitly do so in their conduct and unstudied judgments. Theoretically, as we have seen, a man can hold anything and make out a case for the most absurd views, while in moral beliefs he can so stifle conscience that their emotional appeal ceases to have any force. But such apparent exceptions do not really run counter to the obvious, though often disregarded, truth which I have stated. And so we have at least one initial canon: in what concerns the foundation of thought and action in human life, the expert has no superior authority over that of the normal man or humanity as a whole.

This canon, once stated, needs to be safeguarded from a too-free interpretation. Knowledge and wisdom do not arrive full-grown like Athene from the head of Zeus. Aristotle long ago pointed out the necessity of wise legislators and wise teachers in a State, and it does not follow that, because I have as a man the requisite means to distinguish right and wrong, love and hate, body and mind, I have no need of education and nothing to learn on these subjects. There are many problems to be unravelled, and mistakes are sure to be made owing to confusion of mind. But what I learn will be a clearing up of this confusion, a development of the initial truth and not a suppression of it, and therefore I can always test whether my expert friend is talking sense or nonsense by his ability to articulate or deny this truth which is somehow evident to me. Plato, it will be remembered, while cross-examining the professional, retained a great respect for the good, unreflective and common-sense man; he felt that there must be something wrong in a view which contradicted that good man's actions and beliefs. And this respect is justified so long as the beliefs are of the fundamental nature I have described.

If in reply to this it be said that the fundamental cannot always be separated from what is contingent or conventional or ambiguous, the difficulty has to be admitted. But all that this comes to is that no general rule can be given which will save us all pain of thought in particular decisions. There are cases in which it will be obvious that the expert is trespassing on what is fundamental; there are others in which doubt will arise, and then extra caution will be called for. As is well known, the border-line between philosophy and science is often vague, and time has shown that science can, even when claiming too much, take with it when driven off some of the booty of the philosopher. For instance, work in the laboratory cannot touch the problem of the freedom of the will; nevertheless, it has served a good purpose by indicating to the layman and philosopher where precisely the problem does lie and teaching them not to underrate physical and psycho-physical factors.

Having separated philosophy from science we can now make divisions within science. The name belongs by right to what are called the physical sciences, but it has been appropriated by students of living organisms, historians and scholars. For convenience' sake, in what is to follow physical science will be used to include biology and the other studies of an animate matter and to exclude all else. Now it is especially in these physical sciences that the expert calls the tune. The subject-matter has become more and more abstract and abstruse, the methods and processes more accurate. The result is that a large number of people believe that if truth is to be found anywhere it is in physical science. The experts work behind closed doors, and when they make a state-ment they are greeted as if, like Moses, they had come straight from the presence of God. Nowadays the same honour is being paid in some quarters to other kinds of experts for the reason that, as knowledge advances and its contents and methods become more and more organ-ised, the same cleavage between the amateur and the professional begins to manifest itself. The historian, with his critical apparatus, his linguistic attainments, his comparative methods, naturally sets himself above his fellows and is tempted to take their beliefs as a playground for some original hypothesis of his own.

The conveniences of possessing methods whereby large quantities of evidence can be tested, and tested by means which are themselves careful generalisations from experience, are so great as to need no defence. Papers and magazines and controversialists quite rightly quote the verdicts of distinguished scholars and scientists. By their work they have corrected or added to the common stock of knowledge; there are certain questions which have been so threshed out that nobody in his senses disputes the conclusions reached—certain discoveries about the body, the movements of the heavens, the characters and deeds of dead kings, philosophers and statesmen and poets, like Alexander, Plato, Cicero, Hildebrand, Frederick the Great, Dante, Milton. But it should be noted that outside the conclusions of the abstract sciences, the certainties are not due simply and solely to the verdict of expert judges. The jury of the world has also been in attendance, and has signified its approval. And so we are here relying, not so much on the authority of one scientist or a group as on the tests of time, universality and good sense, or on what, in an earlier chapter, I have called the unity of indirect reference.

In history and in kindred sciences a temptation which has beset the expert is to treat a subject-matter which is the product of free acts as if it were reducible to natural laws. I know that some contemporary physical scientists are inclined to admit freedom even in nature, but there is a confusion here between spiritual freedom of choice and contingency. However that may be, there is no

doubt that any expert opinion in history that is domin-
ated by some theory which is deterministic, whether
the form it takes be that of cycles or economic materialism or evolution of an idea, has stepped beyond the
bounds of history and has no right to command the assent
of the reader because of the erudition contained in it.
The trouble is that rarely can a historian keep away
from some fascinating theory, which seems to serve
as a torch in the dark. I shall not at the moment enter
into the question of the advantages and disadvantages
of a bias in historical writing—that concerns the relation
of desire and intellect—but it is obvious that one has
to discriminate carefully between the learning of such
writers as Sir James Frazer, Harnack, and Dr. Coulton,
and the value of their inferences.

Historians and writers on kindred subjects are
naturally more prone to prejudice than experts in the
mathematical sciences. The former, having to deal
with less abstract material, have often enough to act
as historical, textual, and art critics all together. Rarely
do so many gifts belong equally to one man; the expert
may be a master in Israel in one department and
woefully deficient in another. In the study of Homer
and the Bible, for instance, much German and English
erudition has been brought to bear. The learned world
at one time, with exceptions like the literary Andrew
Lang, favoured the composite character of the *Iliad*.
Now a reaction has set in, and the poet Homer is left
with his genius. But it is important to notice that all
the while that the experts fought and expostulated, the
ordinary intelligent man was capable of reading Homer
for himself and forming an opinion. He could not
compete with the expert in learning, but he might
reasonably take into account the impression made upon
him by his reading. The expert, even when he possesses

taste and insight, does not monopolise them. This licence to dispute the verdicts of connoisseurs does not, however, form an excuse for independence of judgment in all things. The *Iliad*, for the reason that it tells one story and is written in a language fairly well known or well translated, is not unlike a play of Shakespeare, or *Paradise Lost*. The Bible, on the other hand, is composed of many books, and in a tongue which few know and few have translated accurately. We are here dependent on authority all along the line, and I should say that even if we are without religious belief we ought to give ear to the claim, though it be no more to us than a hypothesis, that they are written from a special point of view and with a mind which is alien from that of our ordinary standards.

I have already dealt with the interpretation of massive contents of history, maintaining that it is possible to reach certainty about certain persons, events and periods. Here, once again, we are not at the mercy of the expert; the irrelevant or circumstantial detail cannot upset the unity which the mind is able to perceive in the data. This valid form of interpretation is not, however, possible in the mathematical and physical sciences, or at any rate it is confined to those who are already thoroughly familiar with the subject-matter. The special sciences have become more and more separate and self-governing, and this makes them more exact and at the same time less subject to control by the Aristotelian gentleman, who was supposed to be expert in one subject and cultured enough to be able to listen intelligently and criticise the arguments of other investigators. Few there are who would be prepared to discuss intelligently with a scientist the subject of vectors or the work of Schrödinger and Einstein. We are bound to make the assent of authorities in these matters our court of appeal, and our assent will be of the kind we give to our doctor or a council of the Medical Association.

There are, however, certain cautions to be observed even here. These scientists, as I have said, dwell in a region inaccessible to the public; they have a plot of land to cultivate which has its definite boundary-mark, so that there is less likelihood of their meddling in their neighbour's affairs or publishing ecumenical letters containing new revelations on the world and man and God. Present-day scientists, moreover, are to their honour singularly modest. Unfortunately their warnings too often go unheeded, and their discoveries are exploited by those who have some axe to grind. The public, which has lost its old grounds of authority, is easily gulled and forgets the nature of the subject-matter with which the scientist deals. The prodigy of learning and the precision hide the fact that the victory has been won at a price, the price of complete truth. What is irrelevant in mathematical physics is not, therefore, non-existent or irrelevant to life, and what the scientist calls truth may be an expedient and successful hypothesis for corre-lating data, which vary from facts to convenient symbols, and not at all an account of the real object with which we are acquainted. Schematic generalisations are requisite and invaluable, but the test of their truth is consistency, and we have already seen what degree of consistency is necessary to pass from probability to certitude. A scientific consistency has rarely if ever the degree of complexity involved in our everyday certainties; the data are almost always abstract and therefore removed from contact with facts of another department of life, and the number of data varies with different pursuits. To illustrate this, compare the evidence to be gathered in the study of comparative religion with the evidence available for a knowledge of prehistoric man. In the latter case that evidence is so scanty as to deprive a hypothesis of any assurance of truth; but just for that reason an investigator who builds much out of little is greeted with the greatest acclaim. He is indeed to be praised for his ingenuity, and he approaches to that ideal of interpretation already signalised where, in a few significant data, the genius can read the whole. But there is a difference, despite the supposed resemblance. In the one the detective, shall we say, discerns from data which are sufficient, though they do not suffice for many onlookers, in the other the scientist reconstructs in the light of some hypothesis where the data are in themselves insufficient, and is praised for the skill of his reconstruction. The truth is that his theory is thin and of very little value, and he has no right to proclaim it from the housetops with authority and in the name of truth.

A further confirmation of the transiency of hypotheses as compared with the truth of those facts which form the common wealth of man is to be found in the history of science. Great as are its achievements and its claims on our reverence, it is strewn with the wrecks of past systems which, in their day, won almost universal allegiance. There is no warrant for saying that science has now built what Plato called a raft seaworthy and safe for mankind to sail upon. Each new theory ought to bring us nearer to the truth, and if we measure the advance of knowledge by epochs and not by change of theory there is no denying our privileged position as contrasted with that of our ancestors. But so far as any one particular theory is concerned there are too many factors active in its generation for us to trust it because it is the latest. An important discovery is almost sure to be able to fill the heaven and for a while to blot out other stars, and after the long reign of one theory the reaction to it when it comes tends to take an exaggerated form. It has, for instance, taken nearly a century for Evolution to be restricted to its proper size and extent, and to have its content examined in a critical spirit. The same may be the fate of current *tesserae* like Relativity and the Unconscious, while in Behaviourism we have a theory which is a throwback in philosophy whatever be its utility as a method.

These last reflections lead on to the second part of an inquiry into the authority of the expert. Once again there is room for a long and detailed study, for which only one or two suggestions here must suffice. This part should cover the limitations to which the experts are themselves exposed. There is naturally a close connection between those of the subject-matter on which we have touched and the attitude of mind of the expert dealing with it, because it is not the fault of a discovery that it leads to error but the undue excitement of scientists over it, a glee which spreads like wildfire in a learned body. I am not referring to the well-known personal equation of scientists; that is supposed to be corrected by a system of averages. The supposition is, however, at times optimistic, because when a new apparent vista is opened by a theory, and reputations are at stake, each member in a whole school may suffer from the same form of blindness. This fact stands in the way of accepting too blithely a prevalent theory even when it is supported by numbers. In everyday matters the witness of a group of independent persons may make dissent irrational; in scientific matters a body of opinion should have weight, but suspence of judgment need not be irrational. The unanimity may be more apparent than real when scientists sing in chorus, because opposition may be ridiculed and snobbery is not absent even from such circles. They are, moreover, interested in believing a new theory, seeing that the field of science has many barred gates, and when it is rumoured that one of them has been opened the temptation is to follow a leader and make for the gate.

We have to allow, therefore, for human failings, for vanity and opinionativeness, for credulity and pride and the herd instinct. Pure science is thought to be the most free from such failings. There the interest of the scientist is concentrated on one subject, which has been abstracted from all that might evoke emotion or prejudice, and a consensus of opinion should be unimpassioned. The ideal no doubt which most of us have in this regard is of some far-off garden of the Hesperides where no evil winds of prejudice blow, no sound of strife is heard, where the gardener can work in a pure atmosphere in a plot that is entirely his own. But this cultivation of one's own garden is, alas! very rare and, these Hesperides resemble more an iceberg than a garden, so cold and inhuman are they. The pure scientist as a consequence rarely remains freezing and content; he brings back the human nature which has been expelled and he is as quarrelsome as a theologian and as prejudiced, as apt to generalise on everything as his cousins engaged on more familiar and common affairs.

From these and many other considerations it ought to be possible to appoint the place of scientific authority in belief. That experts have and ought to be trusted we are all agreed. We cannot attain all knowledge by personal experience and investigations. I have already dealt with authority under its more general aspect, and in the preceding paragraphs have confined myself exclusively to the beliefs imposed on us in the name of modern science. There is no question here of authority in the sense of a power with jurisdiction, of a sovereign with the right to command and subjects with the duty of obedience. The habit of mind disciplined to obey is no doubt connected with modesty and reverence for wisdom, but obedience of the will does not directly touch the subject of belief, and no scientist would wish to play the part of a philosopher-king and enforce respect for his opinion by penal laws. He stands forth as a witness to truth which is of its nature difficult of access to his fellows, and he ought to encourage his hearers to test both the importance of the department of truth with which he is concerned and also his own character and attainments. Before we decide to follow him, therefore, we shall do well to formulate for ourselves a few fairly obvious but often forgotten canons of criticism. First, the expert is relying usually on a hypothesis which will bear the marks of the age in which he is living. Secondly, the more abstract it is the less likely is it to be infected with prejudice; at the same time this abstract character attained on the principle of *divide et impera* lessens its applicability to nature taken as a whole; hence it is likely that the more comprehensively an abstract hypothesis is applied, the greater will be the caution needed in accepting it. Next, a scientist who is an authority on his own subject is not necessarily even the equal of the common man in his judgment on other subjects. An Isaac Newton silences criticism when he writes on physics, but need not be followed in his comments on the prophetical books in Scripture or in his search for the philosopher's stone. Again, the scientist is always tempted to extend the methods peculiar to his own study to subjects where they may not be available, and may therefore use scales already weighted when estimating the elusive forces which cannot be measured. All, scientist and labourer, tend to unify their conceptions of reality; they are interested in it and they judge it, and the danger is that they judge its look and their lot from the narrow angle of their chief preoccupation. As the simple bushman thinks of his gods as black, so the mathematical scientist fancies the world to be one great mechanism, or if he allows a God, he suffers him to be a great mathematician or geometer. Thus we carry our failings into our presentation of the truth and make idols of our own predilections.

CHAPTER VIII

BELIEF AND RELIGIOUS EXPERIENCE

Ce qui est trop bête pour être dit on le chante.

[RELIGIOUS enthusiasts who] travail their fleshly hearts outrageously in their breasts and hurt full sore the silly soul and make it fester in fantasy feigned of friends.

Cloud of Unknowing.

Ce que je sais de Dieu?
Exactement ce qu'en dit le catéchisme, rien de plus et rien de moins.
PAUL CLAUDEL.

AND the third kind of monks is that very disgraceful kind of the Sarabites, who have not been brought under discipline by any rule. . . . These are they who, being by twos and threes, or indeed singly and without a pastor, enclosed not in the Lord's but in their own sheepfolds, take for law their own whims, since whatever they think and choose they say is holy and whatever they dislike they esteem unlawful.

The Rule of St. Benedict.

CHAPTER VIII

BELIEF AND RELIGIOUS EXPERIENCE

IN many quarters religious experience is contrasted with scientific truth as a mode of reaching knowledge. Indeed, the appeal to experience cannot be dissociated from the premium put upon the experimental sciences. That there is need for a sober estimate of the range and authority of science seems abundantly clear, and here particularly where the interaction of science and religion may be discerned. Liberal and Modernist religious thinkers have largely abandoned the grounds of belief given by the older tradition of Christianity; they have felt it incumbent on them to admit that the scientist has the exclusive right to reason, and have thereby been forced to find a new form of defence for religion. The chief causes which have contributed to bring this about are the decadence of philosophy before the Renaissance, the separation of faith from reason by Luther and the invention on a large scale of the physico-mathematical methods. Owing to the decadence of metaphysics philosophy tended to pass over into the hands of its successful rival, physical science, which therewith appropriated to itself the name of the philosophy of nature. In the old, scholastic divisions the philosophy of nature was, after the model of Aristotle's Physics, a branch of what now would be called metaphysics. It dealt with the ultimate notions inherent in that of change, and covered, therefore, the ultimate constitution of material bodies, qualitative change, organic growth, generation and decay, time and space. From the Renaissance onwards the interest changed, and in place of the analysis of these notions the student was set to observe and experiment and was taught to consider that the only subject which it was worth his while to consider was the visible or what could be treated as if it were visible. Now the visible was what we see, and we handle the visible by means of parts which are divisible, which can be numbered and treated by mathematics. The effect of this method was miraculous, and the belief in it was helped out by the plain fact that in all our thinking, no matter what the subject, we do represent it to ourselves in a sensible way. If we think of a spirit we always carry an image of it which is, so to speak, the materialisation of it, just as, *mutatis mutandis*, we call a feverish state of the body a temperature of 102 degrees. Philosophy, as I have said, fell in with this way of thinking, and a long line of English philosophers taught a system of Empiricism, meaning by that, that all our knowledge was sensible, being derived from sensations and reproducing these impressions in terms of ideas. The truth contained in this belief is that we have to represent to ourselves reality in mathematico-physical terms, though we mean far more than that by reality. The confusion, therefore, is between representation and significance.

It is easy to see that with these antecedents the prestige of men of science increased. What they said, so it was thought, revealed to us reality in so far as it was knowable, and all other forms of thinking were forms of charlatanism. But the reality so revealed, consisting, as it did, of atoms and molecules or electrons and protons, was exceedingly disappointing, and no universe for a gentleman to live in. It is surprising that for so long this view was welcomed and that folk who lived happily

amid colour and sound and variety could commit
themselves in seriousness to the abolition of all these,
and to a philosophy of rigid determinism. Dissatisfaction showed itself at length in the reaction of Bergson,
in a new belief. Scientific concepts were relegated to a
very inferior place; they were nothing more than a
mechanical device used for purposes of convenience. We
cut up or cut off a section of an ever-moving stream, a
living force which is grasped by a vivid realisation called
intuition. This revolutionary change affected the outlook of science and was valuable at least in this, that it
made the scientist and the philosopher more critical of
the physico-mathematical methods they were using.
The effect of this can be seen in modern works in which
science is called merely descriptive and its conclusions
pointer-readings, and in the attempt of Whitehead to
furnish a metaphysical background to a method which
is, he thinks, desperately in need of justification.

On the other side the religious writers were forced,
owing to their self-denying ordinance, to rely more and
more on experience. Towards the end of the eighteenth
century they made serious attempt to construct a
defence of religion out of the deepest feelings of the
heart, and fortunately Kant, who gave the password to
the science of the nineteenth century, lent them also a
helping hand. Kant had demonstrated to his satisfaction against Hume that the judgments of mathematical
science were valid, and in doing this he claimed to lay
down the powers and limitations of human knowledge.
All knowledge which was a brew of sensible experience
and intellectual forms was palatable and digestible,
but there was no such thing as mere sensible experience,
and pure intellectual knowledge lay outside the limits
of the human mind. Thus Kant consecrated the
methods of physical science and signed the death-warrant

of metaphysics. But this was not all. He had no intention of deserting religion, and part of his object was to rescue it from the attacks of Empiricism. He thought to obtain his end by limiting the scope of science at the same time that he affirmed its competence. Science was in the saddle as long as the subject-matter was phenomenal, but in other matters it must relinquish the reins. Now God and religion did not fall within sensible experience; nevertheless, they were necessary as postulates for the moral order. They were, therefore, to be restored, and their majesty could not be injured by reason.

This conclusion was treasure trove to theologians of the Protestant faith. They could now go straight ahead without interference from science. That, at least, was the hope, but it did not work out that way, for the epoch which followed saw the signal triumph of science and the twilight of religion. Nothing daunted, religion retired more and more into religious experience; it profited by the reaction of Bergson, devised a subtle and alluring distinction between truths of value and truths of fact, and in recent years has been exploring anew the specific nature of what is given in the so-called religious experience. The present tendency, therefore, is to make two divisions of truth, knowledge by experience and knowledge by reason. The latter is the concern of science and is restricted to what is quantitative and numerable. The former covers quality and value, and has, therefore, for its domain the moral, the æsthetic and the religious. Beliefs which are dependent on experience are not necessarily less true than those which are attained by reason; they are different and that is all that can be said about their relation.

From the foregoing it can be seen that the importance attached to religious experience is due to a partition made in the past between religion and reason. There is no reason why this assumption should be accepted, and in fact the Catholic Church has never accepted it. Nevertheless, the question of the validity of this experience bears on the subject of belief, and it is worth inquiring whether a belief founded on it can be justified. This is not an easy question to answer, for the reason that the term "experience" is exceedingly indefinite, and many of those who use it do not trouble to tell us what they mean. As a beginning, therefore, we must distinguish the chief senses in which the word can be rightly used. The Oxford Dictionary under its first heading gives as synonyms "test" or "trial"; under the second "experiment." These we can ignore. The third sense is "the active observation of facts or events, considered as a source of knowledge," and the fourth "the fact of being consciously the subject of a state or condition or of being consciously affected by an event," or "a state viewed subjectively." In a subsection the religious use is given and described as "a state of mind or feeling forming part of the inner religious life." One other use deserves mention—that of "knowledge resulting from active observation or from what one has undergone."

These divisions do, I think, cover the proper uses of the word, and it is easy from them to show their interconnection. First, experience is individual and direct, as opposed to hearsay and opinion and indirect knowledge. This general use is made more definite by emphasis on those acts of ours in which the directness and individuality are conspicuous, that is, the acts of sense—what we call sensible experience. But now in sensible experience we have sensation, and sensation is recognised to be passive as well as active. To taste mustard by mistake for custard is an unpleasant experience, we say—and similarly we listen to good music and enjoy its effect upon us. This passive element leads to a further division. Our feelings and emotions are due to the effect upon us of facts and events, and so they are spoken of as experiences; this resultant state is contrasted with knowledge as interior or subjective. Here, then, is the connection which shows the slender unity of meaning in such diverse statements as "experience teaches," "he knew it from his own experience," "the night passed in the cold was an unpleasant experience," "he guides his life by inner experience," and "the mystic state is the loftiest experience man knows."

If this were a treatise in psychology many more distinctions would have to be introduced; our awareness of a sensation is not the same as the sensation itself, and the word "feeling" is ambiguous. But all can recognise the broad sense of experience here described, and that will suffice as a beginning. It is necessary, however, to draw attention to one point. In sensible experience we have the evidence of the senses, and this direct perception, so far as it goes, provides a firm basis for knowledge. I can be sure that I see blue, that I hear a sound. It does not follow that I am always right in attributing what I so experience to reality. I can, however, be sure on occasions, and I am always sure that I know something; that is to say, the quality I perceive is the quality of something and I am therefore in contact with objects, though I may go wrong in thinking that the quality belongs to this or that particular object, or that this sensation was caused by hot water and not by cold. When we turn to sensations which are, so to speak, more subjective, and to feelings, the so-called experience becomes less trustworthy. We all know this in practice, and are all of us ready to tell our friends not to trust their feelings. The feeling is unmistakable, but our judgment on it is very often in the dark. In sensible perception we are in direct contact with the real order, and such knowledge is the foundation on which all science is built; the subjective experience is the foundation of religious belief according to the Modernist contention, and it looks an insecure foundation compared with that of science. We must therefore regard it more closely.

The interior state is generally an effect, for whose cause we look. I say "generally," because certain religious writers deny this in the case of religious experience. Some would maintain that the language of cause and effect is inapplicable, that the experience is *sui generis* and has a value of its own. It is a fact, they say, that we are conscious of the need of justification, and this may be followed by another interior state which can only be described as one of liberation and union. The experience is one of immense value, and that value stands for a truth whether there be any fact, any liberator and object of union, or not. They separate, that is, value from fact and attribute to each a special kind of truth. They would consider it unimportant, for instance, from the point of view of religion whether Christ really existed and was crucified. The truth of these facts belongs to history, and history is incapable of settling the fate of religion. In the world of religion the story of Christ has a unique value as symbol and expression of the highest that man can attain in religious experience. Another group of writers proceeds in a different way. They hold that all religious experience is mystical and that the mystic is aware directly of the divine. Having intuition, the religious mind does not argue from effect to cause.

In so describing the views of this second group I have

taken the liberty of stating what I think to be the logical conclusion from their own words, though they do not usually employ the word "intuition." They are inclined, I fear, to talk somewhat loosely and to gather together under one heading the strongly-felt beliefs of the churchgoer, the emotions felt by sensitive souls in the presence of sublime natural beauty, vivid and passionate faith, and the mystic states of such diverse persons as St. Plotinus, Francis of Assisi, Shelley, Blake and St. John of the Cross. It is this confusion between quite different acts and states which makes so many discussions of the question a waste of time. An able writer like Mr. Joad, for instance, gravely informs us that both moral and religious experience are ineffable, that they have nothing to do with reason, and his appeal is to the greatest mystics, who confess that they can only babble of what has happened to them. I cannot believe that he is claiming to share their experiences; they are rare souls who have undergone a long religious discipline, a dark night of the soul, before they have emerged on the shining plateaux where they have experimental union with God. To identify their experience with that of the poet's, with that of the vast majority of religious persons who are now alive or have ever been alive, is the grossest of errors. And yet Mr. Joad and the many others who write in the same strain as himself are bound either to include in one all the earnest believers in God and the mystics or to deny to the former all right to call themselves religious. The first alternative is simply opposed to the facts; not all the wand-bearers are Bacchants; and if he takes the second alternative he makes a desert of a world where religion thrives, and incidentally deprives himself of any right to say anything on the subject. Only the person who is like Plotinus or John of the Cross will have the experience, and, as it is incommunicable and unintelligible, Mr. Joad, who does not claim to be a John of the Cross, ought to be silent (though for the matter of that Plotinus, too, ought to have been silent). It really is a distressing fact that so much should be written on mysticism by those who do not seem to be aware of the state of the question. There is an immense literature stretching down the ages, and this and the carefully thought out science of the spiritual life in the Catholic Church, with its vast evidence, its carefully drawn distinctions, have been completely ignored. I am not asking that all should agree with the conclusions of Catholic writers (there are different schools amongst them, and points still in debate); my complaint is that in a subject full of pitfalls the writer must, if he wishes to add anything profitable, acquaint himself with the literature and the evidence and take into account at least the acquired wisdom of a Church which has counted Augustine and Bernard, the Victorines, the contemplative Orders, Master Eckhart, Tauler, the Spanish mystics, and all those enumerated in Brémond's monumental volumes, and could bring in witness a large number of contemporary men and women from every country who enjoy the highest religious experience. Is it not a remarkable fact, and one worthy of attention, that the masters in the mystical life have been able definitely to mark out various stages in the ascent, and to apportion the part to be played in this ascent by the senses, the reason, the emotions and all the activities of the soul? Is it not remarkable that the cold intellectualism of Aquinas proved a word of life to Ruysbroeck, Suso and others of their school, that the philosophical conception and mystical experience bear each other out, that Teresa of Avila found that her experience of God's presence in three ways was identical with the analysis of the theologians whom she had not read?

Such facts could be multiplied, but to treat further of mysticism would be a digression. The argument from religious experience cannot depend upon it except indirectly. The mystic condition is not a common condition, and it is mere confusion to identify it with what is ordinarily meant by the religious experience. It is this latter which must be justified. The defenders of religion are thinking of themselves, their neighbours and all those who say that they know God and can enter into relation with Him, and their argument is directed against the rationalist for whom science covers all forms of knowledge. To bring the mystic as evidence might be useful indirectly on the ground that by his fruits we can know him. He appears to gain and grow and not to lose, and this suggests that he must be in contact with some form of higher life. The argument, it will be noticed, is indirect, and by itself it is not convincing to all; it cannot be direct because the presupposition is that this experience is ineffable and cannot be communicated and that the rest of the world, ourselves included, has no such experience. But clearly what we want to prove is that what most men call religious experience, which is different from the mystic experience, is valid, that our own feeble faith is not in vain. We must therefore turn back to this and examine its credentials.

In a normal act we distinguish stimulus, effect, cognition and response—for example, a spring of water, desire to drink, cognition of this and the spring, and our resultant action; or again, a remark which hurts when we are aware of its meaning, and resultant anger. These are simple cases of cause and effect, but we know full well that we are frequently unable to assign the proper cause of our feelings, sensations and emotions. They may be complicated and obscure. Psychologists have given much attention to an analysis of the precise differences between conation, cognition, the affective state which can be active and passive, and the feelings of pleasure and displeasure. There is, I think, general agreement amongst them—an agreement which substantiates common experience—that the feeling and the affective state are no sure index of a present cause proportionate to the effect. The malaise has its cause, but it may be very difficult to account for it, and it is safer to attribute such states as that of well-being with corresponding optimism to organic conditions. Experiments have proved, as James pointed out long ago, that many of the highest states can be simulated by artificial means. I am not saying that all affective states belong to the sensitive side of the self. This would be a serious exaggeration. There are rational desires as well as instincts and sensitive appetites, but the two are so closely connected that it is almost impossible to separate them in consciousness by introspection. Those, however, who set out to cure mental diseases are bound to assume the existence of them both, and whereas it is by suggestion and similar means they succeed in putting right the sensitive appetites, they can gain their end with the rational by means of argument and appeal to reason. This is decisive, but it does not allow us to trust our affective states. Enthusiasm, joy, ecstasy and all the emotions which are to be found in a religion which offers immediate and felt conversion as the supreme test of truth may prove treacherous allies. In his treasury of common-sense and wisdom, the *Imitation of Christ*, Thomas a Kempis warns his readers not to judge by present feelings. The revels of the night look differently in the cold, grey light of morning, and the overmastering sense of confidence or salvation needs to be controlled by the reflective reason.

The examples I have chosen in the preceding paragraph are not wholly relevant, in that they follow on an attitude of belief and are not quoted to prove that belief. It is no injustice to certain Protestant sects to say that they place great reliance on the Spirit, meaning by that that they take their spiritual states as evidence of God's working in them. This is by no means the same, at least in theory, as the position of the defenders of religious experience whose views I am examining. These latter maintain that the experience is a legitimate foundation for the belief, that it is a way beyond that of reason of getting into contact with God. God exists because of the fact of religious experience, whereas in those sects they believe in God and test His wishes with regard to them by the effects of His grace in them. The difference, however, is perhaps greater in theory than in fact. Some of those sects take over a goodly part of Christian tradition and teaching; they accept the fact of the authenticity of the New Testament and the truth of its record. This gives them a background of belief, but if challenged many, I think, go the whole way and claim that their spiritual life with its experience of God, of Christ and His gospel, entirely depend upon their experience. If they say this, their view is relevant to the problem before us. It should be noticed that whatever view of the two they hold they depart from the Catholic tradition. I hope to show later that the first act of the Catholic, the act of faith, is in no wise an irrational act or one which relies exclusively on an interior illumination. In the Catholic's spiritual life, again, the experience moves within a scheme of life which is intellectual and moral. The experience may be said to be secondary; it has to be controlled by orthodoxy and by the test of virtue. "If you love me, keep my commandments." This rule must be observed whether the religious person be a neophyte or a mystic, and there are many cases where the religious experience of apparently highly gifted souls has been set on one side by Catholic authority. I think anyone who is acquainted with the varieties of religious experience must admit that in so doing the Church has acted with wisdom. Mystics themselves, like St. Teresa, urge the necessity of caution, and the caution is to be found in the Gospels. The monks in the desert learnt to their cost the truth that the devil could behave like an angel of light!

So far I may seem to have been throwing cold water on the possible truth of religious experience. It would be more true to the argument to infer an attitude of scepticism towards those who claim that religion is exclusively an affair of religious experience. That it plays a part not only in the life of the mystic but in that of every believer is undoubted, and it would be cruel to decry its value to the multitudes whose lives have been refreshed by religion. All that is needed is counsel and discretion. In any healthy religion, as Baron von Hügel pointed out, there is sure to be a combination of hard thinking, love of the heart, organisation and external discipline. Thus it is that the Catholic worshipper may know by reason that there is a God, and by faith that that God is leading him by truth and grace into a union of love with Himself. This knowledge guides the devotion, directing it to true objects of worship and affection and informing the mind with the way in which they should be loved. The grace within helps to understanding, and with understanding the affections grow on soil which is well prepared. Nevertheless, throughout the growth in the spiritual life there are perils. The emotion has often to be enticed; if it is forced, it may do harm to the equilibrium of the self;

if it is indulged in, it may attach itself to other motives or waste itself away, leaving the mind dry and depressed. There are, as I say, many perils both in the active and the passive life of devotion, and there is far more need to take advice from some fount of wisdom in the spiritual than in the moral life.

From what has so far been said, religious experience is to be reckoned as of secondary importance. But we have not yet explored the meaning given to it by many modern thinkers. They would probably admit that religious experience is capable of mistakes, like every other activity which helps to knowledge, and they would agree that in all the minor experiences, the random life of the feelings, the ebb and flow of the emotions, the vicissitudes of taste and appreciation, there is no sure foothold for truth. Many would be content just to register the fact that there is an experience which is not like any other, one, therefore, which has for object some reality unique and indescribable. That is all, and they would shrug their shoulders at the attempts of definite religious bodies to argue from the minimum laid down to the truth of their own complicated beliefs and superstitions. A half-way house between this position and that described above is taken up by many Christian writers. They will not suffer the control of dogma, and they distrust the undiscriminating reliance on experience. They hold, therefore, that belief is originally an experience, but it must be verified by further experience before it can be accepted as true. Thus, for example, the fundamental doctrines of Christianity are the outcome of experience and also the living residue of a long and searching tradition of experience. They are, therefore, the abiding values of mankind and can be accepted with confidence as true. I had better examine this Christian *via media* before passing on.

The view has been put as tersely and as definitely as possible. The definiteness is, however, deceptive. We are told that there are fundamental Christian doctrines, but we are left in the dark how to recognise them except by experience. Unconsciously these authors have applied another test, and that a rational one. The effect, however, of the application of the test of experience is to rob even these fundamental doctrines of distinctness. Their number varies with different writers, and in the last resort the appeal is not so much to traditional as to personal experience. This explains why their thought is apt to clothe itself in unverifiable phrases: for example, that the sacrifice implied in the old orthodox view of the Redemption is "alien from modern Christian sentiment." As the largest body of Christians in the world believes wholeheartedly in this sacrifice, and as they are supported by the next largest body, the Eastern Church, and by many high Anglicans, it is a little difficult to see on what ground this statement is made if it be not that of the writer's own personal feeling—and such a criterion spells rank individualism and anarchy. The trouble does not rest only there. Not only do the doctrines of Christianity vary, coming and going according to the choice of each individual, but the meaning of each doctrine turns into a smudge. One writer quarrels with another because he dares to apply attributes to God; the status of Christ becomes uncertain, and the Cross is evacuated. No wonder if the scientist and unbeliever are led to think that there cannot be any truth in Christianity, and so the very truth for which they stand is turned into an image, cracked and defaced. Much more could be said about this theory as it is held by many God-fearing ecclesiastics, who combine with it a belief in a sacramental system and a hierarchy. They are, I think, in a more anomalous position than those who frankly confess their faith to be Modernism; but for both the outlook is disastrous.

Of the frankly Modernist view a representative expression can be found in the volumes named *Adventure* and *Reality*. In *Adventure*, in the synopsis of the essay by Professor Macmurray, we find the following: "The fundamental error commonly made lies in considering faith as a kind of knowledge. This error appears in various forms. (*a*) Faith may be opposed to reason with reference to the same problems and issue in a *credo quia impossibile* in defiance of logical thought. (*b*) It may be held that faith and reason draw upon different sources of knowledge. Faith is then identified with some form of intuition, and the appeal may be to instinct, to experience or to authority. (*c*) Faith may be grounded upon mystical experience, in which case the appeal in matters of faith is really to primitive modes of thought and feeling. Faith, however, is not a kind of knowledge, but rather a practical attitude of the will. The view that faith is a faculty of knowledge is derived from the old distinction between 'certain' and 'probable' knowledge, which finds its classical expression in the philosophy of Locke, and which has been modified and developed by the work of Kant and the romanticists of the nineteenth century." He then goes on to say that experimental science has disproved the view that knowledge can be achieved only by demonstration and that all else must rest on probability and faith. Science does not rest on knowledge but on belief, and it lives by the experimental testing and remodelling of these beliefs, and he therefore defines faith as an attitude of will, as a way of acting in the face of our ignorance.

Dr. Streeter, on the other hand, finds a place for faith by contrasting mechanism with life, the static with the dynamic. The one is the affair of science, but it does not exhaust reality. It leaves out quality and it treats what is living as if it were dead. Therefore "if we make the assumption . . . that the fundamental element in Reality is of the nature of Life, it follows that Reality can only be partially understood by the methods of pure science. The experiment, therefore, must be tried of supplementing knowledge of the purely scientific kind by inferences drawn from the nature of Life—in other words, by a method of anthropomorphism scientifically controlled." Different as these two views are, they have much in common. In both the function of science is limited and corrected by an adventurous and dynamic attitude towards reality. Of the two, however, Professor Macmurray seems to me to present the stronger case. I will leave out criticism of his classification, though it invites attack. He denies that faith is a kind of knowledge and defines it as a practical attitude of the will. By knowledge he means that of which we have certainty, but he causes confusion by contrasting will with knowledge. By the violence of the contrast he seems to suggest that another activity is engaged which is not a form of thinking, namely the will; and this suggestion is strengthened by the further remark that the old distinction between certainty, which is confined to demonstration, and probability and faith has broken down and is unsound. But he cannot mean this, for all that he does is to offer in their stead the method of science, which consists in making some hypothesis and then verifying it. Now this surely is a way not of willing but of knowing, in the broad sense of that word, and it contains at least three elements; the conception of what may be a truth, the determination to try it and the verification of it. The will is shown, I suppose, in the determination to experiment with it, and in the

Q

feeling of confidence which supports one; but the intellect is also present, and in the old forms which were said to make a wrong division. There is first the possibility that the content thought of may be true; secondly, as the evidence grows, a stage in which it becomes probable; and for all I know there might come a third stage, as happens in experience, when the theory is verified by such a wealth of evidence that the mind becomes certain. If, then, Professor Macmurray wishes to carry out to its logical conclusion his example from the sciences, he should be talking of probability and, possibly, of certainty, and his definition of faith as the practical attitude of the will must be abandoned. I do not think, however, that this is his real thought. The truth is that he has been caught in his own snare. Looking at the sciences, and with an insufficient knowledge of the divisions of ancient philosophy, he fancied that he could kill two birds with one stone. He could tell the scientists that they worked with faith, and blame former philosophers and theologians for having omitted to take account of this faith, telling them that this omission and the recourse to antiquated distinctions stultified their attempts to justify religion. But his shot misses the mark and is fatal to his own theory. It is simply not true that former thinkers neglected faith and affirmed that the only form of knowledge was by demonstration. For proof of this one has only to refer to the indemonstrable principles, the theory of synderesis in moral philosophy, and to the definition of faith in, for example, Aquinas, where it is said that faith is an act of the intellect commanded by the will and most certain.

The real interest of Professor Macmurray's view lies in this, that it does seem to represent the attitude of many towards religion. There are many who, confronted with a choice of ways in life, have taken the highest as it seemed to them, have, for instance, embraced a way of suffering and unselfishness, and they learn by experience that it is more blessed to give than to receive. Similarly, I suspect that there are some who have adopted Christianity in some form and found peace of mind in carrying out the duties and counsels which they think belong to it. I admit that this may be the faith some have pursued, and as a method, not a theory, the advice may be excellent; to act the truth is a way of learning it. But there is a point where certainty, where what is Christian faith proper, intervenes. Professor Macmurray has stopped on the road and mistaken his stopping-place for the terminus. And even in his account of the journey he belittles, I believe, the part of reason. He says that the assent is a practical attitude of the will against a background of ignorance. There is uncertainty in human ventures, as when Ulysses set out to find a better world, but normally there is some ground for hope; our trust in a man is founded on some already acquired knowledge of his inerrancy, his prophetical powers, his wisdom in guidance. Where this faith is without reason, as in the loyalty of a mad lover to the good name and promises of his beloved, it is at its furthest remove from that scientific faith to which Professor Macmurray has likened the religious. But granted the correctness of the analysis of natural faith, it is nevertheless utterly distinct from that of divine Christian faith. Professor Macmurray appeals to the New Testament and would have it that Christ and St. Paul confirm his view. "Christ's use of the term makes it impossible to conceive it as a kind of knowledge. He uses it to describe an attitude of mind which produces practical achievement. He frequently sets it in opposition to 'fear.' St. Paul

similarly contrasts 'faith' and 'law,' and identifies it
with 'freedom.' It is practical and creative spon-
taneity." This incursion into New Testament exegesis
is not successful, and, be it said without offence, Professor
Macmurray does not show himself well acquainted with
the literature in which the meaning of πίστις and
πιστεύειν has been thrashed out. Not to quote Catholic
authors—Dean Inge is emphatic on the presence of
knowledge in St. Paul's use of the word, and both in his
work on faith and in his presidential address in 1925 to
the Modern Churchmen he attacks the kind of language
about faith which Professor Macmurray uses.

From the beginning Christianity set its face against
such a view, as a parody of Christ's teaching. St
Augustine has been quoted as advocating a view of
faith which would make it first an irrational adventure
and then an experience progressively justifying it.
St. Augustine's view is rightly summed up in the words
credo ut intelligam, but the correct interpretation of this
summary is markedly different from the modern view
which it is supposed to favour. To see the truth of this
let us turn back to the Gospels. We have there to
distinguish within the use of the word two senses, which
are in fact often inseparable: faith as the acceptance of
Christ, His authority and His word, and faith as a
reliance on and complete confidence in Christ. The
second meaning follows on the first, and is equivalent
often to the virtue of hope. Thus, according to the
Gospel narrative, St. Peter was told to walk upon the
waters, and on his failure to trust the word and command
of Christ was chided for his lack of faith. On another
occasion he is praised because, when others refuse to
accept without question and demur the words of doctrine
preached by Christ, he answers "To whom shall we go,
for thou hast the words of eternal life?" In this latter

incident faith implies the complete certainty in the truth of what Christ is saying, and the motive of the faith is the authority of Christ. Not only have we a double sense in the word "faith," but there is a twofold attitude which is praised according to the circumstances. Those who do not as yet possess the gift of faith are praised if they stretch out towards what they fain would have. Man, who knows not yet the road to life, must wager on the best that he can see. This search, which involves the choice of private judgment and a willingness to trust, is what Professor Macmurray defines as Christian faith. In reality it is but the prelude and the anticipation. Faith comes when Christ is recognised as divine and His word becomes the way and the truth and the life. From now onward there is no waiting on verification by experiment; such an attitude would be an insult to God, would be at one and the same time a confession of God and a denial of His veracity and His words. Naturally, therefore, we find that Christ demands of those who have faith the most implicit obedience, the most unswerving loyalty and the completest certainty. I need not quote the many passages in which Christ demands or praises an unquestioning acceptance of His commands and doctrine, nor the words of His mission to His apostles that they should teach and that those who heard them heard Him.

It is with this background of the Gospels that we must look at St. Augustine. The doctrine contained there is expressed in his own way when he says *"Errabant adhuc et patriam quarebant; sed duce Christo errare non poterant. Via illis fuit visio Dei"*; and when he contrasts the *credo* with the *intelligo* in the saying *credo ut intelligam*, he did not mean that his *credo* waited on understanding to be certain. He meant rather that belief was necessary for understanding, that it was not till the mind was illumined by faith and looked out at the world with new eyes, the eyes of one who has the mind of Christ, that the world could be understood in its proper perspective and in its deep-laid purposes.

Christian writers do indeed make a distinction between faith and wisdom, which resembles that of Professor Macmurray; but the resemblance is superficial. Faith can develop and be realised in successive degrees. The saint has a delicacy of apprehension and a quickness of hearing which is denied to the somewhat nonchalant worshipper. But this is not to say that faith is dependent on realisation or verification for its certainty. There is a growing intensity heightened by love. The love does not change the nature of the act of belief; it adds fuel to a fire already existing. In the other view the act of faith is not a form of knowledge, but an act of the will, and it depends on verification. The difference between the two lies in this, that one believes in God and the other thinks that he does, but does not. Hard as this saying is, I must insist on it, for the reason that failure to see it is responsible for much of the talk about religious experience. If God is God and infinitely richer in reality than ourselves, and if He communicates a word which is rich with His own life and truth, spelling gain for us, it is essential that we on our part should submit to be mastered by it, to be drawn up into it instead of dragging it down to ourselves and interpreting it by our own measure of life and experience. That is to say, the test of a divine message is that it should command us and work its way in us without gloss and contamination; and the most disastrous temptation that we can suffer is to desire to test it by our own experience. Immediately we do this, like Orpheus, we grasp no longer the substance of the loved object but the shadow; like Psyche, in our curiosity we lose the authentic presence of the divine lover. This truth has been put excellently by a writer in the *Hibbert Journal* for July, 1929, and I cannot do better than conclude this criticism of the view of faith by experimentation with one or two quotations from his article. " 'It is one thing to be God, and quite another to be a humble partaker of God,' said St. Augustine in his day. There will always remain a great residuum in religion which obstinately transcends our attempts to arrange and master. It is precisely that which refuses to be mastered—but insists on mastering and transcending *us*—which can most properly be called the stuff of religion. Assuredly it is the more impressive and influential part of it, if we take the long historic view. It is that frontier line where we intellectually comprehend no further, but 'suffer the Infinite.' It is the inevitable emotional expression of our 'sublime dependencies,' of which in his deepest hours Wordsworth was our completest modern exponent. It is man at his noblest and most helpless, aware at last of his condition, face to face with his status and his fate, but not defying it—rather exulting in it. When he is most weak, and most aware of his weakness, then he is most strong; strong, however, not simply because he is recognising adamantine facts and is practically and sensibly adjusting himself, but for a greater reason, that he is *glorying in That which dwarfs him*, yet has produced him. Thus the last defeat and humiliation of his intellect and his empiric will may (in a moment by a turn of the soul) become the supreme success of his spirit. When his half-gods go God can arrive." And again: "The tamed forms of sub-Christianity, of relatively modern genesis, are a softening of the demands of reality, a compromise with the ultimate. Religion becomes desupernaturalised, all-too-human. That which should be sovereign over us is shorn like Samson, and put to turning our pet mills."

The argument of Dr. Streeter is, as I have said, like and unlike that of Professor Macmurray. Scientific methods, he says, "must be supplemented by an intuitive knowledge of the inner quality of life akin to that employed by the artist." He fights shy, however, of trusting to some religious experience comparable to that of the artistic. Like several other distinguished modern writers he sees the danger of relying on the argument from experience. He is evidently in agreement with the criticism which Dean Inge, in the Conference already referred to, delivered against the reliance on an emotional, felt or pragmatic faith. Instead, therefore, of following out the promise contained in the distinction of scientific knowledge and aesthetic experience, he says that our intuitive apprehension of life should be used concurrently with the control of science. I do not find the account very clear. We are told that reality contains both matter and life, and that we have an intuition of this life. Next we learn that the concept of life is in the last resort anthropomorphic, and then that our conception of life must be controlled by science, which before was said to be concerned with matter and not with life. The appeal 'in the last resort' seems to be to science, and if that is so religion must take the second place, a situation which takes all the worth and dignity out of religion. This may well be too adverse a comment, but it is difficult to see what religion has gained in the argument. Indeed, the whole position seems to me an odd one. It looks as if Dr. Streeter had assumed that science is the basic and controlling kind of knowledge. This I have already shown to be a blunder, due to historical causes, which has already been corrected in many quarters. A view which starts with an antithesis of the Victorian era between mechanistic science and a Bergsonian life is unlikely to command

authorities. C. H. Valentine, in a review in *Theology* of Dr. Tennant's book, quotes some of them: "We find so eminent a psychologist as Professor Leuba saying, that 'for the psychologist who remains within the province of science, religious mysticism is a revelation not of God but of man.' And the same conclusion has been reached independently by Dr. Waterhouse and Dr. Matthews, to mention no others. 'The argument from experience,' says Dr. Waterhouse, 'naïvely stated, as if the subjective experience guaranteed the truth of the experient's own explanation, carries no weight. Dr. Matthews is equally emphatic: 'I am inclined to wonder whether advocates of an uncritical acceptance of religious experience have ever troubled to learn by introspection what religious experience really is. It is surely a complete misreading of the order of events to suppose that experience comes first, and afterwards gives rise to beliefs about God and the world. . . From the beginning religious experience is indissolubly connected with affirmations about the universe, which are capable of philosophical and critical interpretation.' "

All these criticisms go to the point and insist that it is incumbent on those who argue from religious experience to ally it with reason and reflection. No one ought, I think, to deny this; only there is reflection and reflection. If it is meant that an experience is useless until it is taken over by reason as a step in its argument, this may well be going too far. All that is required is that experience should be passed by reflection, where reflection means judgment. This judgment may be instantaneous with the experience or subsequent to it. When I perceive, I perceive something. On reflection I may decide that I did not perceive what I thought I was perceiving, but I shall also decide that in percep-

tion I always perceive something. Here I have settled
once and for all something of the nature of the act of
perception. Similarly, with religious experience. Of
course I have to look at it and decide whether it is
valid—unless, as some might claim, in the very act I
know and judge that it is true—but I may be able to
decide that in it I came into contact with an object
which is divine. If this can be ascertained, then one
can say that religious experience has as such a certain
validity. This is the minimum required. In other words
the question to be settled is whether religious experience
in any sense of the words has a specific and objective
content. Many distinguished writers have answered
in the affirmative. If what they say is true, then just as
aesthetics has come to be accepted in modern philosophy
as a legitimate branch of it, so religious experience will
take its place alongside aesthetics and morals.

In expounding this argument I will not use the forms
in which it has been expressed by Otto, Cook Wilson,
A. E. Taylor and others. They are well known, especially that of Otto as developed in his *Das Heilige*. He
has been criticised for neglecting the intellectual
element in the experience, and the criticism is not
without foundation. If there be any truth in the contention of these writers, the success cannot be due to the
invocation of some mysterious faculty. For this reason
I will try to state the argument in the strongest way
possible, and in doing so I will keep closer to Cook
Wilson than to Otto. The first premise is that knowledge
is of reality, that is to say, the contents of our knowing
are not made by us but are determined by the nature
and qualities of what is external to us. Thus it is that
we call different things by different names, that men
from the beginning of recorded history have been in
fear of fearsome objects and felt joy and love in the

presence of what is delectable and lovable; thus it is that the idea of dead and living things arose, and the distinction of father and mother and friends and enemies. It is because different beings existed with different attributes that we have specific ideas and emotions. Now, from all time man has had an idea of the divine, and if we turn to history we see that it was in the presence of some awe-inspiring scene or person that the feeling of awe was evoked and the mind stirred to adoration and worship. If the emotions aroused are distinct and appropriate to some one kind of object, if the emotion is rational and not a mere feeling, if the idea is different from a pure ideal or chimera or invention, we are justified in claiming that religious experience has some unique and real being for its object. On analysis all these suppositions can be verified. Awe and reverence are indeed used to express an attitude towards things and persons which are in no sense divine; but it is an applied sense, and the proof that they are not the primary cause of the attitude is that even when we have recognised that they are not fit objects of worship the attitude remains. The worship of false gods is an indirect proof that there must be some true God, even as a mistaken morality is evidence of the native distinction between good and evil. In religious experience what we find is an idea of an adorable object, an emotion of reverence and an impulse to worship, and be it noticed that this worship implies the complete subjection of the self and dependence of it on the power with which it is brought into contact. No finite object that we are aware of could be the sufficient cause of such worship, and certainly no finite object, when it was recognised as such, could continue to be adored. Therefore, to complete the argument, must it not be said that just as it is the objective character which makes us differentiate between an inanimate object and a living being, a stick and the hand of a friend, just as it is the terrifying aspect of the tiger and the gentle look of a fawn which cause in us distinct emotions, just as it is an objective moral order of right and wrong, good and evil, and an objective world of beauty, which inspire our moral appreciations and our aesthetic emotions, so it is the existence and presence of a power which is adorable that make men believe in religion and in all places and at all times impel him to bow the knee or prostrate himself in awe and worship?

Such is the argument, and as can be seen it does not claim more than a minimum of awareness, a floor, as it were, on which altars can be built. No particular form of religion, no particular religious experience, can shelter under the wings of this argument. It says no more than that there is existing an adorable object and that this is what is common underneath the errors of the primitive worship and the analyses and constructions of the theologian and the mystic. It claims, moreover, to rest on knowledge and not on some necromantic power. Nevertheless, it is in this very claim that it is open to criticism. Otto and Lutoslawski and many others allow the mind and reason a very small part, and I can think of no one save Cook Wilson who stoutly defends the intellectual character of the experience. To Cook Wilson religious experience is parallel to that of moral experience, and as in his theory we have the power to apprehend the rightness of a particular act, so in certain situations we are able to apprehend the divine. The suggestion is attractive, as it calls attention to an experience which is at the same time a judgment and an emotion, a fact guaranteed by the language of mankind, which uses without discrimination the words "sense" or "feeling" or "judgment" to describe conscience. But though religious experience is similar to moral, there are differences so great that the apparent light thrown by the comparison may serve only to produce a greater darkness. In the first place, moral apprehensions are of actions which are in themselves of a right and wrong character, whereas the divine is not a character of any act or situation. It is furthermore singular, whereas the moral order contains many subdivisions and many types of goodness and badness. It is, I think also possible to give an explanation why we are able to appreciate moral distinctions. They have a bearing on our end. If by the force of our nature we are carried on to a determinate end, that end will be our good and will serve as a standard for judgment. But it is extremely difficult to maintain that the divine is apprehended directly in any tendency of ours. I say "directly," because an indirect knowledge in this way may well be possible.

These preliminary criticisms lead on to still more serious difficulties. The realist theory of knowledge on which this argument from religious experience is based is too apt to assume that the content of our experience must be an objective reality immediately apprehended. We have already seen that the divine is not on all fours with the good, and it would be easy to show that the objective character of aesthetic experience does not help us. It is necessary now to ask what can be the object which is defined as adorable, what is the nature of our apprehension of it, and how the emotions of awe and reverence testify to it. It is strange that if we do apprehend God directly we should apprehend Him in so impersonal a way as something having divinity, and that the developed thought of God should depart as much as it does from this first apprehension. Grant that the developed notion contains a core of the primitive, does not the difference argue that the primitive cannot be a direct apprehension? The likelihood of this is increased when we consider more closely the act of knowledge. From the way that some of the defenders of the view criticised expound the argument, it might be supposed that we have an intuition of God. No doubt they lay stress on the directness of the apprehension in order to make it clear that they are not proceeding by means of inference from the unknown to the known. The divine, they say, is a datum of experience. But the history of religion and the history of philosophy and the universal consent of mankind are all against this. We do not see God; our trouble is that we long to do so and cannot, and if intuition is taken in its strict sense this is what ought to be meant. The alternatives to this are inference, interior feeling, a peculiar form of knowledge, or what I have called interpretation. Let us dismiss inference, as defenders of the view are all anxious to do so. Interior feeling, to be valid, must, I think, turn into inference. If the reverence does not accompany a direct awareness, we are bound to say that we are conscious of this reverence and cannot account for it save on the hypothesis that an adorable object has somehow caused it. In this case we are not directly aware of this adorable object, but we trace the relics of its passing or presence within us and this seems to be a clear example of inference. The fact that all writers put the stress on the emotion and not on the awareness—as if the awareness did not suffice of itself—favours this interpretation of the experience. We are told nothing of the way the divine is present. The next alternative is that we are confronted with a special form of knowledge. This would seem a desperate attempt to justify the experience, were it not that a parallel or analogy is offered. This is the knowledge we have of ourselves. We have no intuition of our own substance; nevertheless there is no knowledge of external objects which is not accompanied by some degree of self-knowledge, and what we do know of ourselves is given to us in our operations. Just as the self in in a certain way a datum in all knowledge, and just as we know ourselves in our operations, so we know God, indistinctly perhaps, in and through all knowledge, and certainly in certain situations when we are aware of Him in and through His works. This is an ingenious argument, and has much in its favour. Against it is that the analogy does not hold strictly. We know ourselves in our operations because our operations have no meaning except as the operations of a subject or ego. The relation between the two is not one of two separate beings. But, unless we are Pantheists, we cannot say the same of the relation of God to nature and to ourselves. Both nature and natural objects and we ourselves have a definite character or being, however close the intimacy between it and the Maker of it. Even supposing, therefore, that our knowledge of ourselves can be distinguished from inference, it does not follow that our knowledge of God can likewise be so distinguished. Another difficulty is that without sense-experience, memory, and accompanying phantasm, it is probable that we should never be able to be fully self-conscious. In our knowledge of God, if sense-experience enters in, as it surely must if we are not talking of the highest mystic flights, it cannot be attributed to God, and it cannot play the same part as it does in self-knowledge. On the credit side of this alternative, however, must be set the fact that it does help to explain why man has carried the idea of God, as Aeneas bore his Penates, in his journeying through life. He is naturally a religious

R

being and a theist, and he believes and feels confident
in his belief long before he has heard of the rational
proofs for God's existence. No new star swims into his
ken when he accepts these proofs, and the odd thing is
that he may give them only a notional assent, or find
each one in detail unsatisfactory, and nevertheless
retain his confidence in the wisdom and reasonableness
of his conduct in continuing to believe. It helps, moreover, to explain the errors of crude religious worship.
If God is intimately connected with His creation, so
intimately that creatures disclose Him in a way
analogous to that in which our operations disclose the
subject of them, it is natural that simple folk should
tend to confuse the relation and to worship stocks and
stones. When we remember the lowering effect of the
senses on our knowledge, how they make us represent
even the most immaterial and spiritual of qualities and
objects in a sensible way, how even St. Augustine con-
fessed that for years he thought of God as material, it
is clear that a savage might easily think of God as the
sun or the mighty river or as the inhabitant of some
dark grove, just because he is aware in a dim way of the
closeness of God to those forces and that place.

The last alternative is that of interpretation. As
already suggested, this ability to read through the
evidence its meaning and power can be brought to
bear on a number of puzzling certainties. We know
others by their gestures and face, we grasp the meaning
of a text, we light on the unity in induction which holds
together a number of phenomena. If we are asked for a
criterion of our certainty, we have in some cases to
appeal to the quasi-directness and inevitableness of
the interpretation. "Either I am mad or this must be
the same cross-roads I reached two hours ago." In
other cases the certainty rests on the infinite complexity

of the evidence which is afforded by indirect evidence and given to us under the form of unity. Can this serve? It may be that in experience the Absolute is given implicitly. In one and the same kind of act it is seen that what we know has no ground or unity without a whole, and that we interpret this whole not abstractly but as a cause or power or spirit. I do not say, of course, that simple people use terms like "the whole" or "the absolute," but that they do not see the items of the world all disconnected and independent. They have a world of discourse and a universe in which they view things, and they have no difficulty in identifying this unity with a God who is not the universe but the ground of it. They interpret, that is, what they see as the work of a spirit in an analogous way to that in which they interpret the bodily actions of their fellows as the signs of a human will. The growing consistency of this interpretation in the development of civilisation would confirm it, just as the difficulties of an inquisitive age might weaken it. Now just as the beliefs of savages in stocks and stones could be quoted in support of the view outlined above, so the tendency to identify God with the All would seem to support this theory of interpretation.

There is no need to expand this last alternative, because, if it be not inference, it is at any rate hovering on the verge of inference. If any of the alternatives I have suggested approach the truth, they do so only by emphasising the fact that this religious experience is a form of knowledge. Its value seems to me not to consist in any appeal to feeling or interior conviction which cannot be brought before the footlights, nor to some imaginary contact with God by intuition. There is no need to return to the occult to escape the atheism of science. In both science and religion knowledge is used; their distinction does not lie there, but in the spheres of knowledge with which they are respectively concerned. For two thousand years and more philosophers and theologians have based their argument for the existence of God on evidence, and that evidence has been gathered together in the well-known proofs from the finiteness of nature, shown in its dependence and contingency, and from design. These proofs have been challenged, and since the time of Kant it has been customary in philosophic circles to dismiss them as outworn. For this reason, amongst others, a new argument has been sought in religious experience. This fright is, however, unreasonable, for the distrust of the old arguments has never been able to justify itself. Their supposed refutation by Kant depends upon the limitations which he himself imposes on the extent of human knowledge. Once that limitation is proved to be false Kant's main objection falls to the ground, and it is surprising that philosophers who reject Kant's theory of knowledge nevertheless continue to accept his verdict against the proofs for the existence of God.

It would be out of place here to set out these old arguments in their true form, but as it is due to a misstatement of the chief argument that its validity has been often denied, and as the correct statement of it has a bearing on the argument from religious experience, I must briefly indicate the true form of the proof. The wrong way is to begin with the phenomena of nature as they are related to us in science. These are objects which are confessedly nothing but appearances, and by appearances I mean objects of sensible experience which are detached from their context and so arranged as to be susceptible of treatment by the physico-mathematical methods of science. The objects which we meet in knowledge when we are not working as scientists are always sensible *things*, that is to say, they are made up of a sensible and an intelligible content. Because of this we have some knowledge of nature—not very much, but enough to know that we are dealing with a real world. Because we are in contact with the real world we can correct our mistakes and make progress in our knowledge of it. Not only that, we can make broad distinctions in that nature; we know that sense is not the same as mind, quality as quantity, space as time, whatever their connection; we do not confuse death with life, disease with health, man with woman, pagodas with elephants, stones with bread. Kant denied that we have any knowledge of things in themselves; scientists abstract from things in themselves in order to be able to learn more about them. Their whole effort would be stultified if, at the end of their experiments, they had no hope of making any progress in real knowledge. Their methods on the contrary bear out what I have been urging that we know something, that we are looking through the appearances at reality. Once this is granted the existence of God must be admitted without more ado. Like a hand groping in the dark our mind has come into contact with what is, and this reality cannot be suspended on nothing, cannot be a half and half affair. If there is anything then there must be something fully real. The principle of sufficient reason demands this, for we cannot think of a thing which is insufficient and self-sufficient at the same time, and we cannot leave the insufficient as if there were no more to be said about it. The absolute and the contingent, the self-sufficient and the insufficient, the independent and the dependent, go together in this sense, that if there be the second there must be the first, though the first does not require the second. Either, then, in all knowledge we do nothing but know the one, complete, self-sufficient reality—and this we must call God—or, if we know the dependent, we are bound to assert the existence of its source and ground. The question becomes, therefore, one of fact. Do we know completeness in every act of knowledge, or the contingent? To say the first would be to throw us back again on scepticism, a position which, as we can show, it is impossible to maintain. If there be any real meaning in change, in birth and decay, in the variety of nature, any possibility that what now is might not be, then the reality we know is the contingent, a suppliant for its existence and its meaning on what is not itself.

This is the line of argument for God's existence. Great philosophers in the past relied for their evidence on nature. They looked out, confident that what they saw was no mirage, and unmistakenly nature appeared to them as indigent, as crying for an explanation which it could not itself give. Their outlook was objective, and this gave an impersonal character to their argument and conclusions, which has led moderns to turn away murmuring that this is a philosophic God and no religious one, and so make a fatal division between the two ideals. The complaint was a most unreasonable one; they wanted to appeal to their feelings when the argument was intended to reinforce their reason; they fell back on the romantic because the classic conception seemed too cold. (In parenthesis be it said that the greatest religious geniuses have reached the highest religious experiences by scaling the ladder of the mind or keeping near to that inaccessible light in which God is pure Act.) But—and this is why I have dwelt on the inference from contingency—the odd thing is that the closer we inspect this argument from religious experience, the more does it take on the semblance of the old argument. Schleiermacher, in his *Der christliche Glaube*, let the cat out of the bag when he defined religion as "a feeling of dependence." The experience which modern writers on religion uphold is not a direct awareness of God but the consciousness of their own state as creatures. All it seems that has happened is that, whereas the ancient philosophers focused their attention on the outside world, the modern is more interested in himself and has made a discovery that in his own experience he cannot escape God. Religious writing has followed the same trend as other forms of literature. The novel, which at one period took the form of narrative of external events, underwent a change and became, as it is called, psychological. Drama and poetry underwent a similar change, and religion has not lagged behind. There are signs that we are at the end of this phase, a phase which to many appears to have been a symptom of bad health and decline. The kingdom within is bought at too heavy an expense when the external order of things is neglected, and we shall never see ourselves truly if we make of objects so many mirrors in which to see our own reflection. The signs of reaction from this are, as I said, not wanting, and they can be noticed in religion in the change from insistence on divine immanence to agreement about the divine transcendence, and in the growing body of criticism of religious experience. It will be interesting if in the development of this reaction religious experience turns out to be nothing but the old argument from contingency looked at from inside instead of from outside.

With one other suggestion I can leave this question of religious experience. So far I may seem to have damned it with faint approval. One reason for this is that this experience has been twisted to such unjustifiable ends by the apologists for religion, and on the other hand has been used by many as an excuse for taking no interest in religion. These latter are apt to say with a shrug that they have no religious sense, and they consider that this is a good reason for neglecting to worship God. They forget—and they have been encouraged to forget by those who should know better—that sense and feeling are not the criteria of what is duty, and it is in "an act of duty not of experience that religion first consists." In the old books of morals religion is set down as a moral virtue, an obligation on us to behave in a certain way befitting God. The idea behind this is that our behaviour is to be measured by the kind of being with whom we are in relation. A father, because of his relation of parentage to his child, has the right to be treated by that child in a certain way, even though the child is without any tender feelings towards his father. Similarly the king or head of the State ought to receive a degree of respect, even from subjects who have never met him. Now God demands worship, and it is His due. We may be without any religious experience, but if from information of others or from our own reason we can come to have knowledge of Him we are bound to acknowledge Him and to pay respect to Him. Here is a principle which is far more important than digressions on the value of experience, a principle on which the welfare, not only of religion, but of all behaviour depends. It states that knowledge should be the source of action, that we must do what we know to be right, even thou no interior gladness or appreciation accompany the knowledge. As a matter of fact action based on truth usually creates the appropriate emotion. If we live according to justice we shall come to love justice; if we live the truth we shall in time learn to love it. Therefore, those who are ready to admit that intellectually they do not find serious difficulty in admitting God's existence, but dispense themselves from worship on the plea that they have no religious sense, commit *lèse-majesté* in their neglect of God's rights and are as foolish as a boy who refuses to regard a masterpiece in music or painting because, at the time, he feels no pleasure in it.

Religion, above all, requires to be lived before it can be experienced. I have already pointed out that it is of the essence of the Christian religion that man should, in the words of Denis the Areopagite, "suffer divine action," that he should be wrested out of his experience into an orbit which is higher; and for this to happen he must resist the temptation to bring the divine down to the test of his experience. In all prayer and worship it is better to fix the mind away from the self and its experiences and concentrate them on what is known to be the truth and reality of God and His revelation. Just as love should be disinterested and consider the beloved object for its own sake, without any self-regard, so in prayer and worship it is God's will which comes first, which should be the object of our "naked intent." The cry of religious experience starts only too often from self and ends with self, and God becomes an almsman of its desires. That this is not an exaggeration the evidence of modern discussions of God proves. Time and time again the nature of God and the truths of Christianity are weighed in the balance; God is denied this attribute and that, and all that He says and is, is made to fit the needs of man, and lots are cast to decide what will be preserved. The scientist may have remarked that he had no need for God, and the irreverence can be excused by the half-truth that God is outside scientific hypotheses; but we live in a world with topsy-turvy standards when remarks such as, "I don't want God," or, "I wouldn't accept God on those terms," can be heard frequently in conversations and discussions.

I cannot conclude without mentioning one advantage gained by this recourse to religious experience. It has served to bring out God's intimacy with and closeness to us, which were sometimes hidden in the statement of the old arguments from causality. The height and depth of the notion of creation are more than we can appreciate in any one glance. Our relation of dependence is such that God is at the beginning of our thought long before He is reached explicitly at the end of it. Only God can create, that is, only God can make of nothing a living thing which is at the same time most dependent, and in that very dependence most itself and independent. All that man can do is to make a statue or a robot, and that neither has a life of its own nor is completely its maker's. The desire for the perfect act is well illustrated by the story told of Michelangelo how standing before his statue of Moses he struck it crying, "Speak!" The true philosophy of God accepts all the consequences of His dominance over and in His works, seeing in their relation to Him the marks of the highest union it can conceive of naturally—God upholding all by a never-ceasing act, confiding His power to the weakest and the strongest without diminution of their finite nature! But the most supreme way in which we can conceive of this relation is in the movement of all creation to rise to its final end. If one speaks after Dante of this unconscious and immanent love of God in inanimate nature, the language may be accused of poetry (though I do not see why, if scientists are allowed to concede freedom to atoms, love should be excluded), but in human beings the language is literal. *Pondus meum amor meus*, St. Augustine cried; and it is true that the good, which is God, touches the soul to life from slumber under the guise of finite and passing shapes. God is the final cause and responsible, therefore, for the first act of man, for the direction in which he moves; He is the unseen arbiter and companion of all our journeying and of our good fortune.

If this be so may it not be that He is felt in consciousness as spring is felt in the earth, when all that was overlaid with frost and ice is quickened with a promise now to be fulfilled? "Eye hath not seen nor ear heard what things are prepared for those that love God." It is no exaggeration to find an analogy to this expectation of Christians in the consummation of human desire. The pagans, as St. Paul noticed, built altars to an unknown God, and it is God who is felt across the conscious interest in perceptible joys. As the artist creates patterns in a vain effort to catch a beauty which escapes him, because it is behind his thought and never realised in what he sees, so the love of God beckons and draws the soul of man, though he has never heard the sacred Name. He is aware only that something within him leaps, like a child in the womb, in the presence of anything fair and good, and he is aware of a want and a helplessness and not of the answer and his destiny. All other living things seem to have their end and to be satisfied with it, but by experience he knows that his own end stretches illimitably beyond his known desires, that he might be more than he is capable of being, that his deserts are small and his longing immense. If this is a true portrait of man then it is possible to find a new meaning in religious experience. What he feels is not God but God's shadow, or the reflection of his end and of God's designs in his own act of living and striving. Thus a place can be found in belief for desire and love without the disadvantages which attach to the ordinary pragmatic and modernistic accounts of their influence on knowledge.

In any and every defence of belief knowledge must stand fast and bind belief to truth; nevertheless, as the good and the true converge in the end, the right movement in the direction of the good may assist when the end is not visible to the intellect. Whether this is so and how it is to be ensured we must leave for another chapter.

CHAPTER IX

THE LIMITS OF BELIEF

FOR were it not better for a man in a fair room to set up one great light or branching candlestick of light than to go about with a small watch-candle into every corner?

BACON.

> Dunque nostra veduta, che conviene
> essere alcun dei raggi, della mente
> di che tutte le cose son ripiene,
>
> non può da sua natura esser possente
> tanto che suo principio non discerna
> molto di là, da quel che l'è parvente.

DANTE: Paradiso XIX.

CHAPTER IX

THE LIMITS OF BELIEF

IN this chapter we must gather up and enforce the conclusions of the preceding chapters. The main problems of belief have proved to be its relation to truth and knowledge, what factors go to constitute it, and its range. Belief is by many supposed to be a substitute for knowledge and to be all that man can compass. On this view it may be a high probability, a faith which is waiting on verification, a reason of the heart, a tonic against gloom and scepticism, or finally nothing but a "rationalisation"—a by-product of matter, like the fumes of coal gas or the pallid ray of the glow-worm. Against all such heresies I have argued that the mind can know truth because the mind is immaterial and so active and diaphanous as to be able to view other natures for what they are. All variations on knowing, such as opinion, scientific faith and surmise, depend on the existence of some certainty for their meaning and existence. Their light is a reflection of knowledge and they start from knowledge and are, in their respective degrees, approximations to it. Until this is granted all discussion is waste of time. Sceptics are such as would devour their own vitals or swear that they did not exist, while all the time they are consuming the energy of what they are denying in their very denunciations. On the other hand, once the existence of some certainty is granted the problems of belief fall into their places and we are face to face with the chief and proper concern of philosophy, the questions of the various degrees of knowledge, of error and of the mind's limitations.

The explanation of the limitations of knowledge is naturally to be found in the way in which a human being knows. In mind man has a faculty which is heaven-born and godlike, one which carries out its function impeccably; but it is not the mind which knows but man, and man has a finite measure. He intrudes himself necessarily into his knowing, not so as to spoil it—for then it would not be knowledge at all—but so as to cramp and, at the same time, dissipate it; he can also interfere by choice and wrest his knowledge to his desires. The limitation imposed by his nature is marked in two ways: first, he has to start with his senses, their experience; throughout his mental life he has to image and repre-sent his thought by the help of sense. He cannot, for instance, think of what is spiritual save in terms of the material, and when he thinks of any nature it is only universally and abstractly. This first defect is partly responsible for the second: Man has no intuition, every act of judgment is synthetic, in that it reunites in one indivisible act subject and attribute, particular and universal, sense and thought. The human mind is distracted, it looks before and after, it wanders around, it talks and discourses, it does not fully *see*. That is why even with what is self-evident it can make mistakes or, at least, withhold its assent, as experience proves. The distinctions which I have been trying to make here are in Newman's mind in his analysis of assent. He, like many other great observers of human nature, had not much faith in logic, in the neat conclusions drawn from notions. He, therefore, divided real assents from notional assents and claimed that a conclusion from inference was always radically different from a cate-gorical assent. Much of what he says is invaluable and

I have tried to incorporate it in this study. Nevertheless I have felt it needful to lay more stress on reason than Newman did, for two reasons; first, because I think that his antithesis is partly due to a false tradition of philosophy from which he borrowed his terminology, and secondly, there is a pressing need in these days to bind belief with the cords of reason. For too long a time the balance has been tipped over in favour of the irrational in our judgments, and literary critics and religious apologists have hailed with satisfaction the appeal to feelings, sentiments and processes which may be above reason or below reason but are too facile to be soberly rational.

What Newman called the illative sense can be taken under the charge of the mind without impoverishment. The word "rational," as I have explained, suffered in its meaning during the ascendancy of science. It was equated with the methods employed in the scientific methods of the day. Independently of the effect of that fashion there is to-day a chronic misconception of its range. It is taken for granted that the one test and assurance of reason is proof, and by proof is meant mediate inference. Now, as Professor A. E. Taylor pointed out in his illuminating presidential address to the Aristotelian society, no proof can be given of first principles. They are as indemonstrable as the facts of perception, and willy nilly the scientist is bound to use these principles every time he looks at evidence, weighs it and makes hypotheses. I have suggested that what is currently put outside the work of reason is unmistakably the work, if not of the inferential reason, at any rate of the mind, and that we are using a method of *interpretation* every day of our lives—in our knowledge of our friends, familiar objects, in the reading of the newspapers, in reading biography, history and literature. It is this faculty of interpretation which covers the illative

s

sense and is admirably shown in just those decisive examples which Newman takes, our knowledge that England is an island, that England is governed by a Parliament, and so forth. The mind is here eminently engaged on its proper business, reading through data to the meaning revealed, and, in the examples of absolute certainty, seeing infinitely complex and consistent data, by means of indirect reference, in terms of unity.

If this be true then the vagueness with which we use the word "belief" corresponds with a vagueness in our view of what makes certainty. Those who hold that only what is demonstrable is knowledge call all else that is above the level of opinion "belief." There is a more soundly based tradition according to which belief is contrasted with vision: what we can see as evident for ourselves is vision, what we derive from others is belief. This is a valid distinction and does not of itself determine whether belief can be certain or not. As, however, belief is taken by so many to be necessarily second-hand and fallible, I have found it necessary to argue that it covers certain knowledge as well as the probable. If we say, for instance, that we believe in God's existence, this may imply that we, as particular persons, are not convinced by arguments of God's existence, but nevertheless are strongly persuaded to hold it; it ought not to imply that His existence cannot be a matter of certainty, that it cannot be proved. The difference is enormous between these two positions. In the first we are like one who says that he has not yet been able to satisfy himself by rational demonstration that certain mathematical equations are true; in the second we assert that those equations cannot be reached by reason. When we find ourselves in the second position we set out to find other means than that of reason for getting what we want. There are parallel experiments in the matter of religion, and it is because of these that I have been obliged to inquire into the validity of experience and of the place of desire in our affirmations of reality.

Many have complained that to put the knowledge of God alongside that of mathematical equations is a travesty of the facts, because it ignores the vital distinction between truths of existence and truths of value: the God of religion is not the abstract being of philosophy. To this I would answer that this distinction is not to be neglected, but cannot be pressed into a defiance of reason. It may be that feeling and experience help us to realise truths—it is undoubtedly true that certain objects just because of their nature are apt to incite in us an attitude of fear or reverence, hate or love. But it is necessary that we should let the object be understood before we respond to it in the way that the emotions suggest. By all means let us benefit by the goodness, the loveableness of God and his creatures; we are aware of these characteristics as belonging to their nature, and our own attitude is normally one in which thought and feeling are blended in one act of appreciation. All this is not only permissible but right—on one condition, and that condition is that our mind is never cozened, is never beguiled by the Delilah of desire to desert its duty, which is to superintend all the elements in our experience. For this reason I have tried to analyse the part that desire can play in knowledge, and distinguished between the choice of election and the choice of selection. In the latter, desire should never get in the way, for the plain reason that it is the determinate nature of the object as seen by the mind which must provide the evidence for judging. In all the prerequisites, in the preparation for the act of judging, desire can serve most nobly and efficaciously. As we know full well, it is our estranged faces which make us miss the truth offered to us. We are not sufficiently interested to look and see; we prefer to sit under a fig tree reading, we turn away bored before we have given ourselves time to understand, and we let other considerations enter in to distract us and to prejudice our judgment. Here is the half truth which Plato maintained—that all wrong choices are due to a lack of knowledge. This would be the whole truth if we were to add that our initial attitude has been affected by our choices and runs over into our decisions.

There may be cases in which the will or desire may be still more intimately conjoined with knowledge, and this question will be considered later. For the moment we must hold fixedly to the rule that the deciding factor in all judgment must be the intellect and not an experience which can in any way override the mind. Above all is this rule necessary in our relations with God. Thought here—philosophic thought—is an astringent against the heat of the emotions. At the bottom of so-called religious experience lies a brood of false fancies. The history of religion has shown how easily superstition, crudities and anthropomorphism have intruded themselves into belief. Facile emotion must be cured by the cold spray of reason, and emotion rid of its projections by dry philosophy. "Dry" philosophy I have called it, but this is an unjust epithet, for as philosophy reaches out it can tell from afar of a Being who is no abstraction, despite the lameness of its human terms. The highest object of philosophy is to be a true handmaid of revealed religion and stir the intellectual appetite, the while it trains the emotions to be its own ancillaries and to doff their sentimental habits.

To return now to belief and its meaning and validity. The conclusions we have reached are that belief may fall in with truth, be in fact identical with it if it is used loosely to cover knowledge which is self evident, or like the existence of God, demonstrable by reason; that if it is used for a mode of appreciating reality, which I have called interpretation, it can again be valid in many cases. I have tried to enumerate some of those cases, and, in doing so, to justify the judgments of common-sense against the authority of so-called scientific experts.

Of course, it is necessary to use the word "common-sense" with some accuracy and to determine at the same time its limitations, and correspondingly the extent and limitations of the jurisdiction of the expert. An excellent example of a very common use both of belief and of science is to be found in *My Early Life* by Mr. Winston Churchill: he tells how at Bangalore he began to be interested in books and to educate himself. The first result of reading Winwood Reade, Gibbon and Lecky and many a book on science and religion was to make him react violently against what he had been told as a boy at home and at school. But this phase passed. "I came across a French saying which seemed singularly apposite. *'Le cœur a ses raisons, que la raison ne connait pas.'* It seemed to me that it would be very foolish to disregard the reasons of the heart for those of the head. Indeed, I could not see why I should not enjoy them both. I did not worry about the inconsistency of thinking one way and believing the other. It seemed good to let the mind explore so far as it could the paths of thought and logic, and also good to pray for help and succour and be thankful when they came. . . The human brain cannot comprehend infinity, but the discovery of mathematics enables it to be handled quite easily. The idea that nothing is true except what we comprehend is silly, and that ideas which our minds cannot reconcile are mutually destructive, sillier still.

Certainly nothing could be more repulsive both to our minds and feelings than the spectacle of thousands of millions of universes—for that is what they say it comes to now—all knocking together for ever without any rational or good purpose behind them. I therefore adopted quite early in life a system of believing whatever I wanted to believe, while at the same time leaving reason to pursue unfettered whatever paths she was capable of treading."

Here, I think, is the expression of a point of view very common among intelligent classes of people who are alive enough to recognise the value of religion. The sophisticated will sneer at it, and the orthodox be somewhat dismayed. But it may well be interpreted as the expression of a truth through the fog of modern language and ideas. Mr. Churchill seems to me in this passage like a Gulliver who will not be bound by the strings of the Lilliputians. Hence he is right in his conclusions, though the assumptions he takes over from his reading make his premises all wrong. It is no wonder when reason is supposed to have given the *coup de grâce* to God and to the contents of the Creeds and nothing remains but a distaste for the prospect left, that belief should be made an affair of the heart. Here is an illustration of the so unhallowed influence of suggestion and the creation of a false antithesis. Men like Mr. Churchill can fight their way out of it and form for themselves a view of life which if not consistent is practical; but others who have nothing of the corsair in them find it hard to survive the scuttling of their ships. The language of the heart is of little avail when the reason is gone.

Still, we may ask, what is the right way of escape from the dilemma proposed by Mr. Churchill? His own answer is, I think, wrong more in word than in fact.

Contained in it is the belief that science occupies only one section of the battlefield and that the rest of the world, if inarticulate, is not without knowledge and experience. Their testimony is consistent with far more facts than are those of apparent reason. If this is so, then it is not so much because he just wants to believe what he likes but because the reason of the heart has evidence of infinite variety and extent, that Mr. Churchill is justified in trusting it. This conclusion would bear out what has already been written on the limitations of science and scientific authorities and fall under the argument from interpretation of infinite complex evidence. Both on account of the prevailing tendency to restrict the use of the word "reason" and a failure to see that detective work, diagnosis of symptoms, interpretation of texts, and convictions formed on testimony about past events and persons and geographical facts are to be reckoned modes of knowing, it has been supposed that the word "belief" which is used to cover these operations is not rational. All the argument of this book has gone to show that this supposition is a mistake.

One objection remains over which has yet to be answered. Belief may not always be a reason of the heart, but in fact it very often is, and to seek to justify it on any occasion is to open the way to every kind of falsehood. Be it answered, first, that abuse does not make a proper use any the less justifiable, and secondly certain cautions and safeguards can be laid down. Assuredly no safeguard can save a man from erring, and the richer the subject matter, the more it appeals to him because of its worth. The hard-bitten philosopher reckons his gains in knowledge every day and finds them very small; he is content to say that he knows some well-worn principles, some immediate deductions, mathematical truths and direct experiences at the time they happen; he feels bound on his principles to dismiss history as a study of shadowy figures and events, to put a mark of interrogation after all his neighbour's statements, to call the fact of his birth an opinion and the event of his death a likely contingency. That he is wrong I have no doubt, though, unless some mode of knowledge such as that I have described as interpretation be accepted, I do not see how he can be refuted. Let us, however, leave this question as I have already tried to deal with it, and frankly admit the surd in human thinking which renders the conclusions of mankind so erratic. To call attention to this is only to repeat what was said at the beginning of this chapter: the real problem of philosophy is to give a perspective of human knowledge in which limitation and error find their proper place.

A lack of intuition defines the condition of human thinking, and that lack leaves room for error. The positive causes of error are, however, to be sought not in this lack but in the interference of other factors. In very few acts does the mind work singly and aloof. Interest is almost always, if not always, present, and feelings and impulses are aroused. In the growth, therefore, of human knowledge, patterns are woven which can be called loosely habits of mind or ways of looking at things. They are composed of affective, impulsive and rational threads united together into one whole. That such patterns are of inestimable value is a fact few would care to deny. Brought up as we are to think that the solutions of difficulties come from correct observation and reasoning we take some time learning by bitter experience what dullards we are in the presence of unfamiliar material. Most detective stories contain an amateur hero who is as quick as a Sherlock Holmes and much quicker than the police. Unfortunately the amateur rarely comes off best. And this holds true even with material which is apparently common to expert and laymen alike. In a discussion on free will or immortality there are moves to be made and to be avoided just as much as in a game of chess. There are few moments more trying than those in which an ignoramus will insist on leading off a discussion on to an irrelevant issue. If this be the case on topics which are general, much more is it so in pursuits which are specialised, in art and morality and religion. Here practice, discipline and apperception are required, and the pattern of one kind tends to interfere with the understanding of the pattern of another. The north countryman thinks the ways of the southerner outlandish, the Englishman constantly misunderstands the motives of an Irishman and the man of business brushes aside impractical ideas as mere poetry. A pattern may easily lead to bigotry as love begets hate.

We have here to face a difficulty which is well known, and has been put in the question whether an historian ought to be biassed or not. For the moment let us not discuss the duties of the individual. The consideration of past writers shows that a bias does direct the attention of the writer to evidence which would be normally neglected and to the apprehension of the significance of some of that evidence. Mommsen's love of Caesarism has left us with a magnificent historical portrait and Grote's democratic leanings assisted him to appreciate Athens. In directing a writer to evidence affection and hate have, therefore, a definite value; the evil they do does not lie there but in their influence on the final judgment of that evidence. They sin not by discovery but by leaving out. If there existed a love so universal that it was fair to all sides we should have perfection, and it would be a perfection in which the pattern had played a predomi-

nant part. We may go further and say that the proverb
that love blinds while it illumines does not hold true in
every field. A liking for the good is a prerequisite in
morality. As Aristotle pointed out in decisions of what is
right for us to do we are moved by desire and controlled
by the reason and it is in the fascinating interplay of
these two, in what he calls a reasoned desire and desired
reason, that a moral act comes to be. Not only this but,
as he insists, the youth of a city must be trained in good
habits from the beginning, and in mature life the decision
must always follow from a formed habit helped out by a
perception in the concrete of what is right here and now.

So, too, in our general outlook on life there are degrees
of excellence. Young people often are crude in their
admirations and in their tastes. The boys and girls of a
city fancy that it is the noblest of ambitions to make guys
of themselves in dress and deportment. When another
love is substituted for this there may be no loss but all
gain; high ambitions succeed to low, and true loves are
broadened out so as to embrace not only family and city
but country and other civilisations. In the highest love of
all, the love of God, all legitimate human affections gain
in depth and permanence.

If now we supplement what has been said about truth
and knowledge by this conception of an internal pattern,
ever in process of formation and ever active, we can
complete our study of belief. In the last resort the reason
why belief is used so often to express an attitude which is
felt to be not quite the same as knowledge and inference,
is, I think, due to the fact that belief is influenced by the
pattern. As I have explained, the pattern is made up of
various ingredients of which the affective is one. Hence,
some people speak loosely of such and such a view being
their religion or philosophy of life or say, "those are my
sentiments," "that is the way I feel about it," and they

naturally contrast this with their state of mind in studying mathematics, reading legal evidence or umpiring in
some dispute. The make up of this pattern should be
such as to help reason and not obstruct it, and this can
happen as we saw in the preceding paragraph. All too
commonly, however, *trahit sua quemque voluptas*, the
passion or interest bears away the reason captive at its
saddle bow. There is a beautiful commentary on this
text in one of St. Augustine's sermons. He distinguishes
between the love which is a rebel against the best interests
of the self, and the love which is a messenger of the final
good of the soul. This latter is no traitor to truth but its
disciple. "For if the poet have leave to say: '*trahit sua
quemque voluptas*,' speaking not of compulsion but of love;
not of obligation but of pleasure; how much more ought
we to say that every man who is gladdened by truth,
gladdened by goodness, gladdened by justice, gladdened
by everlasting life, is drawn to Christ, who is all these
things." Here we have again in short the distinction
between a pattern which is coloured and woven by true
desire and the many other types which hide as much as
they reveal... As a general formula we may say that the
mind must judge its own inclinations, its spontaneous
verdicts, and fight against narrowness. The majority of
men can only do this in part and they have to fall back
upon another test, conscience, or the will to do what
appears to be the best. We all admire those whose
judgments are the outcome of a life nobly led; they may
not be philosophers and they may be easily entangled in
an argument, but their judgments are the expression of
their active pattern, of the direction of their lives.

A simple illustration of the working of the pattern can
be found in judgments on the impure and the obscene.
Here, very often, the wrongness is measured by the
feeling of repugnance or disgust. Many young persons

are at first shocked when they hear the facts of nature, and they learn to adjust their attitude by means of reason. At various intervals a controversy breaks out in the newspapers when works of art and literature are banned for their obscenity. The authorities and the public are told to cease being like Mrs. Grundy. Very rarely do the moralists give a reasoned defence of their action; they are probably unable to do so because they have been relying on a sense of what is fitting. Lord Brentford did indeed defend the action of the legal authorities in the affair of D. H. Lawrence, but he based his defence on the laws of the land and the only inter-pretation of them which, in the circumstances, was permissible. I might add that the assailants are no better off; they sling epithets at the moralists and make a pretence that no artist or writer could ever have had a bad motive, that the scandal must be pharisaical. Such humbug, of course, tends to make these controversies valueless. But the point I wish to make is that from the beginning of civilisation one of the tests of the wrongness of certain actions has been the repugnance they arouse; that this test is traditional and necessary, but that it needs where possible to be justified and corrected by reason. And for those who are interested in this matter it must surely seem a striking thing that a moral philo-sophy based on sound principles should be able to control the spontaneous aversions and train human nature to apportion the proper emotion to judgments of reason.

Other examples could be cited, and it is a painful incident in most men's lives when some person or object that meant much in their lives loses for a while, or permanently, all appeal. The object may be known in a cold far-off way to deserve our love, but we have it not and after a time darkness seems to descend even on the

and he can usually point to some superb triumph in the domain of science to bear witness to his teaching. Facts and life, however, sooner or later escape this hard and narrow unity, and philosophers turn a somersault and create a kingdom in which all is spirit or mind. So difficult is it to do justice to the mysterious order of reality with its multifold ranks and stations, its multiplicity of tiny but indelible indifferences! All that these and other philosophers have done is to rub out some of the important details from the canvas or splash it all over with one colour and call the result the last word of truth. Similarly in morals and theological speculations. Now it is a hard and forbidding sense of duty which turns with averted eyes from all forms of pleasure and desire; now it is frank hedonism, and in theology the agnostic and the anthropomorphist take it in turns to hold the public ear, advocating either a mysterious absolute or whole or unknown X, or a tribal God and superhuman man.

Thus it is that we are brought by philosophy and history to a portrait not so much of final truth as of man himself, a being "builded for pride, for potency, infinity," and yet successive unto nothing, truth-begetting and sworn to belief and sayer of dark sayings in a thousand tongues, high priest of nature and iconoclast—to him can the words of Lamb be truly attributed: "and it would not taste of death, by reason of its adoption into immortal palaces; but it was to know weakness and reliance and the shadow of human imbecility; and it went with a lame gait; but in its goings it exceeded all mortal children in grace and swiftness."

CHAPTER X

DIVINE FAITH

THE first step to be taken by the soul who enters upon the straight way and desires to draw near to God, is to learn to know God in very truth and not only outwardly as though by the colour of the writing. For as we know, so do we love: therefore if we know but little and darkly, if we reflect and meditate upon Him only superficially and fleetingly we shall in consequence love Him but little.

BLESSED ANGELA OF FOLIGNO.

THOU art the Love with which the heart loves Thee.
JACOPONE DA TODI.

AND yet he is a weakling who does not test in every way what is said and persevere until he is worn out by studying on every side. For he must do one of two things—either he must learn or discover the truth, or if that is impossible, he must take whatever human doctrine is best and hardest to disprove and, embarking upon it as upon a raft, sail upon it through life in the midst of dangers, unless he can sail upon some stronger vessel, some divine revelation, and make his voyage more safely and securely.

PLATO: Phaedo (Fowler's Trans.).

State contenti, umana gente, al quia:
 chè, se potuto aveste veder tutto,
 mestier non era partorir Maria;

e disiar vedeste senza frutto
 tai, che sarebbe lor disso quetato.

DANTE: Purgatorio III.

CHAPTER X

DIVINE FAITH

IN this chapter I may seem to take a flying leap from the rational beliefs so far discussed to a faith without roots because it is supernatural, irrational because it is above reason, and mystical and subjective because it depends on some kind of interior experience. This prejudice, as I must call it, against divine faith is very widespread, and to dissipate its assumptions one by one would require another book. It is not my intention to argue the case for Christianity, but to make use of the conclusions we have reached to show that what is called faith is another instance, and the highest instance of all, of interpretation, that it is not an interlude, a distracting side issue, but the curtain raiser of the final and divine interpretation of life.

The preceding chapters have led us to see that we are constantly engaged on interpreting natural objects, friends, the worlds of politics and art and history, and that we carry this habit of mind to greater problems, to an interpretation in fact of the whole of reality. Only here we find that the task is too much for us, that we are not sufficiently well equipped to give an answer. We are encouraged to find, nevertheless, that knowledge is a trustworthy guide, that sympathy and understanding go hand-in-hand, that the latter increases with familiarity, and that there is a correspondence between our own integrity and pattern and the perception of unity, direction and pattern in the universe. To return to an old example, the interpretation of the work of a master in music or painting comes out right and unmistakable when we have assimilated his mind and made it our own by affectionate understanding. As experience shows, a creative artist takes time to be understood. At first he has to meet with hostility, if not derision; his generation interprets the work by its own uncriticised standards and is puzzled to find any meaning in it. After a time, however, familiarity proves a good mistress, interest is awakened and understanding comes. Is it not, then, possible that there may be an interpretation of the whole of experience, strange and foolish to those who enjoy their prejudices, but to the once initiated, the wisdom and power of God? It is the claim of Christianity that it is the living document of God, that it can put an interpretation on life which is final and compelling. Nor does it make just idle promises; the credentials are there for all to examine, proofs are offered, and we have the striking fact that all those who possess this faith are utterly persuaded that they have ceased groping and now see. I do not mean that they have instantaneously the explanation of everything, that they enjoy a vision which removes all tears from the eye. Faith is not vision, if by vision we mean comprehension and intuition; it is rather the beginning of a new life, the discovery within and without of a new order, of a new and final definition. It is as though the eye had been trained to look through a telescope; at the first glance objects in the dim distance of normal sight take a shape, and trust in the instrument and knowledge fuse in the same act.

I have now to indicate how the complete and crowning interpretation of life, one in which love and truth meet, is verified in the act of divine faith. And I must beg the reader to allow me to do it in my own way and to bear with apparent irrelevances. The truth is that the subject must be handled with the greatest caution and delicacy. Ignorance is fatal and has been responsible in the past for a number of false problems and false solutions. The greatest minds of Christendom have for centuries been concentrated on this subject, and they have left behind them a number of fine distinctions, which may seem over-fastidious to the amateur, but are requisite for a proper appreciation of the various facets of faith.

I will begin, therefore, with a definition of the act as "that whereby we believe without doubting whatever God has revealed." This has been enlarged and summarised as follows. "We make an act of divine faith in any article of our creed when we take God's word for it. Faith is belief on the authority of God revealing. The motive of faith is the truthfulness of God who speaks. Faith is an act of submission of the intellect to God; it is a venture upon God's word; and at the same time it is a laying hold of some truth which He has revealed, inasmuch as He reveals it and vouches for it." The act furthermore has these properties, that it is firmly certain and free, rational and supernatural.

So far all Catholics are agreed, but in the explanation of the relation of part with part there is much diversity of opinion. On the motive of faith, that it is the truthfulness of God, there is no divergence. In the summary above there are, however, added the words, "Who Speaks," and not all are agreed as to the manner or mode of this speech. To save unnecessary discussion I take these words to include such various modes of communication as the words Christ uttered to His disciples, the preaching of St. Paul and the Church, the signs whereby the words of Christ could have been recognised as divine and, lastly, the signs, such as miracles and holiness and others, which serve to reveal the presence of God's truth. This wide interpretation is justified by facts. A spoken or communicated message is, as we have already seen, made known to us by signs; we behold the meaning through the language or music or gesture in its unity. There are, indeed, differences which some would designate as natural and artificial signs or as signs and symbols. That does not matter as long as we are in fact able to get to the message. Christ, for instance, deprecated signs and wonders, not because they were inefficacious but because they were forcible and indicated a darkness of understanding in his hearers. The footstep of the bridegroom at the door should suffice, and if he has to knock loudly and repeatedly, it is evidence of a regrettable supineness and insensibility within. A miracle and sign in the sky are therefore just as much tokens of the meaning and truth of God as the holiness of the speaker, the authority with which he speaks, or the message itself. In the latter case, be it remarked, the original message can reach directly the mind of the hearer whether it be spoken by the author or delivered through an intermediary. If Romeo sent a love letter to Juliet through boy or friar, or even a message to be spoken, Juliet would have had no difficulty in recognising the authentic tones of her lover. Or, to take another example, a person listening to a musician playing a piece of music would have no need to assure himself first of the credibility of the player, for the simple reason that he would be able in the opening bars to recognise the mind and genius, say, of a Beethoven.

One other point before proceeding. The last examples show that there is a certain proportion between the external evidence and the interior disposition. This proportion is evident in our ordinary experience, and has already been touched on in the discussion of the influence of desire and pattern. Our education in manners and discipline is based on it in that it has for its end to perfect our taste and judgment. In the doctrine here under discussion we have to become like to God before we can judge with His judgment; that is to say, in more technical language, grace gives us the power to be the sons of God, and this power is not just an external help but an interior strengthening. Hence, when we are confronted by the word and work of One whose ways are mysterious and divine, we need an interior illumination and a taste for the divine beauty and good before we are able to seize their proper significance and to know the message as our way and our truth.*

So much, then, for the motive of faith. Secondly as to the object of it, there is again a divergence of view within what is common doctrine. Some say that it is God, others that it is the *Deus absconditus*, God as above natural reason; and there are many other alternatives offered. I take it to be God revealed to us through Christ as our eternal life and truth, so that it is summed up in the word "gospel," the good news of our destiny by our union with Christ. Such an object would contain within it primarily the doctrine of our union with God by means of the Incarnation and Redemption, and, as implicated in it, all the other contents of the Creed. Some readers may think that very little hangs

* This elevation is expressly asserted by Christ in his words to St. Peter : "Flesh and blood have not revealed it to you, but my Father who is in heaven," and there are many passages to the same effect in St. Paul and St. John, such as, that "the eyes of your heart be enlightened, that you may know what is the hope of his calling, and what are the riches of the glory of his inheritance in the saints" (Ephesians i, 18). This correspondence between the internal and the external must be kept in mind in the sequel.

on these distinctions, but that is not so. We have to keep in mind the fact that both the learned and the unlearned may have faith, and therefore it is important to be able to state the minimum. For instance, St. Paul says that "without faith it is impossible to please God, for he that cometh to God must believe that He is, and is a rewarder to them that seek Him." In this text some knowledge of God and belief in His goodness is declared to be necessary for justification. It is the common opinion that other beliefs also are required. In the view I have just exposed it can be seen that the central point of faith is in the good news of eternal life in God through Christ, and this carries with it all the other doctrines of the Christian religion, even though some of them may be only implicitly known and imperfectly grasped. It throws light also on the habit of faith and on the fact that it is a virtue. The words of St. Polycarp, in his Epistle to the Philippians, hold true of all good Catholics: "The faith given you, which is the mother of us all when hope follows and love goes before." The love and hope give Catholics the power to sense what is right in dogma, or at least to be so obedient, so knit to the will of God, that they are only too glad to have the word of God taught to them. They re-echo the words of St. Peter: "To whom shall we go, for thou hast the words of eternal life."

Faith, therefore, is seen so far to consist in the believing of truths on the authority of God. They are not judged on their evidence apart from revelation, but on the word of God who is the truth. We have now to develop this explanation by stating what are the principal properties of this faith. They are four in number: the act of faith is supernatural and rational, certain and free. To give a complete account of the meaning of "supernatural" is impossible within a short compass. A rough idea, however, may be gathered by the consideration of the different orders of reality. The life of a fox-terrier is higher than that of a foxglove, and the life of a man is in turn above that of a dog. Let us suppose that a dog were for several hours of the day allowed to live the life of a human; it would then be exerting powers which were above the capacity of its nature. Now in fact what we mean by the supernatural is that human beings can receive from God a power (or, better, a quality) which makes them sharers in what is so much higher than themselves as to be justly called divine. If it may be said without irreverence, they are made so perfect that they can enjoy the intimacy and insight of the domestic life of the Holy Trinity, as analogously the fox-terrier might be said to enjoy on an equality the friendship of a human family and share the secrets of the family circle. Or to put this from another angle, the mind of man sees reality truly, but even at the highest moment of our existence that reality would still be seen in terms of ourselves, through human eyes, in human expression. The gift of the supernatural removes this radical imperfection; instead of a self-consciousness we are to have a God-consciousness; instead of seeing through our own eyes we are to be so united to God as to see Him and all else with His eyes. This new end of life, unspeakable love and union, is the message of good news which is the object of faith. It is by an act of faith, however, that we learn of it and make towards it, and not by vision or experience; and the reason is that being persons of free will we must have a period of testing during which we can co-operate with the grace of this life or refuse it. The essence, in short, of supernatural faith is that instead of our human pattern and order we are given a divine pattern and swung into a new order.

Despite this supernatural character the act of faith remains eminently reasonable. Reason does not abdicate because the Author of reason takes control and guides. Nevertheless, it is not too easy to assign the parts in this one act, which can be explained and defended on rational evidence and yet includes in its definition something above reason. The same difficulty occurs again when we put side-by-side the properties of certainty and freedom. In our natural certainties, as already shown, the mind must not allow the will or desire to determine its judgments; it is the evidence which satisfies, which determines the intellect to say "That is so, and I know why it is so." In faith, on the other hand, the mind is never appeased in the same way; it has not the vision of God and His truth before it to convince by their own intrinsic power. All the same, it is certain, and its certainty is gained by a confederate act of intellect and will. The will for once has a direct say and a decisive function which does not lead us astray. As St. Thomas said, faith is an act of the intellect under the command or direction of the will.

This being the general nature of the act of faith, it is now possible without risk of misunderstanding to consider its meaning more closely. It is not, let me repeat, an act of confidence, not what is commonly called a religious experience, not a natural assent in which the belief is a mixed act based partly on antecedent grounds for confidence and trust in the word of another. If the reader is convinced that the Christian faith is similar to one of these, he need not come with me any further, for I am assuming that it is different, an act, that is, such as I have tried to describe, a unique act about the existence of which all Catholics from the beginning of Christianity have been agreed. As in modern times, many attacks have been made upon it, principally on the ground that it cannot be a rational act; a number of distinguished thinkers have, so to speak, plotted it out, hoping thereby to prove that at each stage it was rational. By showing its genesis they wish to certify its validity. The graph is nearly always as follows. It can be proved that God exists and that by our natural reason we can know something about Him. It is easy to pass from these conclusions to others, for instance that God might reveal further knowledge about Himself if He chose. The question, therefore, now is whether He has communicated such further knowledge to us. We find when we look at the history of the human race that man left to himself has made a bad muddle of religion, and that, nevertheless, he has always longed for some deeper and more intimate relation with and knowledge of God. This suggests that it is probable that God has come to the aid of mankind and taught the truth about His wishes for mankind and the way to realise them. We now turn to history, and in history we find that the founder of Christianity made the claim to be the messenger from God bringing a revelation of good news, and that the Catholic Church has unfailingly reiterated that claim. The next step is to examine that claim, since it is not impossible and is, indeed, even probable. An examination of it can end only in one conclusion, that it is made out. The historical evidence, the previous history of the Jewish people, the holiness and authority of Christ, which rule out the hypothesis that He could have been a dupe or deceiver, the miracles He worked, which are too closely bound up with the narrative of His teaching and character to be inter- polations, the Resurrection, which has never successfully been gainsaid—all these facts can lead the reasonable inquirer to only one conclusion: Christ is the messenger of God or God. This once granted, the rest follows irresistibly. What God says is true, therefore whatever Christ taught must be accepted on the authority of God Himself.

After this argument it is held that the act of faith in the doctrines of Christianity is thoroughly rational. It is not maintained that all converts to Catholicism move along this line; men are moved by different pieces of evidence, but whatever the genesis of the act, after the act the rationality of it can be defended against all comers. But the theologians who have thus traced the logic of conversion are aware of a difficulty, and it is only fair that it should be mentioned. In thus emphasising reason they have made less obvious the place of the supernatural and of freedom in faith. Various solutions have been given of this difficulty, of which I shall mention a few without comment. Some say that as the supernatural is imperceptible in experience, being known only by the teaching of Christ, it can be omitted in the account of faith. There is a difference between the assent of the man who has reached his conclusion by the reasoning given above and the assent of faith, but to all appearances they must be the same, as the assent of faith is no whit less rational by being supernatural, and the supernatural, affecting as it does the mode of knowing and not the reasoning, cannot be stated. Others are not content with this, and point to the manifest fact that the assent of reason is given on account of the force of the premises, whereas the motive of faith is the authority of God speaking. They endeavour, therefore, to mark the stile where the change or crossing is made from reason to belief. Suarez, for instance, says that in the process of reasoning from the premises we are assisted by the Holy Spirit and illuminated; we then desire to assent to the conclusion not because it is necessitated by reason, but on the authority of God's word. Either can be chosen, and in the choice both the supernatural and freedom can be seen. This theory has been developed by many distinguished writers; they insist that there is a crucial distinction between saying "it appears to me to be true from history and from all the evidence that Christianity is true" and the personal act of self-surrender which exclaims "My God, I accept what You say because You say it."

In these views the common premise is that by reason a conclusion can be reached which is as certain as the act of faith, though it differs from it. Reason runs parallel with faith, and at a certain place the man of logic leaps over from one parallel to the other. A large group of theologians are dissatisfied with this. One party, for instance, denies that the premises in the reasoning could ever without faith bring the certainty required. For their part they believe that the recognition of the fact of God's revelation is not the result of premises, but an immediate act. We may know for certain that whatever God has revealed is true; we cannot know by recourse to evidence alone that God has revealed any definite truth. Hence, before faith supplies this lack there cannot be a certainty of the kind to force our assent. We are free, and it is grace and the authority of God which, when faith comes, move the will to assent without hesitation. By this means a loophole is discovered for the supernatural and for freedom. With this view few agree wholeheartedly, though many take the hint and look for a loophole, which a large number find not so much in the lack of evidence that God has revealed a particular truth as in the fact that the revelation is mysterious: no matter, they say, how sure we are of the authority of the witness, if what he says is obscure and beyond conceiving, a

U

cloud of doubt will hang over the mind until it is cleared away by faith.

There is, I think, something in our experience of natural beliefs which corresponds with the distinction here made. How often it happens that we hear an argument and can find no flaw in it, yet retain an uneasy feeling that there may be something wrong which we have missed. This occurs especially when the argument is deductive, when from some general principle conclusions are made to appear like rabbits from a conjuror's hat. Our suspicion, we remember, has been justified by mistakes in the past, when metaphysicians were apt to get out of their general principles more than they contained, and I think that it is this attitude of suspicion which accounts for the failure of the arguments for the existence of God, the soul and immortality to convince all hearers. We can also grow so conscious of the unknown factors and circumstances of nature that we can become habituated to reserve our judgment when apparently decisive arguments are propounded, when cures are wrought and spiritual and mystical phenomena declared to be above nature. We feel that we know too little to say that every other cause except one has been eliminated. There is, too, a mood, which only faith can clear away, in which we are tempted to say "I wonder if it is all true." When, then, we gaze into the abyss of God's works, our reason even at its best when it seems to be sure is accompanied by a feeling of suspense and giddiness, and this state would bear out the point of view just stated.

Of the views outlined so far all, as I have said, rest on the belief that the act of faith is preceded by a process in which the credibility of the faith is more or less securely established. This process is sometimes called the preamble to faith, and the stages in it are supposed to represent the stages which a man follows who starts out an unbeliever, then comes into contact with Christianity, examines its claims, convinces himself of their rationality and then, in the sequel, receives the gift of faith. I do not suppose that the advocates of this view maintain that all converts are bound to follow some such course; God's ways with men are manifold, and this is an ideal or representative portrait. It is, too, dictated probably by apologetic purposes; it is a reply to the question "How do you know that the Church is right or that you are acting rationally?" The answer to this question, as can be seen, is a strong one, but it has in turn given rise to a further objection, to this effect. A convert enters the Church by use of his private judgment and bases his assent on the evidence of reason; it follows that all his later acceptance of authority rests ultimately on his private judgment; and this judgment is no stronger than the original evidence. Some of the replies to this stock difficulty have been already given in outlining the views of the relation of reason to the supernatural. Without returning to these I may give in untechnical language some examples of knowledge which may serve to show that the objection is not nearly so strong as it may seem at first glance. The most famous is that of Newman in his comparison of the lamp. The lamp of private judgment is needed to find the way; once we have reached home there is no need of it. The knowledge of faith varies from what is antecedent to it as possession from quest. In a hilly country I may try to find out from the valley in which I am standing which is the best point of vantage from which to look down on the surrounding country. This is a very unsafe method, though better than none. If I am a scientist I may by calculating distances and heights work out what is the highest point, and in my journey to this point I may become more and more convinced that I was right. But when I am there and look around, all the previous calculations are wiped away, for now I see. A parallel to this is if I walk in a large garden with many intersecting paths; I am puzzled by the design, and may need to keep all my faculties about me not to lose my way. If afterwards I look down on this garden from a window, its design lies clear and certain before me. Similarly, all the wisdom gathered in my search for the truth of God's word, all my patient reasonings, are left behind as human gropings when God illumines my mind and gives me the substance of things hoped for. That this is so we know full well from the testimony of many converts who are hardly able themselves to understand their state of mind before the gift of faith, so different was it. Louis Veuillot, for instance, in a letter in 1841, wrote of the change affecting even the appearance of natural objects. "Objects have changed colours . . . there is in nature a voice which I understand . . . This sea I am looking at, which used to present to me the sterile portrait of my eternal restlessness, to-day is the fair mirror, the calm image of my profound peace."

In *Les Cahiers Mensuels* of 1930 and 1931 there are a series of articles entitled *Enquête sur les raisons de croire des Croyants*. They give interesting evidence of the nature of the act of faith and its relation to preceding conditions of mind. One writer dismisses as untrue of his own case any feeling of the need of God. "What is certain is that I do not experience as necessary for my comfort a belief in the existence of God, the God one and three in whom I believe. No doubt, since I believe—well or badly—in His existence, I believe at the same time in His supreme, in His absolute, goodness. That makes part of His definition, and it would be

which we must account. To put us on the right scent it will be useful to recall two valuable suggestions given by St. Thomas. He tells us that there is a similarity between faith and the moral virtue of prudence, and again he says that the knowledge gained by faith is akin to that given to us in morality by what he calls synderesis. Synderesis is defined as that habit of mind which enables us to make primary moral judgments. It corresponds in moral thinking with the power in speculative thinking to recognise primary truths. Thus we have no difficulty in distinguishing good from evil, in marking down obvious acts of justice and injustice, and so forth.

This comparison is illuminating. Prudence, as we know, is the queen of the moral virtues. Aristotle, in his *Nichomachean Ethics*, has much to say about it, and some of his remarks are worth quoting as being very much to the point. He says that "Practical wisdom must be a reasoned and true state of capacity to act with regard to human goods;" and again, "That it is a virtue and not an art," that it depends on an intimate connection between inclination and reason, as the perfection of the virtue is "truth in agreement with right desire." To attain this experience is necessary; young people can be good mathematicians, but without experience they cannot judge of what is good for them, and it is easy to pervert the judgment by the indulgence in false desires. What is said here of prudence has its truth also in the region of faith. Faith is not an intellectual calculation; it is judgment about our last end. Hence, just as prudence can be perverted and at all times depends on discipline and a wholesome education of the inclinations, so, too, as a preparation for faith we have to purify our intentions to attune ourselves so far as is possible to the music of God's message. At most our efforts will serve to remove the obstacles of false ambition, self-satisfaction, to give us the single eye, because the supernatural is no human symphony but the revelation of God's own generous gift. All the same, it is important to insist that the inclinations have to be made straight just as much as the mind must be convinced.

There is, however, one great difference at least between prudence and faith. The former, as we have seen, is concerned with a right choice of the means to the good life. It is the choice of a way, of an alternative, of an answer. Faith, on the contrary, is the assent to *the* way, to the end, to life itself. That is the reason why it has something final and absolute in its act; it is aware that for it there are no alternatives open; a call has come, the voice of the Good Shepherd summoning it to the green pastures of eternal life, and just as the habit of first principles makes certain actions appear immediately as a bounden duty, so faith makes it clear to the soul that for it there is only one life, one way and one truth. Moreover, this certainty comes in one full and complete act and carries with it its own validity. In the explanations given at the beginning of this chapter I pointed out that they all assumed or maintained that everything necessary for faith was present before faith came; they tended, that is, to emphasise, perhaps unduly, the genesis of the assent and to show how in that genesis the mind reached certainty. It cannot be denied that in many cases there is no such preparation, that men pass from a state of disbelief even in God to one of assured faith, and that the cases of the centurion, the good thief and St. Paul have been repeated time and time again. Just as one passes without deliberation from a state of unrepentance to love and supernatural charity, so the act of faith may supervene by grace on unbelief, and a man know without hesitation that the assent is fully rational.

What, then, is the relation of the preamble, as it is called, to the act of faith? I have suggested that the acquisition of such virtues as humility and desire of the good is at least as equally important as the acquisition of knowledge. Certainly knowledge should be sought, but it is difficult to lay down any rules, because individual differs from individual. Some have so long been what the psycho-analysts call rationalising that what they need is a frank avowal of their real wishes and a resolution not to be swayed by them. Such men are kept from the kingdom of God because they have all the time been unwilling to accept it, and have hidden their disinclination under specious and often complicated reasons. Others need the help of further information, being men of good will; while others in a similar condition are held back because their minds have been unconsciously steeped in prejudice. For these latter the main purpose of knowledge is to remove obstructions. On the whole, I think that it can be said that before the act of faith the arguments for Christianity may admit of no answer, but they produce no conviction. What St. Augustine said of the Platonists holds true of many, that they see the truth but from afar off. They do not feel that it touches them. It is therefore an answer, but not *the* answer, a truth which, so far as they see, has no flaw and no alternative—but they do not see why it should not have an alternative. Or it may be that the arguments are accepted as logical and within themselves cogent; what they cannot rid themselves of, however, is a suspicion that there are other possibilities, that the truth they have heard cannot be the august and hidden revelation of God, that there are mysteries which the Catholic apologist has not dreamt

this assumption, and for this very reason the early
Church uncompromisingly separated the divine word
from anything human, and made it its supreme duty to
preserve that word as it was without any human gloss
or contamination. For once the slightest human
contamination could be found in it, it had lost its
savour and been reduced to the state of what it had
been destined to supersede, namely a human message
and discovery.

It would seem, then, that the Modernist doctrine,
however interesting it may be in itself, cannot possibly
be more than a new variant on natural religion, and
that it carries with it a denial of what is specifically
Christian. It would seem, also, that those who hold
this have failed to see the significance of the Gospel
teaching, and that there is all the difference in the
world between their interpretation and the interpretation which is contained in the act of supernatural
faith. The reason for this is, I suspect, that there is at
the last corner of the road to faith a subtle and fearful
temptation. There at the parting from the natural to
the supernatural, where the natural looks most like its
divine neighbour, the soul has to make a sacrifice which
to the eyes of human prudence appears uncalled for;
it has to surrender its glory, to change its shield and
throw away the very weapon which has won for it its
safe journeying so far. For the natural man reason and
private judgment are inalienable rights, and now, as a
lover does to his beloved, but with how much greater
wisdom, he has to give up his most cherished possessions
and have no word but "Speak, Lord, for thy servant
heareth." That this must happen I am sure, though I
know that to many who are excellent Christians it is
an undreamt of contingency and even an abhorrent
ideal. It serves, therefore, to show the vast abyss

which separates many who profess the same doctrines and wish to call themselves by the same name, and it serves also to show how different the act of faith is from all that precedes it. The essence of faith is exemplified in the words "My God and my all," and in those of St. Paul when he speaks of "destroying counsels, and every height that exalteth itself against the knowledge of God, and bringeth into captivity every understanding unto the obedience of Christ." Finally, though I have stressed the fact that it seems against flesh and blood to make such a sacrifice of the private judgment, it is from another point of view an obvious choice and one most profitable; for one is not destroying one's judgment, but handing it over to One who is the truth; in other words, the human pattern is forsaken for a divine one, and the way is open to contemplate and enjoy not a human counterpart of the beauty and love of God, but that beauty as it is without any disguise.

These last remarks will not be wasted if they serve to distinguish faith from all other acts of the mind. The arguments which precede faith are not its title-deeds; for these one must consult the act itself, and my contention is that the act carries with it its guarantee and certitude, and is therefore right independently of all the acts of private judgment which, as some think, have provided the premises for the assent. As one example of this mistaken form of accusation I may refer to that which relies on the Higher Criticism. It is argued that the belief of a Catholic rests on, must stand or fall with, the current estimates of the Gospel record. Now, it is the opinion of some scholars that the documents have to be accepted with many reserves and that our information about the first century is so slight and unreliable that at most a probable hypothesis can be built upon it. Hence, the grounds of faith are taken away. No Catholic will admit this argument, and an overwhelming case can be made out for the credibility of the New Testament and for the interpretation which has been put upon it and upon the history of the first century by Catholics. But I adduce this criticism to show how idle it is, resting as it does on a completely mistaken conception of faith. The Catholic has no need to go anxiously back to the first century to be sure that he is right in his belief. He does not live in the past but in the present; he is not at the mercy of every breeze of expert opinion; he has not to keep looking back to a far distant event to see whether it still preserves its ancient appearance. The truth of Christianity is as obvious now as it was to the disciples of the first century. The city set on a hill can be seen now in its majesty overtopping all human edifices and designs and manifesting in its glory the handiwork of a divine architect. In other words, there is present evidence for the living Christ, sure signs of the Word of Life for those who seek with all their hearts to find and hear it.

I will conclude now by trying to show how in the assent of faith all the parts are there to make it an act which is at once supernatural, rational, certain and free. To do this I must recapitulate some of the main conclusions reached in former chapters. In order that their relevance should be clearly seen it will be well to take the saying of Christ, "I am the way, the truth, and the life," as the point of universal reference. This is just because the figure of Christ dominates the whole of Christianity. It is His word which summons us to eternal life, it is His truth which communicates to us certainty from within and from without, and it is not a life of goodness which we embrace but the life which is divine. Now in treating of interpretation we saw that it enabled us to grasp what was signified by the

signs, single or manifold, of its presence. Thus it is
that we are able to recognise familiar friends, see the
answer to puzzles, take in a situation, and gather a true
impression of a historical scene and period; and it is
especially our mainstay in the appreciation of the
meaning of art and communications of others to us or
to the world. We see the meaning and unity of a
number of signs, and as the meaning dawns on us a
multitude of hitherto unnoticed signs also comes to the
foreground. Incidentally, if we are looking for the
wrong thing, because of habit or prejudice or false and
unworthy desires, we may easily miss the evidence,
though it is staring us in the face. The purposes of man
are written across the surface of the earth in every age,
and we have no difficulty in discerning his mark; as, for
instance, when we gaze upon the long dead civilisations
of Rome at Herculaneum or of Crete at Knossos.

Now, not only do we exercise this power of interpretation in the multitudinous details and incidents of
life, but we form an impression of the world as a whole.
Each one of us has a point of view, a personal outlook
on the universe, varying according to his pattern; or
rather, I should say that each has at least a provisional
outlook, for the truth is that some settle down into a
comfortable or exasperated attitude, which they will not
have changed, while others are ever looking beyond
what they see, "and their hearts are restless" until the
meaning of the universe and their own destiny shine out
in commingled truth and goodness. We may say,
indeed, that the attitude of man in the presence of his
universe is not unlike that of the visitor looking down
upon some long-perished, dead city of the plain. The
visible remains are signs to him of thought and design,
but he may be too far removed in habits of mind to
understand the message written in the sand and half

up his lips and waits while another whistles the notes of the octave, at the note to which the configuration of the lips is adapted a corresponding sound will be spontaneously emitted. Again, if a log is thrown into a stream it will itself move to a rhythm set by the dance rhythm of the stream. Still better as an example of a pattern: it is easy so to prepare a room that a visitor has the illusion that he is near to a bunch of flowers in a certain design of colour, and it is only when he stretches out his hand to them that he discovers his mistake. His sight has spontaneously represented to itself a sense-pattern. The same happens sometimes when we converse with another and see him before us, though unawares he has left our presence. For other cases in point the reader has only to consult his own experience. I hope he has noticed how dogs take on a curious likeness to their masters and mistresses. The aged gentleman and elderly spinster are sure to have a decrepit old dog with an air of decayed respectability; the blind man in the street is sure to be accompanied by a dog with an appealing countenance, a very monument of mendicancy, and there are, of course, "flapper" dogs and military dogs, and many a one which has its nose in the air after the manner of its master. To return to human beings, the adaptation of body to environment is too well-known to need illustration. On a higher plane we have to acknowledge that curious sensitiveness that certain people have which shows itself in the quickness with which the troubles and experiences of lower animals as well as fellow human beings are felt and interpreted. This sensitiveness may reach to such a degree that in a family one member can tell almost always what another is feeling or thinking.

The illustrations of this truth could be indefinitely